abortion

abortion: THE WHOLE STORY

Mary Kenny

Quartet Books

London New York

First published by Quartet Books Limited 1986
A member of the Namara Group
27/29 Goodge Street
London W1P 1FD

British Library Cataloguing in Publication Data
Kenny, Mary
Abortion: the whole story.
1. Abortion
I. Title
363.4'6 RG734
ISBN 0 7043 2576 4

Typeset by MC Typeset Limited
Chatham, Kent
Printed and bound in Great Britain by
Nene Litho and Woolnough Bookbinding
both of Irthlingborough, Northants

CONTENTS

FOR R.L.W.
– who chose life

'Some women will have an abortion even if it kills them. And it *has* killed them.'
Dr Fay Hutchinson, recalling back-street abortion

'The foetus has a right to life. But only the mother can protect that right.'
Professor Peter Huntingford

'I was aware that I had deprived somebody of his or her life.'
Teresa Guillaume, a young woman recalling her abortion experience

'Human experience cannot be transmitted. Everyone has to find out everything for himself.'
Alexander Solzhenitsyn

ACKNOWLEDGEMENTS

There are many, many people I have to thank for help and advice with this endeavour. First, I must thank the many women who spoke to me, wrote to me and shared their experiences and their feelings about abortion. There was hardly one encounter in the course of these meetings and communications that I did not find touching, or which did not send me away more reflective than before. I might add that I should also like to thank the men who communicated their thoughts too.

I must especially thank Lynn Reed, who wrote an article called 'Shall I Have an Abortion?' and the *Daily Mail* for publishing her piece – which brought in over 500 letters, many of them deeply-felt documents drawn from many women's experiences. Where I have quoted from them, I have tried to get the writer's permission to do so and this has nearly always been forthcoming.

I would like to thank Dr David Paintin at St Mary's, Paddington, Dr Alan Rogers of the London Private Nursing Homes and Dr Roslyn Stephens of the London Temperance Hospital who discussed, explained and demonstrated techniques of abortion with remarkable openness. Miss Pamela Simms, a consultant gynaecologist in Northumberland, has been unfailingly helpful in explaining gynaecological terms to me. Thanks are also due to Professor Ian Donald, Dr Mary Belton (of Let Live), Dr Peggy Norris, Dr K.L. Oldershaw, Dr Wendy Savage, Dr Kay Hutchinson (of the Brooks Advisory Centre), Dr Timothy Black (of Marie Stopes) and Dr Shirley Bond, and to many other doctors and nurses who responded to questionnaires and letters, including my own helpful GP, Bill O'Neill.

Very special thanks are due to Dr Mary Lucas, genetic specialist at University College Hospital in London for her patient tutorials on genetically inherited defects. And I am greatly indebted to Professor Peter Huntingford, who read large sections of this manuscript and suggested corrections of a technical kind. He disagrees strongly with the basic attitude of this book, but he was hugely helpful just the same.

I should like to thank the abortion counsellors who gave me their time and their reflections on their experiences, notably Valerie Wallace and Hilary Greenwood of the Samaritan Hospital for Women in London, Pat Garrard and Barbara Chandler from PAS, and Anne Dibb, chief caring officer for Life who has seen all the problems of women facing a crisis pregnancy.

I am grateful to Diane Munday from BPAS, to Madeleine Simms who supplied documents and papers, and to Dr Colin Brewer who lent me some extremely valuable books.

Phyllis Bowman and everyone at the Society for the Protection of the Unborn Child have been a constant source of knowledge and support. Elspeth Chowdharay-Best has kept me supplied with some of the voluminous material which continues to flourish in the political conflict over abortion. Nuala and Jack Scarisbrick of Life supplied me with endless books, papers and hospitality.

I would like to thank Debby Sanders of Women for Life, for sharing her knowledge and her personal experience, and Marion Keogh of the National Abortion Campaign for her honest conversations about feminism's commitment to choice.

Thanks are due to Marie Turner and Frances Holmes at the Catholic Crusade of Rescue for their superb knowledge of adoption past and present. And to Jean Thompson of Hammersmith Borough's adoption service for her helpful interview. I would also like to mention Angela Hamblin, the editor of a now-defunct but very useful publication, *Jigsaw*, which charted stories of natural mothers and their babies. And to Margaret Fogarty for drawing my attention to this area.

John Keown of Linacre College, Oxford, gave me enormous help with historical papers on birth control and abortion in past times. Professor Gerald Bonner of the University of Durham provided me with a rich background on the Christian traditions of objection to abortion.

Aurora Grove in Spain provided me with background research from there: Gisela and Ferdi Picker sent useful comparative studies from Germany; and Mavis Arnold in Ireland did a thorough job of comparing data on maternal health in the Republic. My thanks too to Orjan Landelius of the Swedish Embassy in London and to

Andrew Brown for translating Swedish medical papers.

Thanks to Ann Kaye, producer of the Radio Four programme 'Does He Take Sugar?', who helped to put me in touch with handicapped and disabled people, and especial thanks to those of them who wrote to me. Acknowledgements of assistance to Annie Morgan from Yorkshire Television's 'Where There's Life', and acknowledgements to the independent film-maker Gina Newson, whose Channel Four film about abortion, 'Mixed Feelings', provided many insights. I'd like to acknowledge the help of the *Manchester Evening News* and *Nursing Mirror* through whose pages I reached many correspondents.

I would like to thank Geoffrey Simmons for sending me helpful material on animal behaviour, and my friend Valerie Grove for special kindness.

For the poems quoted in Chapter 10, I would like to acknowledge thanks for permission to the following. To Gwendolyn Brooks, for her poem, 'The Mother', published in Britain in 1979 in *The World Split Open: Four Centuries of Women Poets* (Women's Press); to James MacGibbon, the executor of the Stevie Smith estate for permission to quote her poem, 'But Murderous', which comes from *The Collected Poems of Stevie Smith* (Penguin Modern Classics), and to D.M. Thomas and *Encounter* magazine for permission to quote his poem 'The Foetus'.

I have not been able to contact David Sutton or Maurice Kearney to seek permission to quote their poems 'Not to be Seen' and 'Bargain', but if they would care to contact me I will be glad to do so in any further editions of this book.

Thanks and acknowledgements to John Vernon Taylor, former Bishop of Winchester for permission to quote his 'Prayer for Abortion'.

For various suggestions, information, contacts and general acts of friendly encouragement and co-operation, I would like to thank Anne Sharpley, Shirley Flack, Bernard Cartwright, Kate Anstey, Joyce Jeale, Peter Zelles, Clodagh O'Reilly and Hugo Brunner. I would like to thank Mary Taylor and Mary Warner for their practical help in getting the manuscript typed. Pat Kavanagh of A.D. Peters has been loyal and patient with what has always been a difficult and controversial subject. And Rana Kabbani at Quartet has been an editor of outstanding sympathy, understanding and dedication.

Although many people have been very helpful to me with this book, any errors in it are of course mine.

abortion

INTRODUCTION

I cannot say that I grew up with any sense of trauma about abortion. It did not haunt my youth. Indeed, I had never heard the word until I was twenty years old, and then I was introduced to it very liberally. I was living and working in London in the 1960s, first as a secretary, subsequently as a journalist. A friend got pregnant, much to my surprise since we were all aware of various methods of birth control, and she had an abortion. My recollection of this was that it was hard luck on the girl but it only proved what we thought: that the chap was a swine anyway. Abortion was not quite legal but there were ways and means, if you knew the right people. It did not shock me in the least. I was glad that my friend was able to be rescued from a difficult situation. I also thought the swine got off pretty lightly by only having to cough up 150 guineas.

I was vaguely aware of a campaign to legalize abortion when another friend took me to a meeting conducted by the then Labour MP Lena Jeger. Lena made an impressive speech, saying that rich women could get an abortion because they wanted to have a ski-ing holiday, but poor women couldn't have an abortion even if they had twelve children and lived in a slum. I found this persuasively sympathetic and I joined the Labour Party on the spot.

However, I took little further active interest (beyond

general agreement that abortion freedom of choice was a Good Thing) in the fight to legalize abortion in 1967, largely because I think I assumed it was merely a formality. Among my own contemporaries, the battle was well and truly won: abortion was here to stay. This feeling was, as it turned out, politically and socially accurate. Gynaecologists, such as David Paintin of St Mary's Hospital in London and the campaigning Peter Huntingford, remember that the 1960s were a period during which the pressure for abortion became irresistible. Professor Huntingford actually began his medical career by being anti-abortion, and was a member of the Society for the Protection of the Unborn Child (SPUC). As a young doctor in the 1960s, however, he received more and more requests for abortion, and some were very hard cases. He began to carry out those he really felt were justified. Then he realized that he, a man, was sitting in judgement of women, and that his judgement was not always right. He would refuse a schoolgirl, and do an abortion for a mother of five children. Afterwards, he came to see that it was entirely possible that he had made the wrong judgement: the mother of five very probably could have coped with another baby; the schoolgirl's life was shattered by having the child. He told himself that he would have to come to a principled position: either he would agree to *all* abortions requested – or to none. He decided that he would do all abortions, and became famous as the doctor who said he would abort any woman at any time just because she wanted an abortion. It was a logical position; you must either accept abortion as a woman's freedom to choose, he says, or you must accept no abortion at all on the principle that human life is to be respected. There are only two consistent attitudes to abortion: one is the extreme feminist one; the other is that held by Roman Catholics. The middle way, that abortion is all right sometimes, depending on the circumstances, and justified by situation ethics (i.e., it depends on the situation), is morally and logically absurd. Moreover, the middle way is judgemental of women. If you take the view that abortion is always wrong because it takes human life, you are not discriminating against anyone in particular; you are simply holding a general principle, without discrimination. If you take the view that abortion is sometimes right, you are judging certain women by saying that *their* case for abortion was not a good enough one. You are falling into the trap of pronouncing abortion as OK for the overburdened mother, but jolly well not OK for the promiscuous schoolgirl.

As I have mentioned, abortion was practised by my generation in the 1960s with confidence, and it was seen as a remedy when contraception failed. I have since heard harrowing stories about hapless young women having washing-up liquid squirted into their wombs (any irritant may cause miscarriage, though it is dicing with infection and death to try it), and of women being admitted to hospitals with botched abortions. A gynaecologist such as Wendy Savage of the London Hospital became converted to the abortion cause because she was sick of seeing young women badly damaged or even dead, from criminal or self-induced abortions. A friend of mine who was a nurse in the Royal Free Hospital – then in north London – recalled an Irish Catholic woman being admitted with a bad case of haemorrhaging from incomplete abortion. It was touch and go, but they saved her life. As she was being discharged, my friend said: 'Now for heaven's sake, don't get yourself into this mess again. Use a contraceptive.' The girl was shocked. 'Oh, I couldn't use contraceptives,' she said, 'I'm a Catholic.' Tragic? Yes, but we laughed over stories like that in our youthful, heartless way. Actually, it is an interesting tale because it reveals much about attitudes to abortion and contraception: abortion may be a sin, but it is a one-off mistake. Contraception shows premeditation, deliberate intention, forward planning. This mentality is by no means confined to Catholics, and is one of the fundamental reasons for the sometimes surprising failure rate of birth control: some women do not like the feeling that they have planned a romance, made provision for falling in love, or been prudent about the possible results of spontaneity.

Abortion was not a strong point in the canons of

women's liberation in the West in the late 1960s. It really emerged as a feminist issue only in the 1970s when the Americans turned to legalization. In the early '70s, I had recourse to abortion myself. It was a self-indulgent little drama, and everyone was frightfully good about it. Two observations remained in my mind. One was the Harley Street gynaecologist saying to me, 'I only do this sort of thing because I am so concerned about the population problem, you know.' Years later, when I read Bernard Nathanson's *Aborting America*, a witty and wise book, he brought this up as a common justification among abortionists. Though how the problems of Africa and India were alleviated by aborting career women in Manhattan, he remarked sardonically, was never quite explained. A second observation was made by critic Philip Hope-Wallace, who entirely approved of all liberal-minded legislation, yet said, 'Everything can be remedied, nowadays, can't it? No one ever has to pay for their sins any more.'

It was not until 1977 that I consciously began to feel real misgivings about abortion. I had had a child and thought, 'What a piece of work is man' as the baby appeared. I had had a miscarriage and thought, 'Ah, so we *can't* always choose. Sometimes it is nature that chooses.' Anti-abortion literature disturbed me much more when I became a mother, whereas before I had always dismissed it as anti-feminist propaganda. In 1977 there was a spate of articles in the papers celebrating ten years of abortion freedom – 'Ten years on and no regrets!' The *Daily Express* was in perfect harmony with the *New Statesman*. I reacted, first, only as a journalist. I am very suspicious when all the media are in agreement; it smells of conspiracy. Now wait a moment, I thought – it ain't that simple. OK, back-street abortion was bad – but did that mean that front-street abortion was good? And who can deny that the nub of it is a human life?

I remember the exact moment when abortion hit me emotionally. It was May 1978. A woman called Joan Paton was seeking an abortion and her husband tried to stop her from getting one. His application was rejected by a High Court Judge, Sir George Baker – an important legal decision, as it set a precedent in case law that husbands and putative fathers had no rights concerning a woman's abortion. I was sitting on the bed with my youngest child, then a baby of four months. The radio newsreader referred to the case and added, 'Mrs Paton has now had the operation.' I remember sitting there and feeling a personal sense of loss. I felt it right in my belly: a pang. I have had this feeling again since, when sitting in waiting rooms and clinics, preparing to interview abortionists for this book. As women have come in, visibly pregnant, I have experienced a sense of melancholy that a life is about to be lost. This is the characteristic feeling of the anti-abortionist. It is not anti-feminist, it is not a desire to control women or to judge them; it is just a feeling of loss. And I know many women share it, whatever their intellectual views of abortion. In April 1983, a young woman called Lynn Reed wrote a short article for the *Daily Mail* under the headline 'Should I Have an Abortion?' She was aged thirty-five, divorced, and unintentionally pregnant by her boyfriend. The letters poured in – over 500 of them. Of these 452 pleaded with Lynn not to terminate the pregnancy, and many alluded wistfully to regrets about personal abortion decisions. The most common theme was loss, the most common coda to each letter was, 'I have never really spoken about this before – please do not reveal my real name.' Fifty-nine letters were ambivalent. Eight letters argued for abortion.

I got in touch with Lynn, interviewed her at length and discovered that she had, in the end, chosen abortion basically for practical reasons. The boyfriend didn't want to know, and she came to feel that she could not cope with a baby alone. She rejected adoption as being too upsetting. The operation was efficiently carried out at thirteen weeks – and that was that. She went through a weepy phase afterwards, and then acquired a cat. (Women often acquire a pet after an abortion. One woman who had had three abortions also had three cats. 'These are my babies now,' she remarked.)

To some extent, I believe that my own odyssey through the abortion landscape has been that of many women – and men, too. I think that the generation of the 1960s regarded the legalization of abortion as a simple matter of de-criminalizing a scandalous back-street practice, and halting the extortionate fees charged by the up-market abortionists. (To be fair, their fees were justified by the risk they might be taking with the law and their reputation.) Besides, the law was flouted on all sides. It seems, though, that we did not think a lot about the matter of human life.

Looking back on the newspaper cuttings of the great abortion debate, the editorials in serious newspapers such as the *Observer* and the *Sunday Times* constantly referred to the foetus as 'a blob of jelly', 'a piece of tissue'. But in the years in between the science of embryology has developed extraordinarily, and the 'blob of jelly' is now known to have human organs all in place after eight weeks and an entire nervous system after ten weeks. I have watched many abortions taking place, and in the early stages the operation is so swiftly destructive that nothing can be properly perceived by the naked eye. Into the second trimester (after thirteen weeks) however, it is evident that this is a very tiny human being. Once past twenty weeks, the baby begins actually to try to resist the needle which draws away its amniotic fluid.

I believe that we have become much more reflective about abortion generally, and that we admit that it is nothing like as simple a matter as was once claimed. Many young women today are much more thoughtful about the termination of pregnancy than my generation was. Although in the UK legal abortion is unlikely to be repealed in the near future, the questions, dilemmas and personal anguish will continue. As the life of the unborn child is revealed ever more to us through new technology, the questions are likely to become ever more pressing.

No long-term follow-up of women's experiences of abortion has ever been carried out because it is thought that this is too distressing for women, disturbing feelings that may have long been tidied away. But many of the women I have talked to have wanted to speak about their abortion experience, in all its complexity, in all its mixture of relief, regret, adjustment, acceptance, misgiving and remembrance.

1

WOMEN'S EXPERIENCE OF ABORTION

'Studies confirm that abortion for the majority of women is not a threat to their physical and/or mental well-being. Most women feel relieved, and they return to as good or even better psychological, marital and inter-personal relationships than before the abortion.' *Abortion and Sterilization: Medical and Social Aspects*[1]

'The mental backlash has been enormous, and in all my consultations, not one person ever warned me of this. Even with the support of a firm marriage and a loving family, I came as close to a mental breakdown as I am ever likely to come, thus threatening the well-being of the family I was so concerned to protect.' Letter to the *Guardian* women's page, 19 July 1979

There has been much mythologizing about the experience of women in abortion. One theory holds that a woman is permanently psychologically wounded. Another claims that abortion is as trivial as having your hair cut – once done, instantly forgotten. Neither of these statements can be said to be generally true, for the experience varies almost as much as individuals vary. I have met a woman who has had eight abortions whose emotional impact rippled over her like water off a duck's back. I have met women for whom one abortion caused such distress that they could not afterwards even say the word 'abortion'. No one can confidently predict what effect an abortion will have upon a woman – and that may include the woman herself.

'No woman knows whether she wants an abortion until she has had one,' says Professor Peter Huntingford, the gynaecologist who has advocated absolute choice for women and championed women's rights vehemently in this sphere. Certainly no doctor can assess how a particular patient will react. 'The true emotional consequences of abortion for an individual woman can never be known to her physician,' says an authoritative medical textbook which also advocates liberal abortion as a woman's choice.[2]

The wise gynaecologist steers clear of predicting anything specific about the effects of abortion, though occasionally women are curious to know what the impact might be. The emphasis in recent years on a woman's right to choose is the consequence of feminist campaigns to make it so; but it is also a useful neutral stance for the physician, who cannot afterwards be held responsible if a decision is regretted, or blamed for encouraging a pregnancy that turned out unhappily. In an anguish of indecision, one twenty-year-old talked for two hours to the doctor willing to perform an abortion whenever she wanted it (she was just thirteen weeks pregnant). 'I kept asking him how it would affect me, trying to get him to help me decide,' she recalled. 'But he refused to sway me one way or the other – he just kept saying: "It can be done if you want it to be done. You must choose."' The man was a very experienced practitioner who may do more than a score of abortions in a session, and was, incidentally, earning over £1,000 a week in 1983. But he was too experienced ever to give advice. She had the abortion. There was an unusual sequel: nine months later she began to lactate spontaneously – milk flowing from her breasts in an unexpected reminder of the lost pregnancy. Not everyone is so exquisitely in control of their bodies, or their emotions, as rationalists would have us believe. And although dependent behaviour is today castigated in women, dependency in fraught emotional moments or in entangled relationships still occurs in all humans.

'*Please* refuse me this abortion,' begged a twenty-six-year-old, pregnant with her third child, to a woman doctor assiduously filling out forms in London's Charing Cross Hospital. 'We never refuse abortions – it's our policy,' she replied, continuing to fill out the forms. In this case, the patient wanted the protection of the doctor while she was under pressure from her lover who wished to avoid a scandal. Feeling pressed into the abortion by her circumstances, the woman went through with it. Not surprisingly, she was pregnant again within six months. (This time, she went through with the pregnancy, had a much-wanted daughter, and her lover had to acknowledge an out-of-wedlock child after all.) Perhaps the doctor should have suggested some further, outside counselling in the first instance.

What a doctor can do, and what a doctor should do, is to lay before a woman an objective account of the physical risks of the termination of pregnancy. Doctors have the right, of course, to refuse to handle abortions on grounds of conscience, as have nurses. They should not be judgemental towards the woman when invoking a conscientious objection here – and the woman should not be judgemental of the doctor or nurse either. The overall risk of abortion, when carried out under medical circumstances, is very low, though all operations carry some risk.

First, death. About four women in every 100,000 (in England and Wales) die as a consequence of the operation. These deaths occur from an air embolism (bubble of air in the circulation causing heart failure), pulmonary embolism (clot in the circulation), intestinal obstructions (bowel blockage after accidental perforation) and anaesthesia. It is very seldom that such deaths happen when the abortion is carried out within the first thirteen weeks of pregnancy.

Secondly: complications which can be serious but do

not lead to death. The overall rate, in the National Health Service, is between 2 and 6 per cent. These fall into three categories: infection, perforation of an internal organ, or haemorrhage. Under thirteen weeks' gestation, the complication rate is just over five per 1,000; after thirteen weeks, about twelve per 1,000.[3] There are slightly more complications within the National Health Service than within the private sector. This is partly because the NHS takes on the more complex abortions anyway, and partly because cross-infections are more likely to occur in hospitals.

These are the immediately perceivable physical effects. Longer-term effects are harder to quantify, show wide geographical variation and are generally more diffuse. One gynaecologist, Mr Christopher Naylor, estimates that morbidity – the indication of disease – after abortion is between 5 and 15 per cent in the long term.[4]

Some women mention problems after abortion which are either written off as 'anecdotal' and are therefore not considered scientific (though so much of past medical knowledge has been gained 'anecdotally' – that is, by noticing case histories), or else they are regarded as symptoms of that familiar old female complaint: hysteria. These include problems with periods, abdominal pain and lowered resistance to pelvic infection. Lynn Reed, whose letter to the *Daily Mail* about abortion brought over 500 personal replies, had her abortion in the private sector of the Health Service, which boasts a low-infection record. But for over six months afterwards she was plagued with pelvic infections which required repeated antibiotic treatment.

Infertility and miscarriage as a consequence of abortion are difficult areas. Until recently, it was thought that there was a small risk of infertility after abortion, but today that is more or less discounted. There is now said to be little evidence of post-abortion infertility – unless there has been an infection. Miscarriage in subsequent pregnancies does present a slight risk, particularly if the woman is very young (seventeen and under) and particularly if there are repeated terminations.[5] One medical report claimed that, in abortion, the rate of injury to the cervix in girls aged seventeen and under was twice the rate of damage to older women. The cervix, or neck of the womb, in a teenager is tighter and less elastic than in an older woman, and with induced abortion it is forced open rather quickly – particularly where the termination is a late one (and younger girls do tend to present for abortion later). This can make the cervix incompetent, that is, liable to weakness in subsequent pregnancies. Nulliparous women (women who have never given birth) who have had two or more abortions treble their chances of a late miscarriage in a subsequent pregnancy.[6]

Consider the case of Astrid, a woman aged thirty-nine who was very anxious to have a baby. She had her first abortion at the age of seventeen, the second at the age of twenty-five. At thirty-three, she was pregnant again and decided to continue the pregnancy; the pregnancy proceded to twenty-three weeks, but she lost the baby. Subsequent attempts at pregnancy also ended in miscarriage, to her great chagrin. She was diagnosed as having an incompetent cervix. On the other hand, women miscarry who have never had abortions, and women who have had repeated abortions subsequently go on to have full-term pregnancies. The journalist Anne Sharpley, a veteran campaigner for abortion rights, told me of a friend of hers who, in the 1950s, had had nine abortions – and went on to have two children quite happily afterwards. However, in this case, the woman was in her twenties when the nine abortions took place. Apprehension about cervical incompetence tends to be more focused on young girls.

Infertility may arise after abortion as a result of an infection, or the perforation of the uterus, or pelvic inflammation. An infection can occur after childbirth, too, and pelvic inflammatory disease is rather more associated with the intrauterine device (IUD) than with abortion, though any invasive technique of the vaginal area can be a source of irritation. An infection may result in the loss of a Fallopian tube which reduces fertility by 50 per cent – ironically, some of the demand for *in vitro* fertilization (IVF; test-tube babies) arises from women who have had a Fallopian infection after an abortion. One of the most celebrated test-tube babies was born because the mother's Fallopian tubes were infected after a previous abortion, and this was the root cause of her infertility – and her need for IVF. Again, much depends upon circumstances. In the Soviet Union, where standards of gynaecology are not – by the Russians' own admission – very good, one study claimed a staggering 20 per cent infection rate among 7,500 aborted women. Of this group 8 per cent suffered permanent infertility. Julia Voznesenskaya, the Russian author and feminist, says that in the USSR the authorities very actively discourage a woman from aborting a first pregnancy because of the widespread fear that first abortions render a woman infertile; thus, the first child – who often turns out to be the only child – may actually be the unwanted child, arriving too soon in a marriage. Russian infertility rates are linked with inadequate standards of maternal and baby care – their rate of perinatal mortality is similar to that of the Third World – but the Russians do have a point: abortions on women who have had children statistically carry less risk. Not only has the cervix already been stretched by childbearing, but it is arguably (only arguably) less of a tragedy for a woman who is already a mother to be unable to have any more children, than it is for a woman never to be able to have children at all. Abortion has been going for a long time, to be sure, and the techniques of abortion were already moderately advanced by the 1930s; but, historically, abortion has more usually been carried out on mothers who already *had* many children. The routine abortion of nulliparous women is comparatively new.

There is also a small risk that subsequent pregnancies (after abortion) may be ectopic (conception in the Fallopian tube, which has to be terminated to save the life of the mother), a slightly higher risk of stillbirth in subsequent pregnancies and a slightly higher risk of premature delivery. These risks are statistically very small – all within 1 or 2 per cent, and some doctors would feel they are hardly worth mentioning. Moreover, any allusion to infertility brings with it another psychological risk. 'Very occasionally,' says Mr Alan Rogers, a Harley Street gynaecologist, 'a woman will become pregnant after an abortion just to check that the abortion has not *made* her infertile.' Fear of infertility can, paradoxically, lead to a further unwanted pregnancy. For this reason, some doctors may not wish to inform women of the small percentage of risks, let alone mention other theories associated with termination, such as the risk of endometritis (an infection of the lining of the womb) or the theory mentioned by one researcher that cancer of the breast could be related to abortion – that starting a pregnancy and then deliberately stopping it is placing the woman's hormonal system on a 'stop-go' circuit, animating the hormones and then cutting the flow. Where do you draw the line between informing the patient fully – or alarming her by talking about risks that are minimal or theories not yet proved? Perhaps it is just fair to mention the statement from the International Planned Parenthood Federation's publication on abortion: 'The long-term risks of abortion include infertility, possible hazards to future pregnancies and psychological disturbances.' And add that there is no proof that these risks are meaningful for the majority. The law in Britain stipulates that a pregnancy may be terminated if it is more dangerous for a woman to continue a pregnancy than to abort; statistically, the risks of motherhood are always greater than the risks of non-motherhood. Infections and infertility may follow childbirth, and it is certain that anxiety levels are raised by the experience of becoming a mother: thus 'psychological disturbance' is easily as likely to occur in the mother as in the childless woman. The abortion law was prudently phrased, for it can be argued that it is always more dangerous to continue a pregnancy than to terminate one.

Psychological effects of abortion? Impossible to quantify, for, as mentioned, some women experience none, and some many. There have been all manner of studies which have tried to chart women's experience of abortion, and there are few definitive conclusions. Some of these studies have been fundamentally political: you can prove anything with statistics. A much-cited Swedish study showed that not only had abortion no psychological effect whatsoever on women, it was very nearly beneficial.[7] Dr Colin Brewer, the psychiatrist who was a founder member of the British Pregnancy Advisory Service (BPAS; an abortion charity), published a pamphlet which said that even late abortion, when the foetus is nearly viable, hardly mattered a feather. An American guide to abortion proclaims that 79 per cent of women are positively 'happy' with their abortion experience, only 1.5 per cent had misgivings. The orthodox feminist view, as articulated by writers such as Gloria Steinem, is that abortion is a 'simple surgical procedure', like having your ears pierced. Steinem writes that she actually tried hard to feel 'some emotion' about her own abortion, but couldn't feel a thing. This was perhaps a 1970s overview. In the 1980s, the feminist line softened marginally. The National Abortion Campaign, which insisted in the 1970s that the foetus had no rights and was of no significance, and that women should have abortions right up to birth if they so chose, shifted their emphasis to underline the fact that to some women abortion was a serious and painful decision, although their basic approach remains that only the woman's wishes count.

Then there are the studies which say that a woman's feelings about abortion will be wholly conditioned by her background, and by the attitude of the people carrying out the abortion. If people tell a woman she should feel guilty, she will feel guilty. If they tell her that abortion is wonderful, she will absorb that point of view too. This is the view of the philosopher L.W. Sumner, who, while arguing for liberal abortion also warns against 'conservatives' projecting guilt on to women. This attitude is also insidiously patronizing, since it assumes that women are a *tabula rasa* on which society can write what it pleases. Thus there was the Danish report which said that 90 per cent of women were delighted with their abortion experience, and the Swiss report which said that half had regrets; the Norwegian study which said that 82.5 per cent of women were 'glad without reserve' about having an abortion, as against the Swedish study which showed that 82 per cent of women refused an abortion were afterwards pleased to have a baby. Then there were the 84 per cent of Japanese women, living in a society which has institutionalized abortion since the Second World War, who having had abortions still felt it was 'morally wrong'.

All these sociological studies are true, in their own way; all have been correctly carried out. Abortion can be such a complicated subject that it is possible to say that you were glad you had an abortion, if you had one, glad you had the baby if you had the baby; thought it necessary to have an abortion at the time, and still feel it to be morally wrong, in some part of you. Women are better able to tolerate ambivalence and contradictions than men, and it is entirely possible to hold all these feelings at once. No subject produces more ambivalence and paradoxes than abortion, and the only thing which seems to me to be erroneous about the sociology of abortion is the assumption that society can predict how women will feel. There are Catholic mothers of six who, having come to the end of their tether, feel no guilt whatsoever about terminating a seventh pregnancy. There are atheistic, feminist rationalists who are devastated by having had an abortion. It is simply not true that 'society' imposes the emotional norms: some of the women who are most devil-may-care about abortion are those who went through the experience in the old days, before it was legal.

The journalist Anne Sharpley, for instance, had her first abortion in the 1950s, and remembers it with real happiness – though she was brought up as a Catholic. 'I recall a sunny morning radiant with relief because the whole spiralling nightmare was over and now I could get on with my life. And for thirty years, I have felt grateful. It was in so many ways a positive experience, and in 1967 [as the abortion act was framed] we seemed at last to be making abortion not only a known, but an available remedy. I thought how wonderful that the fear of unwanted pregnancy could now go. Other women could be free like me.' She later had a second abortion, and has never experienced a moment's regret or remorse, and indeed can scarcely understand people who talk about the sanctity of human life in this context. She watched with amazement the development of the anti-abortion lobby in the 1960s. She could scarcely believe that anyone could claim that abortion meant killing. Not when she looked at nature. 'Nature, always exceeding, always destroying, making a mockery, whose conduct we have to try and remedy for everything from myopia to carrot-fly.' Here was a woman who was formed by religious education and lived in a society where abortion was not legal (though it was practised) and which kept the practice well and truly under cover. Yet it has never meant anything to her but the joy of freedom.

On the other hand, it is not difficult to find young women today who have grown up in a society which accepted abortion legally and socially, who look on the experience with painful feelings of loss and melancholy. Elizabeth is a social worker in Guildford, Surrey. She was born in the 1960s and brought up in a stable, liberal-minded family.. Her mother explained to her about contraception; she was not a victim of ignorance, repression or a negative attitude to sex. Her relationship with her parents is excellent, and she is in every way a responsible and caring young woman, very concerned about the problem families she now deals with. At the age of nineteen, she became pregnant, and had no difficulty in seeking an abortion, which was carried out at about seven weeks gestation. She was treated with kindness by the people at the abortion agency, and her boyfriend was helpful and supportive. In short, Elizabeth's situation was a model of what Anne Sharpley would want for young women today: absolute freedom of choice, absolute freedom of accessibility to abortion. And yet, she said she felt 'rotten' for a full six months afterwards, and not even fully reconciled a year later. The abortion took place in the spring. 'I think I was still very depressed about the whole thing right up to Christmas. I think you feel very lonely because you think "If I'd had that baby, that baby would be mine." I think a lot of people think like that – it's something that's yours, and it's warm and lovable, and ultimately that is the nice bit that you have lost. An incredible amount of maternal feeling came out in me afterwards.' Just as she was pulling out of the depression, she came across some anti-abortion literature with a picture of an embryo and the slogan 'This child is alive'. It threw her back into a bleak mood of depression. It made her wonder if she shouldn't have had the baby and had it adopted, particularly as her work brings her into contact with people requesting babies for adoption. But then she wondered if she could have done that, and keeping the baby would have been extremely difficult. 'Ultimately, it goes down to a bad experience, but in a way it helps me to understand other people in other situations and also to say "Well, my life hasn't been perfect – I can't turn and point the finger at other people."' It has deepened her understanding, broadened her compassion, but she still saw it as a 'bad experience'.

The range of women's experiences in abortion is simply endless; the word most commonly used by every writer or researcher who has spoken to individual women (as opposed to adding up percentages or figures on a graph) is 'ambivalence'. Linda Bird Francke, the American feminist who did one of the first human-angle series of interviews with women after abortion became legal in the United States, tellingly called her own book *The Ambivalence of Abortion*. In 1984, Channel Four transmitted a highly sensitive documentary which stood firmly on the principle of the woman's right to choose – and equally strongly on the point that women have a right to feel hurt, and to express their grief, too, if they want to. Gina Newson, the programme maker, appropriately called the documentary 'Mixed Feelings'.

In this, the voices of women told their individual reactions.

'Nothing prepared me for how I felt.'

'I was against abortion until I got pregnant again last year.'

'I knew I didn't want it, but I still felt torn by indecision.'

'Afterwards I felt relief, mixed with sadness.'

'Deep down, I knew it was the right decision, but I still had mixed feelings.'

From a range of interviews with women, and with abortion counsellors, I can pick out any number of quotes which articulate the full spectrum of reactions.

'I feel terrific.' (An English woman in her late twenties with two children who had an abortion after a revenge affair because her husband had been unfaithful.)

'I feel bad about killing the baby.' (A twenty-year-old West Indian with a poor relationship with her family and boyfriend.)

'I have no regrets at all.' (A westernized Chinese girl with a loving family and an interesting job.)

'A year ago I had an abortion: I was eight weeks pregnant. It was the biggest mistake of my life. No matter what suffering the pregnancy would have involved, it couldn't be worse than the suffering I have had since. I am now desperate to become pregnant again.' (A twenty-five-year-old schoolteacher in a stable relationship.)

'I can't say that I regret it; but I do still grieve – I feel the need to.' (A post-graduate student in her twenties.)

'I feel guilty about not feeling guilty.' (A wisecracking American, aged twenty-one, who had changed her hair colour after the abortion and looked radiant.)

'I now have a baby daughter and it makes me sick to think that I destroyed something as beautiful as she is.' (Twenty-eight-year-old mother, one abortion as a teenager.)

'I could not have had another child. I am glad that I took the decision to terminate. But I can never say, hear or read of that word again, which I can only bring myself to spell out. Don't ask me to say it. I can't.' (Businesswoman, mother of three, aged thirty-eight.)

'After the abortion, I feel my life will never be the same, that I will always be aware of the guilt, and it has made me depressed. My marriage is shaky; part of me hates my husband for letting it happen.' (Mother of a five-year-old, speaking a month after an abortion.)

'Abortion seemed the most rational decision in the world. We had three children, no money and elderly parents to help. We are not religious and I believe very much in the woman's right to choose. But it devastated us. We were full of grief. I was not at ease again until we had another baby.' (Twenty-nine-year-old artist with a very close marriage whose fourth child assuaged post-abortion depression.)

'My child would be seventeen years old this coming Christmas and I wonder with each passing year whether I was carrying a son or a daughter.' (Anonymous woman who said she was thirty-seven.)

'Abortion? What's the problem? I've had lots of them, and it has never cost me a thought.' (Journalist in her fifties, divorced, brought up as an Irish Catholic.)

Women's experiences of abortion are thus unique to each woman, and they are often unpredictable.

The most useful question to ask, it seems to me, is not whether 82 per cent of women were glad they had an abortion, or whether 82 per cent were glad they had the baby (as the counsellor Anna Raeburn has remarked, it is one thing not wanting a pregnancy, it is another not warming to the baby when it arrives) – but is there a pattern to be perceived? Are there some circumstances in which abortion is more emotionally distressing than others? Are there some stages in life when abortion seems more acceptable than others? Here I believe there are general indications to be drawn; they are not absolute, of course, and never certain, but they can be revealing.

On the whole, I believe that abortion hurts older women less than it hurts younger women. Women who have had children, women who have fulfilled their maternal desires and feel quite sure that they do not want, or could not cope with, another baby seem much less anguished about abortion.

As people mature, they become more realistic, less starry-eyed, more resilient emotionally. They know themselves, their own strengths and limitations. And there certainly comes a time when a woman with several children feels she has reached that limit, and just cannot take another child on board.

Olive, aged thirty-nine, has four children under ten. A warm, kindly, energetic woman who is happily married and runs a pleasant, family-orientated home. Her husband is a civil servant and she does some research work for an economic development organization from home. They are not strongly religious, but vaguely observant at Christmas and Easter and also do practical things for the local Anglican church in the way of jumble sales and restoration fund appeals. Olive was on the mini-Pill – yet she became pregnant when her youngest child was ten months old. 'I simply knew I could not have another child,' she said. 'I would not be able to look after my other children, let alone my husband and other responsibilities with a fifth.' When the pregnancy test was confirmed, she simply made arrangements to have an abortion straight away. There was no anguishing about it: she and her husband came to a quick decision, and she also told her mother – who agreed with her decision wholeheartedly. It couldn't have been more straightforward and, without being insensitive in any way, she would not have contemplated any alternative, or admitted to any misgivings.

I have come across many instances like this one. Hilary, aged thirty-three, the wife of an MP, became pregnant (while using a diaphragm) for the fourth time – she had three school-age children. 'Relief' is a word frequently used by women to describe their immediate reaction to abortion, and relief was all she felt. 'It wasn't traumatic, it was just a relief. I went into the clinic feeling really pregnant, sick, heavy and lethargic, tired and exhausted. And I came out the next day feeling like a totally different person. I felt marvellous. An extraordinary feeling – it really was. I've had no regrets, no depression – I've hardly thought about it since.' She did have certain feelings of anger, however, that the National Health Service had kept her waiting several weeks for the abortion, and the pregnancy was twelve weeks when the operation took place. This, she felt, was a scandal, though there is no easy answer to this problem, for bureaucracies are bureaucracies, and some might even argue that as social abortion is not a medical condition, the Health Service should not be asked to give it high priority. Some might even say that MPs and their families earn enough to pay for abortions, which are optional operations. And the private sector claims, probably correctly, that if the NHS put the abortion business out to tender for privatization it would be infinitely more efficient. 'We could take over the whole abortion network,' Mr Maitland Cook of the London Private Nursing Homes group told me, 'and offer an abortion service costing £76 per client to the taxpayer.' Within the National Health, the cost is about £600 per client – though it is not easy to quantify exactly because the economic infrastructure of gynaecology is so complex.

Similarly, a working-class mother with five children, London-Irish, married to a bus-driver, came to a calm decision that she could not reasonably continue a sixth pregnancy. 'I had to talk about it for a while with the counsellor at the hospital, and I was a bit nervous about having the operation. The counsellor even offered to put me in touch with a priest, if I wanted it. But there was no need to do that. I knew that I wouldn't be able to cope with another baby and that was that. There are some things that are just practical. I didn't worry about it afterwards either.'

'Because of my experience, I feel certain that there isn't necessarily any psychological trauma,' says the principal of a famous women's college. She, too, had five children, when she became accidentally pregnant again in 1963. Her youngest was eleven months old and had been very sick as a tiny baby and still needed a lot of care. In choosing abortion, which was readily agreed to by the family doctor in Oxford, 'I knew I was doing the right thing. I felt no doubts whatsoever. I came out of hospital thinking "Thank God". I don't think I ever thought "Well this baby would now be such and such an age" – partly because I find five children is jolly well enough. I just regarded it as a stupid mistake. Mind you, if the pregnancy had been in any way advanced (it was all done very quickly) I would have started thinking about it as a baby, and I didn't leave myself time to think like that.'

However, there are always exceptions, and even mothers who rationally decide to terminate because they feel they have completed their family can be hit by ambivalence afterwards. 'Long after the physical discomfort has disappeared, some of us are left with an aching sense of grief,' wrote Jane Lewis in *Woman's Journal* in January 1980. She chose abortion because she and her husband felt sure they did not want any more children.

'We took a holiday. Images of those weeks in France linger in my memory. Artichokes growing in green fields; starfish and crabs in rock pools; my children running across a golden beach, the magnificent sunsets over the bay when the sky is red and the sea a glistening pink; then the moon rising and seeming larger and closer than ever before . . . All these memories, plus a desperate, continuing sadness and an empty sense of regret. I mourned my lost child, and I still do.'

These poignant images of how nature aroused her sense of loss were evoked by Linda Bird Francke when recounting her experience of abortion. She and her husband were also convinced they had taken the right decision not to have a fourth child. 'It certainly does make more sense not to be having a baby right now – we say that to each other all the time,' she reflected in the immediate aftermath. 'But I have this ghost now. A very little ghost that only appears when I'm seeing something beautiful, like the full moon on the ocean last week. And the baby waves to me. And I wave to the baby. "Of course we have room," I cry to the ghost. "Of course we do."'

Abortion legislation, universally, has been designed with the over-burdened mother in mind, and there is widespread public sympathy for the woman who simply has enough children. There is also, possibly, a feeling – both among women themselves and among the public at large – that mothers have made their contribution to society, that they have fulfilled their responsibilities. That overriding practical consideration somehow confirms that the decision is the sensible one, the right one. Traditionally, women who have had no children, or who use abortion as a means of sexual freedom, have been judged as either selfish or promiscuous. The feminist movement has fought hard against such notions, insisting that a woman has a right to have an abortion just because she wants one – and she does not need to justify her morals to anyone else.

'There is a lot to be said for abortion on demand,' says Dr Sheila Abdullah, a doctor who has championed abortion rights for women fervently. 'There is a lot to be said for the idea that the woman has a right to *demand* abortion whenever she wants it, without having to plead or apologize or justify herself to anyone in authority.'

Here we are talking about a change in moral climate, a change in social attitudes of great magnitude. 'Every child a wanted child' implies a responsible attitude to parenthood, and a concerned feeling for children's welfare. 'Abortion on demand' is to do with women taking control of their own sexuality, without having to answer to any other agency. The phrase has in fact slightly fallen into disfavour because of its aggressive overtone and its implication that the doctor has no right to refuse, and the more moderate 'abortion on request' is now more usually used.

However, a change in the moral climate *has* occurred, and in views of women's sexuality. 'In my young days,' the author Margaret Powell, born in 1878, told me, 'if you didn't want children, you didn't get married. A married woman who didn't want a family at all would have been considered ridiculous, especially in the working class.' And of course, if you didn't get married, you didn't have a sex life, unless you were fast or a 'Bohemian'.

Today, in the 1980s, single women do have sex, and married women do choose not to have children. There is a concomitant change in attitude towards sexuality and children, wrought first by the acceptance of contraception and subsequently of abortion; sex and babies have been separated – in the notorious words of Hugh Hefner, 'recreation' and 'procreation' are now two quite different things. I do not believe they are as clinically separate in women's psyches as the sex-liberationists would have us believe, but that is certainly the theory. And some women *have* very successfully divided the two things. These women – who want sex without children and are certain that they do not want to become mothers – seem to adjust to an abortion experience, or even several abortions, without much anguish. Catherine, a single and dedicated career woman in her late thirties, had three abortions over a period of about fifteen years; each time it represented a nuisance, and each time she asked herself if she wanted to proceed with the pregnancy. And each time she concluded that it was 'not on'. Rachel, a married woman, a musician, became pregnant at the age of thirty-seven after more than twenty years of contracepting successfully. Neither she nor her husband ever wanted children and regarded family life as 'boring'. She didn't hesitate to have an abortion when the pregnancy occurred, and said there were no circumstances in which she would have proceeded with a pregnancy. And although the abortion had no measurable effect on her, she did ask me, out of curiosity, if I had ever come across women who had regretted their decision to remain childless. I told her, truthfully, that on the whole people tend to stand by, or justify, their past decisions, and it is, moreover, psychologically healthy not to anguish too much over the past, since there is not a lot you can do about it. Of course, some people change their minds about what they would or would not have liked to do in life – the author Lynne Reid Banks, for instance, mother of three, has said that she wished she had never had children, on reflection. Just as the journalist Felicity Green told me, in her fifties, that now she wished she had had a family. Women who defer having children, and then find that it is too late sometimes have regrets; women who were discouraged from having babies by unwilling husbands are sometimes resentful towards their partner. But women who have had a firm resolution not to become mothers seem, on the whole, to remain firm in this resolve. Perhaps the definitive example is the writer Simone de Beauvoir, who deliberately chose abortion rather than motherhood and always proclaimed herself pleased with that decision.

A third group of women for whom abortion represents little trauma and only relief are those who become pregnant by a man they do not care for. 'I lived happily with my married lover for five years,' recalled Natasha, childless and in her sixties. 'But in the end, the tension was too much for him and he did go back to his wife. After that, I had a silly, brief affair with a colleague – and became pregnant. I moved heaven and earth to get an abortion. It was pretty sordid, but I couldn't have had that man's child. If it had been my lover, I wouldn't have dreamed of aborting it.' One of the reasons why rape is almost universally accepted as grounds for abortion is that the notion of carrying the child of a rapist, as well as carrying the memory of the assault, is extremely repugnant. (Mercifully, rape very seldom results in conception – see page 49.)

Many are the cases of women who recall seeking abortions because they did not want a particular man's child. 'It had to go,' says Rita firmly, recalling an accidental pregnancy in the 1960s. Later she married and happily had a family by a man she loved. 'Sex was in the air in the 1960s, somehow. At my most active, sometimes it was two or three men a day.'

Where casual partners were concerned, there was no question of continuing a pregnancy. Mary, a student from Liverpool, remembers trudging to London and, without knowing anyone, setting about finding an abortionist in the days when it was still illegal but practised by those who knew how. After much investigation, and borrowing the necessary 150 guineas, she got the abortion. 'I would have died rather than continue that pregnancy – I didn't care for the man.'

Thus, where the man is repudiated and the abortion very actively sought, there is rarely much regret. Ironically, it may have been psychologically easier (if practically more difficult) in the days when abortion was harder to get. 'If you question a woman's request for an abortion, she will usually immediately start giving you reasons why she *must* have an abortion,' says an experienced gynaecologist. 'If you say, you can have an abortion whenever you want one – she becomes reflective and starts to ask herself whether she does really want one.' It seems to me that women born into an age when abortion is legal are more prone to ambivalence, anyway, than women who remember putting up a fight for an abortion. And women openly offered an abortion will sometimes recoil from the idea, even if they had been entertaining it.

Is there an identifiable group of women who *are* hurt by abortion? Of course, again, it always depends upon the individual woman; women with a strong maternal instinct that has not been fulfilled (and each person's definition of maternal fulfilment is different, too) do seem wounded by the experience.

Women who want a child but who feel forced or pressured into an abortion decision by the man's reluctance to be a father may feel doubly wounded – both by the loss of the baby and by the man's rejection. Janet was twenty-five years old, working in her parents' business in Nottingham, when she became pregnant. She is quite a sensible and down-to-earth person, but she had been involved with a married man for over three years. 'When I first found out I was pregnant, I was leaping up and down: I thought – lovely, a sort of dreamy world. I was thinking, we'll get married, live in a cottage in the country. It will be absolutely super.' Then her lover put a stop to her dreams. He loved her, but he did not intend to leave his wife. He advised her, gently but firmly, that abortion would be the best solution; and accordingly, she had the abortion. She was 'fine', after it, and did not suffer any real depression or regret, though it was clear that the memory of it brought back sadness. But she did not want the baby on its own. 'It was the three of us I wanted. Him and me and the baby, not the baby alone.' After the abortion, the relationship continued, though in the end she felt it was doomed and they began to drift apart. It is not unusual for a relationship to break up after an abortion in these circumstances. An abortion can be a vote of no-confidence in the future. And although Janet had no strong sense of misgiving about the abortion itself, it must have remained significant for her, because she continued to observe the would-be birthday of the child, by taking a quiet walk in the country and scattering flowers in a private ritual.

There is a growing body of opinion that more mourning rituals should be available for women who need to mourn either an abortion or a miscarriage. The worst thing that society can do, write the authors Friedman and Gradstein on miscarriage, 'is to deny a woman her sense of personal loss of a real human being'. With abortion the situation is more complicated because the woman may only perceive the child as a 'real human being' if she wanted it. If the woman positively desires the child, it is 'real' from the start, and its loss is mourned as such; if the woman does not want the child, or is not certain, she may not acknowledge it as a human being, or wish it to be acknowledged as such. There is good scientific evidence that life begins at conception, or at the very least, at fertilization, but the mother's recognition of a child's life may depend on many other factors. Women who are wary of miscarriage (because they have miscarried in the past, possibly) often do not allow themselves to believe that the baby is 'real' until the pregnancy is safely established. But again, there is ambivalence even in pregnancies that are doomed. It is not unusual for a woman who plans to have an abortion to leave off smoking and drinking alcohol for the few weeks that she is pregnant; she may be planning to terminate the pregnancy, but she still does not want to harm the foetus while it lives. Curiously, the stage at which abortion is carried out is not something that is much dwelt upon. It seems that every woman would draw the line for abortion just beyond the point she had her. Those who terminate at six weeks say they would not have wished the pregnancy to proceed beyond eight weeks, and so on.

Ambivalence nearly always arises when the woman herself simply has mixed feelings about continuing the pregnancy. Many women altruistically decide on abortion because they consider it the best thing under the circumstances, though it is not their heart's choice. 'I have had two abortions, the first one was out of common sense,' writes a woman in the hotel business. 'My husband and I both had seasonal jobs and were six months in England and six months on the Continent. There was never time to settle down. A few years later, I was pregnant for the second time. When I told my mother, she was most upset. According to her, my husband was now too old and he wasn't earning enough to give a child a decent start in life. It was a difficult time generally. My grandmother was dying, and to complicate matters we had to put down the family dog. Circumstances seemed to conspire against us. To cut a long story short, I had the second abortion because life already seemed so complicated. The abortion itself was nothing and I was all right immediately afterwards. But then, as time went by, resentment began to set in. I quarrelled with my mother, argued with my husband – I took my mistake out on the rest of the world. Two and half years have passed since, and there is still anger but most of all, every day, grief. I am not maternal, but I know that I should have had that baby. My marriage is now non-existent and I feel the years passing me by. It is very unlikely that I will now have a baby to call my own. I am thirty-nine years old. I feel suicidal at times . . . People envy me because I look young and am not short of possessions but they don't realize the hurt I feel inside.'

These are the women, indeed, for whom abortion does represent a great loss: the women who have had an abortion for the sake of others, because of outside pressures, because it seemed 'sensible' at the time. Women should perhaps be told that the best time to have a baby is when their grandmother is sick – one loss should not generate another, one loss deserves compensation by another. There is an old superstition, an old wives' tale no doubt, that for every death in the family there is a birth. It may be worth considering. Life is indeed a cycle of events and perhaps we need to compensate death by new life. It is not so far-fetched.

Counselling can, and should, help women who are ambivalent to resolve their feelings; and the woman who is not certain about having an abortion, even if it seems the most 'sensible' thing in the world, should be supported towards continuing the pregnancy. Counsellors are trained to be non-judgemental, and the best counsellors are; instead they help to bring out the woman's own feelings. At the Pregnancy Advisory Service (PAS), the abortion agency, counsellors say that there are two 'warning bells' which alert them to the possibility that a woman does not *really* want an abortion. One is when the woman persistently uses the word 'baby' when speaking about her pregnancy. The second is when she is curious to know what the sex of the child might be. Both of these indicate that the woman may not truly want an abortion. The woman who is uncertain about her own feelings is at risk of feeling hurt by abortion, and also most likely to have a repeat pregnancy, which is the most usual form of post-abortion consolation.

A lot may also depend upon what happens to a woman subsequently. Sometimes an abortion passes off without much effect, and the woman settles in to motherhood a few years later. Sometimes, the abortion is not really 'squared' in the woman's psyche until after another child is born. This is how it was for Anna, a student, who became pregnant on a ski-ing holiday in Switzerland. It was a holiday romance. She didn't see how she could have the baby and came back to England and quickly had a termination. But a year later she became pregnant, semi-deliberately, by an old boyfriend. 'The abortion had been a kind of dry run. I knew I couldn't have that child, but it awakened my basic desire to have another child.' She continued with the second pregnancy and became a very happy single mother.

Others are not so lucky. A Swedish woman, a diplomat, conceived after a passionate affair with an African diplomat. 'I would have loved to have had the baby but it really was not possible in my job. I always hoped there would be another chance. But there never was.' She never got pregnant again. She was a gentle person, and had 'adjusted' quite well to her situation; yet had remained rather wistful on the subject of abortion. She never married.

Some reactions may come many years later. A woman who had had one child but aborted a second pregnancy because times were hard and she and her husband were fairly poor, forgot about the abortion for many years. Then her only child died at the age of seventeen in a road accident. From the moment he died, she began to regret the second abortion, and started to feel deep remorse. Although not religious she began to feel that the death of her son was a 'punishment' for the abortion carried out fifteen years previously. She also very much wished that she had had a second child as a consolation. It is pointless to accuse people of not being 'rational' in these circumstances, for feelings are not rational.

One of the ways in which the Japanese – a high-abortion society since 1945 – deal with these feelings is to institutionalize ritual mourning. Couples who have abortions place small dolls at a Buddhist shrine as a memorial to the aborted baby. The dolls are inscribed with little messages such as 'Please forgive your bad Mummy and Daddy' or 'We will never forget you'. Couples may go on visiting these temples for years and offer up gifts. Buddhist thinking has it that the spirit of an unborn or stillborn baby returns to haunt the parents unless appeased by prayers and presents. Superstition – or good therapy?

It might be argued that in the over-intellectual approach to abortion experience in the West, we could benefit from such rituals. Occasionally, even a woman who has been certain that she had wanted an abortion undergoes the experience of the 'phantom child'. Jean Saint, a woman who had an abortion in the 1960s just before it became legal, and was certain at the time that she wanted the abortion, nevertheless had visitations from the phantom child. 'I'm not remorseful or regretful about the abortion,' she said, speaking on BBC1's 'Panorama' in February 1980. 'I just felt absolutely relieved, tremendously relieved, and I still do. The only thing is that I've got this strange thing that I've always thought of the child as being a boy, and a blond boy at that, and I occasionally think that he'd be thirteen by now, and I can sort of see him.' Sometimes he just comes and looks over her shoulder – a blond boy growing with the years.

A Christian psychologist specializing in healing therapy, Dr Kenneth McAll, has been helping women come to terms with their abortion experiences for years.[8] Many disturbed women, he found, had never acknowledged lost or aborted babies, and in 'recognizing' them they often rid themselves of troubled feelings. Similarly, in the United States a group of Christian women who have had abortions have been able to work through their feelings of loss by consigning the baby to God, 'safe in the arms of Jesus'. They go through a ritual of naming the baby, and of a process of 'giving' the child to the spiritual world. In Britain, some of the agencies now offer post-abortion counselling, as do some women's therapy centres.[9]

Perhaps the most curious case I came across of this need to 'acknowledge' abortion was that of Ruth, a woman with three daughters in a visibly good marriage. She had had an illegal abortion in 1967, just before the law changed. She was studying zoology at the time. Eleven weeks pregnant, a medical student procured her abortion by injecting a soapy liquid into the cervix with a catheter. He told her to go home and wait for a miscarriage. She did so. Presently, she passed a very small foetus into the toilet and fished it out. Being of a scientific frame of mind, she took the foetus and preserved it in formaldehyde. Afterwards, she married and had her three children, but she always kept this foetus with her, preserved in the jar of formaldehyde. 'Each time we move house, I mean to throw it out, but each time I hang on to it.' She keeps it in the attic and calls it 'Fred'. 'It's funny. I can't quite bring myself to say goodbye. Fred seems to stay with me.' She was not disturbed by the presence of Fred; on the contrary, she rather liked having him with her. By any medical and social measure, Ruth was a woman who had adjusted very well to abortion. But she still couldn't quite let go of Fred.

Women's reactions to abortion are as complicated as individual people are. None of the social studies is trustworthy in that none of them addresses itself to the problem of the individual woman. There is no evidence that women are psychologically distressed by abortion and much evidence that abortion is an event which passes off without sequel in many women's lives. There is also no evidence that women are not psychologically distressed and may not feel that distress for years beyond the limitations of the studies carried out.

When Gina Newson was preparing her programme for Channel Four she happened upon a woman who was exceptionally serene about abortion. The woman was, indeed, almost a model of positive reaction. She had two children and did not want any more. She had very nearly forgotten about the abortion. To oblige Gina Newson she took out an old diary to check the details. 'Took the children to school,' she had noted. 'Left the car in the garage. Checked into clinic for TOP' (termination of pregnancy). As she reviewed these banal events in her well-organized agenda, all of no consequence, suddenly tears began to fall. And then she cried a lot.

Nobody knows what the consequences of abortion are. Sometimes, that includes the woman whom it most concerns.

REFERENCES

1. Edited by Jane E. Hodgson. (For full details of all books and articles referred to or quoted from in the text, see Bibliography, page 303).

2. Potts, Diggory and Peel.

3. Figures for the death and serious complication rate among women undergoing abortion have tended to fall progressively as antibiotics and other medical knowledge have increased. Death is now down to two women per 100,000 abortions in some areas. But the private sector seems to be safer than the National Health: women had 42 per cent less risk of complications when treated privately than when aborted under

the NHS according to a study by the Royal Colleges of General Practitioners and of Obstetricians and Gynaecologists published in April 1985. Patients also tended to stay longer in NHS hospitals, which increases exposure to infection (and incidentally costs the taxpayer more, too).

4. Christopher Naylor, Consultant at the Middlesex Hospital, London, wrote in *General Practitioner* on 11 May 1979: 'Morbidity is . . . difficult to quantify as accurate incidence is difficult to establish, but most authorities would accept a morbidity rate of between 5 and 15 per cent.' Mrs Wendy Savage in the *British Journal of Hospital Medicine*, October 1982, puts it at between 5 and 10 per cent.

5. *The Lancet*, 28 May 1983, reported that 'cervical injury is one of the most frequent complications of suction curettage abortion', especially to teenagers. On 3 September 1983 it carried another article warning gynaecologists of the danger of damaging the cervix of young girls.

6. *British Medical Journal*, 16 May 1981.

7. 'Most investigations do not look deeply into the emotional and spiritual changes in the woman, but simply look for frank psychiatric disease,' writes Dr Andrew Stanway in *A Dictionary of Operations* (Paladin, 1981) in an attempt to clarify the many different findings that studies have come up with. Thus the medical handbook edited by Jane Hodgson cites studies which show that abortion contributes to the prevention of mental illness, by reducing post-partum psychosis, and by reducing population pressure which 'adversely influences human well-being' (page 185). Furthermore, this publication refers to claims that 'where no moral or religious objections exist, even if the legal codes are restrictive, psychological or guilt reactions to abortion are practically unknown'. Yet there are the Japanese studies cited by Callahan (pages 260–61), noting the strong degree of 'mixed feelings' in a culture where abortion is widely accepted. Stanway mentions the Norwegian study which showed that just over 82 per cent of women who were aborted were afterwards pleased. But Gardner (page 266) tells us of other studies where 84 per cent of women refused an abortion were afterwards glad they had the baby. There have been studies which showed that women refused abortions either sought them illegally or their children when born, showed a higher rate of delinquency and maladjustment. However, there are many factors which might be said to contribute to delinquency – including divorce, for example – that complicate the picture, since many so-called 'unwanted' children are also the children of parents who divorce. Suicide, or threatened suicide, was formerly looked on as a 'psychiatric' indication for abortion, but it is now widely accepted that this was a sham – and pregnant women tend to commit suicide less than non-pregnant women.

8. Kenneth McAll and his wife Frances, who practise as doctors in Hampshire, have published in *The Lancet* (16 August 1980) descriptions of how he helped young women out of anorexia nervosa through 'ritual mourning' of an earlier abortion.

9. Post-abortion counselling is available through the Women's Therapy Centre, 6 Manor Gardens, London N7, tel: 01-263 6200. Life, which is against abortion, nevertheless offers professional and non-judgemental post-abortion counselling. Their address is 118 Warwick Street, Leamington Spa, tel: 0926-21587. In January 1986, a new telephone service started for women needing post-abortion support, called Anonymous Counselling, at 01-350 2229.

2

WHY WOMEN CHOOSE ABORTION

'Request for termination arises because the pregnant woman does not want or is persuaded not to want her child.' – Derek Gill, *Illegitimacy, Sexuality and the Status of Women*

'Not all unplanned pregnancies are undesired, nor do they necessarily produce unwanted children. Studies . . . have suggested that whereas possibly a majority of women who have not first planned to conceive experience feelings of grief or anger when they become pregnant, less than one in five remains disappointed and unaccepting throughout the course of the pregnancy.' – Candida Petersen, *Should We Have a Baby?*

'No woman knows whether she wants an abortion until she has had one.' – Prof. Peter Huntingford

'Abortion is usually an altruistic decision.' – Potts et al., *Abortion*

During the writing of this book, I missed a menstrual period, and realized that there was a chance that I might be pregnant.

As soon as the thought came to me, my mind was filled with a score of contradictory feelings. It is often satisfying for a woman to reflect on the fact that her fertility is still in working order. Aged thirty-nine, with sons aged nine and five, I would have loved another child. Indeed, passing prams with babies, seeing pictures of babies, filled me with a sense of yearning and a longing to hold a baby of my own again. It is not such an unusual sensation among women of my age, if my own friends are anything to judge by. 'Polly is pregnant again,' a mutual friend, who had herself chosen to limit her own family, wrote to me. 'I'm *green* with envy.'

And yet, against this instinctive maternal desire were set a hundred anxieties that clouded my imagination. My husband would be extremely depressed at the thought of a pregnancy; he had said to me once, in an unguarded moment, 'If you ever became pregnant again, I would die.' Actually, he would not die; he would accept it, and be kind and patient and, in the end, doting and sentimental; but it would be a major worry, a major problem. I understood perfectly the women who had said to me: 'I'd love to have had another child, but I couldn't possibly *impose* it on my husband.' Imposing on husbands who see themselves as already long-suffering is a worry with wives; women, notoriously, do not like to impose. 'I'd love to have had that baby,' the wife of an immensely rich accountant told me, describing her decision to have an abortion with the third pregnancy, 'but I *couldn't* have done it to him. It would have broken up the marriage.' And indeed, 'he' never even knew about the pregnancy or the abortion. When I visited her several years later, she was looking after the toddler son of a neighbour: a millionairess turned child-minder. Abortions can leave a gap that a woman seeks to fill in other ways, sometimes without even being aware that she is doing so.

In contemplating a possible pregnancy, fear of imposing on a husband who had always been very understanding was foremost in my mind. And then came other worries. How would I continue to work with *three* children? Two are just about manageable – especially once they come to school age – but a baby? As a self-employed journalist, maternity leave was out of the question. How would the continuous flow of bills be met without my income? What would my mother say? Even as a devout Irish Catholic, her practical anxieties would be overriding. She would be sleepless with worry over how I would *manage*. What would my mother-in-law say? She, similarly, would feel it was an extra responsibility that we would find very difficult – and at our respective ages, too (my husband is fifty-three). Older mothers, and grandmothers, are often primarily concerned with the practical aspects of survival. Once babies are born, the maternal instinct of protectiveness usually moves into top gear but, before that, practicalities are the main concern. I even wondered what the neighbours would say. In London, children are generally regarded as a nuisance: noisy, not very clean, troublesome.

And then, at the age of thirty-nine, there was a one in fifty chance that I would have a handicapped child. As a Catholic, I did not feel that I could accept an amniocentesis test with a view to abortion; even women who accept abortion in theory suffer depression at aborting a baby which has been diagnosed as defective. To consider abortion at twenty weeks would – I know myself well enough to know – be impossible for me, for reasons of conscience. So I would have to take the risk, and face the consequences, of bearing a handicapped child.

In considering all these anxieties, I was sick with apprehension as I waited to do a pregnancy test. Even a wanted pregnancy can be very frightening because of the way in which a woman suddenly feels a prisoner of her own body, as the body itself is colonized by an 'outside' force. I remembered the thirty-four-year-old woman who had had three abortions. In each case, she had let the pregnancy run on until the end of the first trimester – always deeply ambivalent about whether or not she wanted the child. In a sense, she did want the child: she just could not bear the feeling of being pregnant. She felt physically sick all the time, and psychologically as though an alien was gradually invading her body. In a recent horror film, *Alien*, a dreadful little creature penetrates the body of the character played by John Hurt, takes him over and eventually bursts out of his stomach, killing him. This is the image of pregnancy that haunts women who feel hostility towards it. 'I'd been in control of my body for thirty years – now this *thing* was taking it over, altering every cell,' she said. Each time she tried to endure the pregnancy for as long as she felt bearable. Each time she felt insufferably imprisoned. Each time she had an abortion. Yet she wanted a child sufficiently to keep getting pregnant.

There is an inevitability about pregnancy which can be extraordinarily frightening. It feels as if one is held captive by some force of nature. Even when one desperately wants a child, the prospect can be terrifying. It can be especially daunting for women who feel intellectually in control of their bodies; it can be very repulsive for a woman who is proud of her figure. 'I love children,' a doctor's wife from Co. Tipperary told me. 'We had two and we're greatly looking forward to another. But I *hate* being pregnant. I hate what it does to my figure. I hate looking like the backside of a bus. I hate being asexual – and don't tell me that pregnant women can be sexy, because that is just not the way I feel. I hate being cow-like. Pictures of pretty girls drive me crazy when I look like a prize elephant.' She was an attractive young woman, seemed happily married and pleased to be a mother; but I daresay given a different cultural background and different opportunities, a woman with such a strong physical dislike of pregnancy might have chosen not to become pregnant. On the other hand, the fact that she could grit her teeth and endure the pregnancy and feel perfectly all right once it was all over also shows that abortion is not the only solution for women who do not physically like the condition.

I happen not to share these feelings: I love being pregnant. When I am, I feel well, cheerful and strong. My arthritis of the hip joint dramatically improves during pregnancy because of hormonal changes. The old wives' tale that pregnancy cures other ills is, for me, quite accurate. And my family is very kind, they always rally round, and a baby can be managed – where there is a will, there is a way, as it were. There are also many sweet friends who lend a hand. Yet even I, with so many reasons to welcome a pregnancy, felt anxious and apprehensive as I purchased a pregnancy test. At that moment, I could easily identify with those women I had seen turn up at abortion clinics who felt they could not go through with a pregnancy. Even I, completely committed to the moral rights of the unborn child, trembled as I wondered what the result would be. My husband was abroad, and I passed a sleepless night before carrying out that test. Would it, wouldn't it . . . I hoped desperately that I would be pregnant – oh, how I longed for it to be positive. And yet I worried dreadfully about what I would do, how I would cope, if it were . . .

As things turned out, I was not pregnant. When the test clearly showed a negative result, I was crestfallen and dreadfully disappointed.

Yet it was, in many respects, a salutary experience, because it reminded me of something which one can easily forget in this matter of abortion: how complicated, ambivalent and diffused our feelings really are about pregnancy; how endless the various social and economic pressures which come to bear on a matter deemed to be one of 'personal choice'; how a woman must agonize before she can sort out what she truly thinks.

'I could not decide easily,' recalled a Hampshire woman, aged twenty-five when she found herself pregnant. 'One day it was yes, I will have the baby and we will marry; another day it was no, and we won't marry; and yet another day it was yes I'll have the baby even if I don't marry.' The putative father was also uncertain: he was twenty-eight at the time and they had only been together for about six months. 'We were lovers and greatly engrossed with each other.' In such a relationship – where the couple has not been together very long, and is still at the intense phase of what is in essence a modern courtship – a baby is certainly an intrusion. This woman also felt 'silly' about having become pregnant by accident because she was a senior nurse and she felt she should have known better. In her indecisive frame of mind she visited her doctor, and it was his attitude that clinched the decision for her.

'My GP was great. I cried and he made me laugh by saying that many couples start married life with pregnancy and that if I was going to have a baby it was time I started. He asked me how the father felt and I cried again. But deep down, then, I knew I could not have an abortion and would have to keep the baby no matter what.' She went ahead. They got married, and had a daughter who is 'the most wonderful, beautiful creature on this earth'. For the woman, the child was simply the best thing that had ever happened to her and she has never regretted her decision – but the marriage was not successful. The man was not ready for fatherhood, resented the pregnancy and has acted sullenly ever since.

For those who might say that the woman was at fault in continuing a pregnancy when the man was clearly against it, consider a contrasting story. A woman from west Glamorgan was pregnant in very similar circumstances. 'I went ahead and had the abortion and later married the man. Unfortunately, the marriage was not a success, and I felt a deep resentment against him when I was told that I was one of the few who, following an abortion, would never bear a child. This was the main reason for the failure of the relationship.'

Have a child against a man's wishes and risk losing the man? Abort a pregnancy to please a man and risk the resentment that may fester for years? Women often wrestle with such dilemmas when faced with an unexpected pregnancy. There are women who go ahead with the pregnancy despite the hesitation or the outright hostility of the putative father; in some cases, the child exacerbates the differences in the relationship; in others, the child proves eventually to be a healing force. 'I had been going out with a man for eighteen months whom I loved more than anything in the world,' wrote a woman from Northampton to me. 'In 1973, I found, to my shock, that I was three months pregnant. I always said that I never wanted children (the screaming brats, I used to call them). I told my boyfriend and he said he was not ready to get married or to be tied to a child . . . I did not know what to do. I had no family, I lived on my own and worked as a typist. I had considered abortion, that would have been the easy solution, but then I thought, "This is a living being" and when I thought that I would be terminating the life of an innocent child that was conceived out of love, I could not bring myself to do it.' The woman was aged twenty-two, and continued the pregnancy through 'some rough times'. She had a baby daughter – 'and I instantly fell in love with her. My boyfriend still came round to see me regularly and at first ignored the baby . . . I was always very loving towards him and I never forced the child on him, but gradually and very slowly he started to take an interest in her. When at the age of six months she became very poorly with a bad cold, he suddenly seemed quite concerned for her welfare.' Little by little, his feelings grew, and two years later the couple married. Now, ten years later, they have five children and are an extremely happy family.

Yet in other cases, the man never relents, and continues to refuse to see his child, which greatly hurts both child and mother.

We often speak of 'choice' as though it were an abstract concept, something which can be arrived at after theoretical debate in a social, economic, and emotional vacuum. But life is never quite as simple as that. People make choices based on all sorts of reasons, and feel forced into choices for all sorts of reasons, too. Contraception does fail – at the Marie Stopes Clinic there was a woman who got pregnant despite using in succession the mini-Pill, the coil, the diaphragm and the condom. And if a woman honestly wants to analyse whether or not she wishes to continue a pregnancy, she might discover more about her motives if she asks herself truthfully if she half-deliberately ran the risk of becoming pregnant; and if so, why. Many women do admit to throwing caution to the wind and inviting an unwanted pregnancy.

This is a complex area because a woman may wish to be pregnant without wanting to have a child; and a woman may wish to have a child without wanting to be pregnant.

The Harley Street gynaecologist Alan Rogers was told by one patient that the contraceptive she used was 'Intention'. What did she mean? 'Well, I know when I intend to be pregnant, and I know when I don't intend to be pregnant. It has always worked.' But she was pregnant now, and was requesting an abortion; what had gone wrong? 'Well, at the time of conception, I intended to be pregnant. But now that I am pregnant, I don't intend to be.' The doctor agreed to the abortion and arranged it. What sort of contraception would she use afterwards, he enquired? 'Oh, I shall go back to "Intention",' she replied. This was what she was happy with and he left her to it.

And people *do* change their minds about these matters. At the Hammersmith Hospital in west London a woman with three children applied for a sterilization. After appropriate counselling she had the operation, feeling quite sure she did not want any more children. A year later she returned, having changed her mind: she now wanted the operation reversed. With great skill, Dr Robert Winston's team was able to reverse the sterilization so that the woman could conceive again, which she duly did. Then she changed her mind yet again; she returned to say that she did not want a child after all – she now wanted an abortion, which she had.

People have many different reasons for making an abortion decision, in short. Obviously, for a large number of individuals, the considerations are practical. Dr Carol Gilligan, an American academic who has studied abortion decision-making in women, says that for most women the considerations *are* practical. Whether they can reasonably support the child and whether their partner will be a willing father are the two practical questions that are uppermost. But even that is relative. An acceptable level of economic support for one person is the breadline for another. I have come across a woman with five children living on social security who decided that, with a bit of sacrifice and careful economic management, she could reasonably support a sixth. On the other hand, public school fees are the reasons for some abortions: journalist

Joyce Hopkirk has written of couples who terminate a third pregnancy because while they could just about manage two boys at Eton, they could not pay for a third. Everything is relative, in this as in all other matters.

A mother of three, faced with a fourth pregnancy, was told by her own mother: 'You're mad to have another baby. Why, there won't be room in the *car* for another child.' Consumer society tends to place the child within the context of acquisitions that one can afford – the deep freeze, the car, the foreign holiday, the 1.8 children – and advertising everywhere reinforces the image of the perfect consumer family with its perfectly planned, carefully controlled two children who fit in with all the other commodities. People, however, do not always fit neatly into the categories assigned to them. One woman I knew deliberately had a third baby because she hated the idea of having 'a TV family – one boy, one girl, in correct order and with proper spacing' – as, by chance, she had already had. There had to be a way of hitting back at prescribed consumerism, she figured, and it was to have another baby.

Not that one should discount the real problems of economic necessity. We know that many women in the past, particularly during the hardships of the 1930s, felt driven to criminal abortion because having a fourth or a fifth child simply meant destitution. Other mothers heroically managed, though with enormous sacrifices: I have interviewed a woman in Dublin who brought ten children up on 16 shillings a week (about £18 in today's values). She had twelve children, but two died of childhood illnesses. Life certainly would have entailed less suffering for her if she had had fewer children – though I feel obliged to add that with her ten children now settled and prospering, she now enjoys a happy old age.

Worldwide, the most common reasons for abortion are economic ones. Many women have abortions – especially in poor countries simply because they have too many children. In the developed world, however, this is less usually the reason for abortion – two-thirds of American women who present for abortion have no children at all and are not married. But economics still play a part. The most common candidates for abortion, in the developed world, are the first and third pregnancies; the first pregnancy where a young woman has become pregnant by accident, usually outside or prior to marriage; the third pregnancy where the couple has decided that two children are all they can afford, or that a third would interfere with the wife's ability to earn money. As women grow older, they become more skilled at using contraception, and fertility declines anyway, so fourth and fifth unwanted pregnancies occur less often.

Objectively, it is becoming more and more expensive to raise a child. By 1977, it was already reckoned to be $54,000 from pregnancy test to high school graduation. Modern children are dependent on their parents for longer than ever before. In the seventeenth century, the average age for children to leave home was fifteen – they went into apprenticeships, military training, domestic service or monasteries. Today, a quarter of all French offspring are still living with their parents at the age of twenty-five, and the cries of despair from mothers about youngsters who just will not leave home are heard throughout the land. Unemployment, of course, and the high cost of accommodation has made things worse. Children today are a very long-term economic commitment the benefits of which are purely emotional; financially, a child is a liability. On the other hand, in traditional agricultural societies a child was not a liability but an asset. On farms, even young children could provide an extra pair of hands, and as children grew up and parents grew old, offspring justified their existence by helping to support elderly parents, and by giving their parents social status and occupation in old age. This is still the case in India. Indeed, possibly one of the reasons why abortion, whether legal or illegal, has not been characteristic of agricultural societies is that children have been easier to raise in the countryside and were welcome there for economic and dynastic reasons. Moreover, food was always more accessible in the country: the Dublin mother with ten children recalled that having cousins in the country was indispensable, for they could always be counted upon to send food. Leaving aside famines or crop failures, another mouth to feed has always seemed less difficult in rural areas than in towns.

But today, even in agricultural societies in the developed world (Italy, France, Ireland) a child has become, from a financial viewpoint, a liability. In old age, parents today are more likely to be giving money to their grown offspring, than to be financially supported by them (many grandparents help to pay for education of grandchildren, for instance). An Australian guide for couples thinking of embarking on parenthood, *Should We Have a Baby?* (by Candida Peterson) compared the arrival of a child with 'an earthquake' in the life of an average couple. The cost was gigantic, the demands terrific, the strain on marriage enormous and nothing would ever be the same again. When one considers what is entailed in having a baby, the responsibility indeed seems huge. 'Just one look at the Mothercare catalogue decided me for years to come,' said a twenty-eight-year-old teacher. 'I could see immediately that we couldn't possibly proceed with parenthood at the moment – not while my husband is still studying. We just couldn't manage.' It seems perhaps unfair to say that the Mothercare catalogue was the cause of the abortion which followed: Mothercare, above all, must be in favour of the production of babies, one might think. But Mothercare is part of consumerism, and it is 'quality of life' which counts in the consumer society.

Not very long ago a baby was deemed to need nothing except food and clothing (only actual hunger was a reason not to have another child in the 1930s). But an inventory for a modern baby might read: carrycot with wheels, buggy, baby bath, plastic changing mat, pram harness, bouncing chair, sterilizing container and bottles, sterilizing pills, disposable nappies, baby car-seat, feeding chair, two dozen babygrow suits, four sets of outer clothes, one dozen vests, half a dozen cardigans, bibs, tights, nightclothes, blankets, sheets, cot, toys, toilet requisites, playpen, rainwear for buggy – and that is only the start! The man who created Mothercare became successful by realizing that as the birth-rate fell, people would be able to have higher standards for the smaller families they did beget.

In sum, practical and material considerations are important; and they are seen in many different perspectives.

One woman with two children decided against continuing a pregnancy (she had got pregnant while using the coil, so there had been no subconscious exposure to pregnancy) because her husband was having a particularly hard time at work, and she felt the material back-up would not be available for her to keep the family together. He needed her, the family needed her income, another child would bring tension and practical difficulties. She was sad to terminate, but resolved that it was the sensible decision; she had the abortion, and felt it was the right thing to do. Two years later she became pregnant again, and by this time, things had improved. Her husband's position at work was greatly enhanced, their children were settled in school, so she continued this pregnancy, because her practical and economic circumstances had altered.

But a parallel situation proved more distressing. Another couple had two children. He was a musician, she worked as a laboratory assistant. When faced with a third pregnancy, they were distraught, and felt that they just could not cope. So the woman had an abortion, but the couple were very upset by it, although neither of them was religious or had strong views about abortion. Fortunately, the woman was able to conceive again. They not only managed to cope with a third child – they coped better, because they were both in a more positive state of mind. People are different.

Economic survival is always a consideration, and it takes different forms. It can be jobs; it can be housing; it can be space (many parents today feel, for example, that a child has a right to room). Economic pressure can come from other people. A woman who was told by her boss that she was a ninny to get pregnant just when promotion was within her grasp felt very tempted to terminate her pregnancy. A career woman who had a series of disasters with nannies (one committed suicide, one was in trouble with the police for drug offences) was crestfallen to think that she had to start nanny-hunting all over again, just when her older children were no longer in need of nannies. Women are often under enormous strain in raising a family, maintaining a job, running a home. For a woman living in a block of flats where the lift has broken, a third or fourth pregnancy can seem like the prescription for a nervous breakdown. Although in the UK the welfare state has greatly alleviated extremes of poverty, the extended family has gone, and some mothers are at their wits' end as far as child-care is concerned. What connotes economic survival is a relative matter, and it is difficult for one person to judge what are acceptable standards for another. Diane Munday, founder of the largest abortion charity, the BPAS, says that 'every woman knows her own limit' as a mother. Nevertheless, the limits may still be set by other people or circumstances.

Abortion is chosen, of course, for reasons other than economic ones. The explanation of why rape is such a compelling argument for abortion is first that the woman has had no choice whatsoever if conception occurs. With normal conception, the woman has had a voluntary act of intercourse and, with the man, bears a responsibility for the consequences. When conception is voluntary a woman can hardly argue that she is 'forced to have a pregnancy'. And secondly, the idea of bearing the child of a rapist is in most cases repellent. This does not mean that the abortion is without distress: 'It was the rapist's baby she didn't want to bear,' said a counsellor who had seen a woman through just such a situation, 'but you see it was *her* baby too.'

However, rape is, mercifully, statistically rare, and conception from rape rarer still. The reasons are manifold. One study (*New England Journal of Medicine*, vol. 297, 1977), showed that there is often no sperm deposit in the vagina. *Sexual Medicine Today*, January 1978 showed 58 per cent 'sexual dysfunction' which made sperm ineffective. Where hormone treatment is administered after rape, pregnancy is almost unknown.

In a less dramatic situation, a woman may simply not wish to bear the child of a particular man she dislikes. A twenty-eight-year-old woman who had emotional rather than moral objections to abortion – she just didn't 'fancy the idea' – nevertheless chose abortion because she 'loathed' the man she had conceived by. To the question of why had she had a relationship with him, one might say that people do not always like the people they go to bed with; or they like them at that particular time and not later. It is not uncommon for a couple to 'expose' themselves to a pregnancy, as the expression goes, just when they are on the point of divorce or separation; it is as if there were some desperate instinct to make one last effort to seal the old partnership. But when conception does take place, in the cold light of day the couple often comes to believe that the marriage or relationship is not a going concern, and abortion is the best decision. It is generally held by marriage-guidance experts that it is disastrous to have a baby in an attempt to paper over the cracks in a disintegrating marriage; the baby exacerbates the problems rather than heals them. It is also generally disastrous to have an abortion in the same situation, for it is the final proof that the relationship has ended, and the abortion becomes a symbolic as well as a literal extinction of life.

For young and for unmarried women, a frequent reason why contraception fails is the 'reconciliation syndrome'. (Birth-control clinics, such as the Brook Advisory Centre, have many such cases.) The young woman will usually be on the Pill, even perhaps the mini-Pill, which requires careful discipline (it must be taken at approximately the same time each day), the relationship then breaks up and the couple parts. The young woman comes off the Pill, since many women do not like taking it 'just in case', and also because most women realize that it is healthy to have a break from it every now and then. Two or three months later, the boyfriend appears once more, and there is a reconciliation, but this time without the protection of the

Pill. The young woman thus becomes pregnant.

Some folks would say that this is what happens in a 'permissive society' – young men and women feeling free to go to bed with one another whenever the fancy takes them; and with such a casual attitude prevailing, it is hardly surprising that there is little motivation to be responsible about pregnancy. It has certainly been well established that teenagers are less stable, more volatile, less reliable about using contraception than older people; the more stable a relationship, the more mature the couple, generally speaking, the more responsible they are towards the whole matter of contraception. But young blood is hot and quick and impatient. Would Romeo and Juliet have paused to use a contraceptive? It is not at all unusual to hear teenagers say that they reject contraception because it is 'unromantic', 'sordid', 'premeditated', that it takes away that feeling of excitement and danger, of being swept along by passion and damn the consequences. Peter Zelles, who has counselled men involved in abortion in Minneapolis, claims, too, that there is a great lack of rites of passage in Western society. Unfortunately, one of the few rites that do remain to mark a passage from childhood to maturity for a young person is that of becoming pregnant, or impregnating someone.

Abortion will often be chosen in these circumstances. Contraception has failed, and behind that failure are further complications concerning emotions, relationships and ambivalence about fertility. Some very young women – by which I mean girls aged seventeen and under – do not always choose abortion in these circumstances however; indeed, they may choose to continue a pregnancy either because they want to, or because they have let the pregnancy drift on until it is too late for an abortion. Younger women tend to present later for abortions because of this problem of 'non-acknowledgement': there is an unrealistic hope that the pregnancy will 'go away' of its own accord. By the same token, the now regular occurrences of new-born babies being abandoned in urban conurbations are usually the consequence of a very young mother who has hidden her pregnancy, given birth secretly – perhaps in a park or a public lavatory – and panicked. Sometimes a younger woman will be pressed into a late abortion by her parents – in this case it is the parents who are panicking – and in abortion clinics it is common to see young girls accompanied by their mothers who have frog-marched their daughters there. This is, it seems to many experienced observers, a very unwise course for a parent to take. Parents (or anyone else) should never force a girl into an abortion: it builds up problems for the future, and quite often invites a repeat pregnancy.

Houses for unmarried expectant mothers (such as those run by Life and Lifeline) contain young women who are continuing a repeat pregnancy. That is to say, their first pregnancy was terminated under duress, and so they seek to heal that wound by actually having a baby.

The reasons for continuing a pregnancy may be as complex as the reasons for terminating it. It is the opinion of many social workers that young women become pregnant to give them a sense of achievement in a world which denies them opportunities for employment or advancement in other ways. It is certain that there is a worldwide correlation between the education and employment of women and the postponement of motherhood; generally speaking, the more educated a woman is, and the better employment available to her, the fewer children she will have and the later she will beget them. And the less educated she is, the sooner she will commence motherhood.

Peer-group pressure can be a considerable factor in what choice is made finally. It has been reckoned that a woman who presents for abortion has already been unofficially 'counselled' by about five people, sometimes including a partner but most usually by friends. And what her friends say and do can be very important indeed.

'I just didn't know anyone with babies,' explained a woman in her late twenties. 'All my friends were very liberated career women who were then deliberately childless. Three years later, they all seemed to have babies – but not when I was pregnant.' A woman who had an abortion in the mid-1970s recalls that everyone she knew was having abortions. 'One friend was particularly good. She had recently had an abortion herself, and really nannied me along. Looking back, I now wonder if in some curious way she wanted me to have an abortion because she had had one. I don't mean this maliciously; I think her help was genuinely well-intended, but human nature being what it is, there is always this pressure to make you conform: the married want you to be married, the divorced want you to be divorced. Mothers want you to have babies, abortees want you to have an abortion.' Similar pressures can happen in reverse. At a high school in the English Midlands in June 1985, no fewer than seven girls in the fifth and sixth forms were having babies. One schoolgirl told *Daily Mail* writer Sara Barrett: 'It's like an epidemic.' Another girl said: 'We know all about contraception. We all started fooling around quite young – about twelve.' Yet none of the girls that Sara Barrett spoke to would consider abortion. Older people at the school gave many different reasons for the number of pregnancies, ranging from girls being denied the Pill because of the Gillick ruling that under-sixteens could not get contraception without their parents' permission – to the lack of entertainment available in the Birmingham area. They omitted an obvious element: it is the *fashion* among teenage girls to get pregnant. The majority of mothers under the age of twenty are now single mothers. Obviously, peer-group pressure has only a limited application, but it is not to be discounted, especially among the young who like to do what their friends do. Example also plays some part; every time a member of the royal family has a baby, the birth-control campaign groups become anxious lest that example prove to be too influential.

We live in social groups and the attitudes of society naturally influence our behaviour. In the past, the stigma of illegitimacy was one reason given by women for fearing an out-of-wedlock pregnancy – and the stigma certainly served to keep women virgins for much longer. There is still a sense of mortification for women in some societies, but today it is no longer the overriding reason for choosing abortion. A survey done by Life (an anti-abortion organization) in Northern Ireland – a conservative and very intimate society, where there are few secrets from the neighbours – found that only 4 per cent of unmarried mothers felt any lack of social acceptance for them or their children at any stage. For most, the problems were unemployment and financial worries. The Irish Pregnancy Counselling Centre in Belfast, which refers women to England for 'social' abortions (abortion is illegal in Northern Ireland except for strict medical reasons) does not list social disapproval among the reasons for why 500 Ulsterwomen chose abortion – although parental disapproval certainly figured.

Reasons for Considering Abortion	*percentage*
Quality of life for self and family threatened	22
Parental disapproval	18
Too young to care for child	18
Too old to care for child	3
Circumstances strongly unfavourable	13
No relationship with putative father	11
Previous pregnancy ended in abortion – prospect intolerable	8
Others	7

This seems a fair enough general picture of the reasons women give for choosing an optional abortion, although hidden within these headings are many other complex situations.

Among some of the most emotionally wounding abortions are those where a married woman has had an affair with a lover, conceives and knows there is no possible way she can pass off the child as her husband's. 'I shall never forget my dear little unborn child, even though I *knew* I had to have an abortion,' wrote a schoolteacher from the north of England. 'My husband has had a vasectomy, so he would have known I couldn't be pregnant by him. The man I love has to stay with his wife and children because she is in very poor health. We *can't* abandon our responsibilities. I had the abortion, but it broke my heart.' In this case abortion was seen as a remedy for extra-marital conception; according to present-day morality it is more correct to have an abortion under these circumstances than to introduce a cuckoo into the nest, the acceptable remedy among many Victorians and Edwardians. (Abortion, of course, can also be used as a weapon in marriage. One woman chose to abort her husband's child as a punishment for his having had an affair.)

There are different attitudes prevailing here, according to class. The usual interpretation of class morality is that the upper class and the lower class are morally more easy-going: it is the bourgeoisie in between who are rigidly moralistic. The upper classes have behaved badly for a long time; the working classes are more tolerant anyway of bastardy, possibly because for people of no property (I am speaking historically) the values of property and inheritance do not weigh so heavily. Bastardy is, of course, usually seen as a threat to inheritance and property.

A working-class Dublin woman, separated from her husband and living with another man, found herself pregnant by her lover. She already had one child by this lover, and two children by her husband. Her mother advised her to take the boat to Liverpool and have an abortion because although the husband might tolerate *one* bastard, he would be unlikely to tolerate two. The reasoning behind this was that everyone was permitted at least one mistake. The woman accepted her mother's advice and had the pregnancy terminated. Afterwards, she was thoroughly regretful: she loved the man by whom she had conceived the child she had aborted. Moreover, there was a neighbour in the housing estate where she lived who had had four children by four different men and no one seemed to mind very much. The kids were lovely, anyway. Difficult to imagine a single woman with four children by four men being so kindly accepted in the middle-class English suburbs.

Sometimes an abortion can be decided for – or against –

because of a kind of fatalistic approach to pregnancy. At the Marie Stopes Clinic, about one woman in thirty does not turn up to have an abortion she has already arranged. What happens to that woman? It can be an insignificant occurrence which suddenly inspires the woman with the courage to go on with the pregnancy. 'It was a lovely day,' said one would-be patient. 'I was supposed to turn up at Marie Stopes at midday. My boyfriend rang and said, "Let's have lunch – you can always be a bit late." We had a merry, and rather boozy lunch – though I knew I should have been fasting – and I somehow felt terrific. And I somehow just never got to the clinic.' She intended making another appointment but felt embarrassed about having flunked the first one. And what with one thing and another . . . the pregnancy progressed and progressed until she gave birth to a son. She didn't marry the father and she probably wanted to continue the pregnancy anyhow but it was that sunny day and the wine-splashed lunch that tipped the scales. Sometimes women have checked into abortion clinics and felt, as they were being prepared for the operating theatre, that they suddenly didn't want the abortion but have continued with it because they thought it was 'too late' now.

The idea that 'fate' can somehow take over and decide on the course of a termination is not confined to those women who cruise through life letting everyone else make their decisions for them. Two of the best-organized women I have ever met became pregnant because of 'fate': they had used a form of the rhythm method, knowing perfectly well that natural fertility control doesn't work unless it is very carefully organized. Why had they let things drift? Well, you see, everything *else* in their lives was so well-organized and so well-controlled that they wanted there to be one thing left which was spontaneous. At least in bed they could, just for a moment, stop being superwomen, everlastingly in control. Being well-organized, very sensible, rational and strong has its disadvantages: sometimes it's nice to see what nature has up her sleeve.

Another curious case was that of a brilliant woman

academic head of a department at a provincial university who was in her thirties and having an affair with an artist – a moody, melancholic yet pleasing man, married, though not very happily. She used a foam contraceptive, but nevertheless became pregnant. She was at the same time very pleased and very sad. She would have greatly liked to have had the child, but she thought the relationship impossible. So she took herself off to an astrologist and had her horoscope cast. The astrologist was disturbed at what he saw in her future, and warned her to try and avoid an event which might happen 'about eight or nine months from now'. That clinched it: she knew it was a sign that she must have an abortion. So she did. Some eight months later her lover committed suicide. So it may not have been the birth of the child, but the suicide of the man, that the astrologist had presumably foreseen. The woman was, naturally, very distressed, though she stood by her decision, and felt that the suicide of her lover would have been a bad omen for the child anyway. Later, she became obsessively keen to have a child and even considered artificial insemination by donor (AID), though, up to the time of writing (some five years after the original abortion) without success.

What is significant about this case is that it shows how a highly intellectual and rational person can use what some would consider a quirky and superstitious method to help her make a decision about abortion.

Such a decision may, indeed, be arrived at by many different routes. In another case, a forthright and confident Italian woman – an active member of the Communist Party, utterly without hang-ups of an emotional or religious nature and rather dismissive of 'sentimentality' in general – used abortion fairly regularly as a form of birth control. She had a daughter from a first marriage and was married again. She simply didn't like any form of contraception – the Pill made her ill, the IUD made her bleed, the diaphragm was uncomfortable – so she decided that the 'rational' thing to do was to have an abortion whenever she needed one. By her middle thirties she had had 'three or four' abortions, though the pregnancies were getting more infrequent as she got older (fertility begins to decline quite noticeably after the age of thirty-five). But at thirty-seven she became pregnant once again and, as usual, she decided to have the abortion. She arranged it and was talking to her husband about collecting her daughter – now aged thirteen – from school that day, when something suddenly occurred to her: perhaps her daughter was now old enough to be consulted? So she asked the young girl if she would like to have a baby sister or brother. The girl's eyes lit up. 'Oh, Mama,' she said, 'I've been secretly hoping and hoping and *hoping* I might some day have a baby brother or sister. Oh, it would be so wonderful!' The mother cancelled her appointment for the abortion. She continued the pregnancy, had an adorable baby son and, so far as I know, they all lived happily ever after. Yet the mother apparently did not make the decision; her own child did.

Strange and unusual happenings can be interpreted by an undecided woman as a 'sign' of which road she should take. A divorced woman living in Kent and working as a secretary became pregnant from an affair with a man she saw occasionally. She hadn't had children from her marriage and took it that she was probably infertile. Her parents were rather strait-laced, but not at all religious and she was fairly sure they would disapprove of her having an illegitimate child. She had her own house, but she had mortgage commitments, and wasn't sure exactly how she would manage with a baby, although her office was generally friendly and co-operative. She took counselling from the British Pregnancy Advisory Service and she took counselling from Life. Both were very nice to her, she said, but she still couldn't decide. Coming home from work, she used to pass a church. She herself was not religious, but she would sometimes go in and light a candle simply because it made her feel comforted.

One morning she woke up early, just before dawn, and as she sat up in bed she suddenly saw something at the end of her bed. The picture became clear – it was, it seemed to her, a vision of the Virgin Mary, smiling at her warmly and radiantly. In a moment, the apparition dissolved and the woman got up, went to the lavatory, and came back to bed again. When she woke up in the full brightness of the morning she knew that she would continue the pregnancy. 'It was just a feeling,' she said, as so many women say when they suddenly know they are going to continue. And she did, and all was well.

A sign from heaven? Magical thinking? The psychologists would say that this is a classic example of the unconscious mind supplying an answer which the conscious mind cannot come up with. The Virgin Mary is an obvious symbol of motherhood; in lighting the candles in church, the woman had seen statues and pictures of Mary. Perhaps some religious people would not rule out heavenly intervention – and neither did the woman herself, incidentally, although she still had no particular religious beliefs.

Fanciful thinking is not that unusual in pregnancy. In Fay Weldon's novel *Puffball*, the foetus 'speaks' to the mother from a very early stage, and throughout an uncertain pregnancy the woman is reassured and guided by its 'voice'. One woman I interviewed tried to communicate with her foetus in the same way as the character in the novel – but her foetus would not talk back. And the fact that the foetus was so unresponsive helped her decide not to continue the pregnancy. If the foetus had 'spoken' to her, she would have continued.

These are just *feelings* that people have, and that defy rational analysis. I have come across women who had a *feeling* that the baby was going to be abnormal, and so chose abortion. They had no evidence – it was too early to carry out any tests – it was just a feeling. Who is to say whether such feelings are not an instinctive expression of some reality? I have also encountered at least three cases where women were warned that their babies were likely to be handicapped – in two cases the woman had contracted rubella (German measles) in the early part of the pregnancy. Yet a 'feeling' that everything was going to be all right carried them through the pregnancy, and all three produced normal babies.

Death and loss can both be reasons why women decide to terminate a pregnancy. One of the saddest cases that a National Health Service counsellor came across was that of a woman who sought an abortion at twenty weeks because her husband had suddenly been killed in a road crash. Her immediate reaction was that she couldn't continue with the pregnancy, although the baby was coming near viability, without the support of her husband; and she said she couldn't bear to give birth to a child who might remind her of the man she had lost. Up until that moment the baby had been greatly wanted. But 'being wanted', which is our great modern criterion for acceptance into the human race (next to 'normality', of course) can be a dangerously shifting qualification. The loss of the husband turned the baby into an 'unwanted' one. The woman applied for a NHS abortion, and got one. What is doubly tragic about this case is that the woman's reaction to her grief was fairly typical: in shock and loss, people often wish to get rid of everything that may remind them of their pain. Counsellors who treat women who have been suddenly widowed say that it is very common for the woman to want to leave her home where everything reminds her of her loss; but this phase passes and, later, what first caused pain subsequently brings back sweet memories. (It is also true in burglary cases, where the shock causes women to want to move but later there is an adjustment.) It is possible that a baby who reminded the woman of her husband might later have been a consolation. We do not know, but it is true in other cases of loss that painful reminders later become acceptable and then pleasurable.

Counsellors at PAS, the abortion charity agency, came across a similar case where a woman applied for an abortion of what had been a much-wanted pregnancy until the sudden death of her husband. What was curious in this case was that the baby was not, biologically, the husband's, but the product of artificial insemination. Yet, without her husband's support and consent, the woman felt she could not go through a pregnancy – although there was no possibility whatsoever of the child physically reminding her of her dead husband.

Loss has a vivid impact on the human psyche, which was born and bred in attachment; and a loss may be very sensitively intuited between members of the same family. A counsellor at St Mary's, Paddington, who has been dealing with abortion requests for seven years, says that a miscarriage or a hysterectomy in a mother seems, on purely anecdotal evidence, sometimes to precede an unwanted pregnancy in a teenage daughter. Fanciful thinking perhaps? One empty womb inspiring another to fill itself? Very fanciful, but in this matter of the causes and consequences of pregnancy, nothing can be ruled out absolutely, since subconscious motives and psychology and even para-normal thinking play such a vital part.

Ambivalence about whether one wants a child or not can run so deep that there is no knowing its roots or motives. 'Do you want to be pregnant?' was the simple question put to Theresa Guillame, a twenty-year-old who turned up for a pregnancy test at a clinic. 'It was meant as a routine question,' Theresa wrote afterwards, in *19* magazine. 'But to me, it was enormous. Indeed, it was a question I had asked myself when I thought of the lovemaking a few weeks before – passionate, intensified by a wild and unfamiliar urge to conceive – and when I thought of the weeks just gone by, when I would lie in bed clutching my tummy as it thickened with protective fluids, trying to protect it further from the threats of my own intentions. The girl looked up at my silence. Then she wrote, "No".' Asked if she had used a contraceptive, Theresa fibbed, yes. 'I wondered if it was others like me, thus intimidated, who were responsible for the statistical failure of the sheath.' (Women do not like admitting they have not used a contraceptive to doctors or authority figures, because it sounds so irresponsible.)

Theresa went ahead and had an abortion at thirteen weeks, after repeatedly putting it off for as long as possible. If she had known, she said afterwards, that clinics do abortions much later than that in London – certainly up to twenty weeks, and sometimes as late as twenty-four – she would have waited longer. For a long time she *couldn't* decide. She was marrying the man by whom she had conceived; they loved each other deeply; he had a well-paid job and they already had a house; there were no urgent money problems. Moreover, she had been brought up in a happy, devout Anglican family, and she definitely felt that she was going against a moral code of some kind. 'There was certainly somebody up there judging me, when I had the abortion.' On the face of things, there was no real reason to terminate the pregnancy, and had the present abortion law worked as it was intended to work, Theresa would not really have had grounds for an abortion. She was in excellent health. She had taken no contraceptive measures. 'I'd done it on purpose, virtually,' she said of the pregnancy.

And yet, voluntarily, with all the options open and almost three months to think, she chose abortion. Not without anguish: 'I definitely feel I have cheated someone out of his life.' Not without regrets, and painful, confused feelings afterwards – a compulsion which she had to fight very hard, to get pregnant again straight away – and a great preoccupation with her fertility. Theresa decided for the abortion – in a sense, made the sacrifice of having the abortion – because she wants to be a writer, and she felt she must establish herself in her career before embarking on motherhood. She felt she would be cheating *herself* if she did not place her desire for career fulfilment before maternal fulfilment, even though she 'can't wait to have a baby'.

It is indeed possible to want to be pregnant but not to want a child. Much failure of contraception is rooted in and motivated by ambivalent feelings about fertility. A year and a half after the abortion, Theresa was still trying to establish her career and still a little sensitive about the termination itself. Moreover, she was using natural family planning as contraception, because she wanted to be 'in tune with her body'. And also, perhaps she still did not want to rule out the chance of pregnancy completely.

The first problem with understanding why women choose abortion is to figure out why, sometimes, they choose pregnancy; yes, sometimes contraception fails, yes, sometimes sex 'just happens', and yes, a few women would prefer to have abortions than to use birth control. Kristin Luker's classic study *Taking Chances: Abortion and the Decision Not to Contracept* made it clear that for some women the psychological cost of contraception was too high for the benefits of the safety it conferred. In her study, ex-Pill users were the highest group of women who became pregnant without wanting to have a baby. A pregnancy has certain potential benefits, Dr Luker points out; the pleasure of confirming fertility is tremendously satisfying for the majority of women. As Dr Fay Hutchinson of the Brook Advisory Centre says: 'The problem with contraception is that it *is* unnatural.' To stop doing what you are doing in order to insert a barrier is unnatural in the act of love; to ingest steroid hormones daily is also deeply unnatural. Maybe we do need a better quality of contraception, but no amount of contraceptive technology or pharmaceuticals will alter the human problems involved in choosing pregnancy: to prove fertility, to bind a marriage, to take revenge, to assuage the thought of age, to punish parents, to cry for help, to defy death, or just to enjoy sexuality without having to plan it all. The woman who told Kristin Luker that the cost of the abortion was worth every minute of the pleasure of her night of love is not going to be reproved for not taking precautions: not taking precautions is what it is all about. Some might say she may be reproved, with some justice, for taking human life so lightly.

Contraception can become too safe. 'Take away even the slight possibility of pregnancy, and making love for a woman can become too sterile in all ways,' wrote Jill Goolden in *Company* magazine. This is another version of the Roman Catholic doctrine that the act of love is indissolubly linked, in the natural order of things, with the transmission of life. Some women undoubtedly become pregnant to prove their fertility (male fertility is much more easily tested, with a simple sperm count; female fertility can really be tested only by exposure to pregnancy). Jill Goolden quotes a friend who is certain she never wanted children, but got pregnant just the same. 'There was never any possibility of me actually having the baby, but it gave me quite a thrill to know that I could.' Even though the end result was destined to be an abortion followed by sterilization, this woman was genuinely pleased to have had the experience.

There is, nevertheless, real contraceptive failure, and perhaps there always will be. Moreover, reasons for abortion vary from one society to another, from one class to another, as well as from one individual to another. There is, above all, the very simple reason that a woman feels she has too many children; that too is varying. 'The number of children a woman has before she turns to abortion varies from culture to culture,' wrote Daniel Callahan. The Chinese are mad about children, yet carry out late abortions without much misgiving, it seems: their sense of shame is much more focused on divorce, which involves family loss of face. Middle-class young women in the Western world, given time to think and to examine their own motives, to develop a sense of reflection and responsibility, are more disposed to anguish about pregnancy and abortion than women on the edge of survival. Working-class people, one counsellor says, are markedly more down-to-earth about abortion and, having decided on it, just go ahead and do it; middle-class intellectuals are the ones who examine their own psyches endlessly. Paradoxically, however, poor people the world over accept babies more easily than do the middle classes. For the poor, babies are just part of family life; for the better off, children are deliberately chosen.

Yet the individual reason for wanting or not wanting a pregnancy remains, still, individual.

3

MEN AND ABORTION

'Hardly any attention has been paid to men who suffer as a result of abortion. It is not our masculinity that is threatened or conquered: it is our feelings that we have done wrong.' – Man, aged twenty-nine, remembering an abortion nine years earlier

'Men are unhappy . . . because they feel they are losing a sense of power they have had over women for centuries. But it doesn't matter how much men scream and holler that they are being left out. There are some things that they are never going to experience fully. I say tough luck.' – Louise Tyrer, vice-president of medical affairs, Planned Parenthood

Do men have any rights in abortion? In law, no. No man can stop a woman from having an abortion; no man can legally coerce a woman into having an abortion; no man can force a woman to have a child. This has been established by case law in Britain and it is also true in most other countries where liberal abortion laws have been enacted.

The Paton case in 1978 (see pages 4–5) was sensational for a day, but provoked little in the way of protests. No men marched on Parliament demanding a say in abortion decisions. The correspondence pages of the newspapers were not filled with fathers calling attention to their responsibilities when a child is born – and thus their implied share in the decision as to whether their child is born or not. It would be easy to conclude that men were indifferent, or even pleased to be let off the hook, and that feminists were gratified that men had been, at last, excluded from the picture – since the feminist position is that abortion concerns only women, and that any attempt by men to influence a woman's decision is an attempt to exercise male power over women, or to manipulate women's freedom of choice.

In abortion, the traditional balance of power between the sexes is reversed. Frequently, in traditional law and practice, men have had power while women have only had influence. But in abortion, in the Western world, women have power – indeed total power – while men merely have influence. A man has no rights in law, but his relationship with the woman, his attitude to her and to the pregnancy will usually influence her decision. In her study, *Birth Control in the Modern World* family-planning sociologist Elizabeth Draper says: 'It is everywhere found that where the father wants the child, the woman will generally go on [with the pregnancy], whatever her fears or the hazards.' Dr Carol Gilligan, Associate Professor of Education at the Harvard Graduate School of Education, did her PhD on decision-making and its relationship to morality. Her first research project was on the question of how women come to make their decisions about abortion, and what struck her were the practical considerations that brought women to their final conclusions.

> The main question these women had in their minds was: could they responsibly raise this child? Would they be cared for themselves? It was emphatically *not* an abstract decision based on the right to life of the foetus – the kind of argument that goes on interminably amongst male judges. Theirs was a pragmatic decision rooted in their *relationship with the father*. [my italics]

If the relationship with the man was good, Dr Gilligan

went on, the woman would not worry about space or the amount of money she might have to spend on nappies. Such things could be overcome.

That point was admirably well-illustrated by Anna Raeburn in her testimony in the 'Mixed Feelings' programme. She explained how she had had her first abortion as a young woman, illegally. The focus then had been on the gruelling mechanics of actually getting an abortion (as was frequently the case for those people who had an abortion before it was legalized). Her mind continually dwelled upon the dangers and the horrors of it. But her second abortion took place after the 1967 Act, and after she was married. 'I was married: I was married to a man I loved,' she recalled. 'It's no good crying poverty to me because I've been poor all my life until relatively recently. I knew that his mother would rally round and my mother would rally round, and people would give me things and we would manage. That's what you do. That's what life is about.'

Anna Raeburn was here expressing the attitude of many couples who, when a pregnancy has occurred which was not exactly planned, cope with it because they mean to stay together. It is often a shock to a woman if, in marriage particularly (since marriage conventionally implies commitment and eventual parenthood), the husband refuses to accept a pregnancy. And Miss Raeburn's husband did refuse, she went on. He told her: 'I'm terribly sorry – I don't think that I can handle that right now.' She was stunned: her husband was saying that he did not want their child and, by extension, that he did not at that time want her as a mother to his child.

For the sake of the marriage, for the sake of her husband, she terminated the pregnancy. 'We spoke about it afterwards, when I turned on him in great anger. "I'm glad you've been able to go through this with so little apparent knowledge of what you have done [she told him]. You really don't know what you have asked of me . . . I am living, and will have to live with, what I have done, and you do not know *what* I have done." I don't remember suffering depression. I do know that it took me several years to make peace with that one.'

Not unexpectedly, the marriage broke down. The breakdown of marriage is one classic consequence of abortion, especially where there has been previous disagreement between a couple. Abortion can be a vote of no confidence in the future of a relationship. It is my own belief that abortion generally is a contributory factor to the ever-rising divorce figures, and it is certainly circumstantially true that the rising divorce rate and the increasing practice of abortion have gone hand in hand in many societies. Others would dispute this point, however; some sociologists would maintain the opposite – that children put stress on marriage and come between the couple.

There are some studies which indicate the strong impact of abortion on a couple. The most thorough study of men and abortion has been done by an American sociologist, Arthur B. Shostak, who spent eleven years surveying more than 1,000 men and their abortion experiences. Professor Shostak's book *Men and Abortion* – published in America – is extremely valuable but its source material is provided by men who came voluntarily to abortion clinics, or who declared themselves to be involved in some way. By definition, it is impossible to interview the men who do not care, who repress their feelings or who simply disappear. Thus it is biased towards 'involved' males. Yet even among these caring men – men who had accompanied their wives or girlfriends to abortion clinics – Shostak found that 44 per cent of the couples broke up their conjugal relationships after the abortion, and 10 per cent were afterwards still trying to assess the impact on the relationship. Only 38 per cent of these caring males believed that the abortion experience helped to bring them closer to their partner.

Yet if 44 per cent of relationships broke up among men who were concerned enough towards their partners to come along to a clinic and involve themselves in counselling, what can be said of the impact of abortion on those who do *not* come to support their partners through the experience?

There is often a divergence between what women say about men's feelings, and what the men themselves say. Listening to women talk about abortion, one hears many accounts of heartlessness, lack of feeling and dismissiveness among men. 'Heaven knows men don't need much persuading to turn their backs on domestic situations that don't suit them,' says a single mother who, despite the advice of her boyfriend to terminate the pregnancy, went ahead and had her baby. 'Even as I neared seven months pregnancy, my boyfriend was still screaming at me: "They will still do it for you at Roehampton if you plead insanity!"' (There are at least three private clinics in Britain where 'social' abortions have been carried out up to twenty-six weeks pregnancy, though the limit now tends to be twenty-four weeks. But, according to my researchers, two are in London and one is in Birmingham, and I have not found such a late-abortion clinic in the Roehampton area.)

The Don Juan figure, the man who takes his pleasure and then takes no heed of the consequence, crops up again and again in women's accounts of abortion experience. 'When I said I was pregnant,' wrote one young woman, 'it just didn't seem to register with my lover. "Well, you can get rid of it, can't you?" he said. I had felt so romantic towards him, so much in love, and I thought our love would be for ever. With the pregnancy, he turned quite cold towards me. I had the abortion, because that was what he wanted, but now our love has turned to dust and I feel very, very sad.'

'Men will come and men will go,' said an older woman sadly, 'but they are selfish creatures at best. A child's love is for ever, but a man's is passing.'

'I sit alone in my rented flat, work full-time to keep myself occupied and think of the child who would be seven and a half now if we had allowed it to live,' recalls a divorced woman in her forties. Her husband had been 'horrified' when she discovered she was pregnant, and he told her that it would make him unhappy for the rest of his life. Reluctantly, she had the abortion under pressure from her husband, but it poisoned the marriage and they subsequently got divorced. 'The worst aspect of the whole business is that he now says he regrets terribly "the baby business". He realizes that he was quite wrong. But nothing can heal the divisions of the past. We are both too bitter.'

'Men are selfish,' says a middle-aged woman who has been married twice. 'They can't help it. They want the love of a woman for themselves. They find it difficult to share that love with a child. But once presented with the child, sometimes they relent. Men, however, have to *see* the child. They cannot envisage the child as a being until it becomes real to them. Women have to make them understand.'

In talking to women, it emerges very strongly that it is extremely risky for a woman to have an abortion *for the sake of a man*, unless she is fully aware of what she is doing, willing to make a sacrifice and to live with her decision afterwards without bitterness towards him.

The rise in the number of late abortions in the 1980s – by 1983 abortions after twenty weeks pregnancy were running at approximately 4,000 a year – is ascribed by some counsellors to the 'male panic' factor. The man goes along with the pregnancy in the early stages; then, when it starts to become visible, its full impact hits him; he panics and says he cannot take it. The panic spreads to the woman and she requests a late abortion.

'Some of the saddest cases I have seen,' says Hilary Greenwood, chief counsellor at the Samaritan Hospital in London, 'are where the woman wants the pregnancy but the man cannot face it.' This is what Jung called the *puer eternis* – the Peter Pan complex – the male who cannot accept the responsibilities of maturity.

Modern contraception has played a key role in shaping contemporary male attitudes to procreation. Until the age of the Pill – which appeared in Britain in 1961 – the most common form of birth control was the condom. In the military services (in Britain men did National Service until 1963) men were issued with male contraceptives as part of the regulation kit. If they contracted venereal disease, they were often reprimanded for not having used a contraceptive. Thus the responsibility for pregnancy was frequently attributed to the man, especially if the couple was unmarried. 'In the 1950s,' says a man who was at Cambridge in 1951, 'if you got a girl pregnant you faced two options: marry her, or fork out seventy-five guineas (a huge amount of money at the time) for a dangerous and illegal abortion. It sounds callous to say so, but it tended to make us very careful about running the risk.' 'Getting a girl pregnant was like joining the Communist Party,' says a man recalling his Oxford days in the later 1950s. 'You could get over it, but it would always be on your record.'

Although unmarried mothers and abandoned, pregnant women were often cruelly treated before the Pill era, there was also much emphasis on out-of-wedlock pregnancy being the man's fault. Stories of guilty men being horsewhipped by the woman's father are many and, according to the writer Margaret Powell, looking back over the twentieth century, there was much pressure on a woman to 'name the guilty man', if an irregular pregnancy occurred.

The Pill shifted the onus of responsibility dramatically on to the woman – a responsibility which women eagerly embraced. Feminists championed women's new autonomy: the Pill (as well as the intrauterine device, and the more traditional Dutch Cap) 'put women in the driving-seat'. It was an important shift of attitudes. And like most social change, it had a negative as well as a positive effect: it removed from men the role of chief progenitor – the impregnator, and thus the one in charge – but it also diminished their sense of responsibility. By the 1980s, some young women were beginning to complain that men just took it for granted that *all* women were on the Pill, or had automatically taken some measure to prevent conception. This also led to the expectation that women were constantly available for sex. By 1984, Family Planning Associations were launched on a repeated cycle of trying to convince men of their equal responsibility for contraception. And with an increase in sexually-transmitted diseases, the condom was once again being recommended. But success in this field is only moderate: many contemporary young men won't use a condom because they feel it diminishes pleasure, is mechanical, and interrupts the act of coitus. Interestingly enough, many young women protect men from having to think of anything as 'squalid' as contraception. A birth-control doctor from the Margaret Pyke centre in London says that she commonly hears young women say: 'Oh I'd never ask him to use a french letter. I wouldn't impose on him any such restrictions.' Kristin Luker's study of the failure to contracept by people who were perfectly well informed about contraception says that many women fear alienating the male by requesting him to participate in the contraceptive act, even limited co-operation such as postponing intercourse until a method such as the Pill is started!

In any case, men are often in a double bind: if they persistently make the choice of using a contraceptive themselves, women may resent it because the man is withholding something (his sperm) in the act of coitus; he is, moreover, 'controlling' the situation by doing so.

One interviewee told me that she found her boyfriend's decision to have a vasectomy (he was certain he didn't want children, and had always made it plain) to be a very 'angry, aggressive' act. Her attitude was not unusual. It is well-established that contraception works best in a stable, long-term relationship where both partners have talked sensibly about such matters, but the balance of power always remains a delicate one.

Social history and contraceptive technology have both conspired to put men at a distance from abortion decisions. Feminists are of course factually correct when they point out that a man can never fully understand the experience of pregnancy. Nature has implemented this by the function of the procreative act itself: a man produces some 200 million sperms on ejaculation. Once these are produced, his biological function is effectively finished. Among many animal species, the biological urge of the male is simply to fertilize as many females as possible. Among four-footed mammals, the male may be protective towards the suckling female, but he may be hostile or indifferent to the young. If 'biology is destiny', then men have very little place indeed in attachment to the young, and a father's love may have to be earned. Yet it seems difficult for men to be at once detached and involved, and it is hardly surprising that in their reaction to abortion men are often bewildered, uncertain or neutral or, sometimes, profoundly distressed.

So, what *is* it that men feel when confronted with abortion? Here is a robust character, Harry, reminiscing in his late forties about his experiences of pregnancy scares and abortions.

'First case: late 1950s, Spanish woman. Swore she was "all right", so we blasted away, all precautions to the wind. Of course she wasn't and what ensued was a real back-street, witch-doctor job, and she was very ill for some time afterwards. Feel? In my youthful confusion, my first reaction was "stupid bitch", followed by a nasty sick sensation in my stomach for having made her suffer so much. Met her again ten years later: no hard feelings.

'Second case: early '60s, English deb. The usual party story, everybody pissed out of their minds, one wakes up the next morning beside a girl whose name one doesn't even know. She says: "You stupid bastard, give me £150!" Then her period arrives on time, and I get my £150 back. Feel? Relief. And it turned into a beautiful affair.

'Third case: Scottish girl, early '60s. Apparent spermicide failure, but big panic. The full gin and bath works, but then period turns up late due to undetected anaemia. Feel? Phew. And next time, see a doctor you silly girl, before you go putting the wind up everybody!

'Fourth case: Spanish woman, late '60s. Condom failure (know the one about the Catholic condom factory with a priest and a pair of scissors? Well, it must be true.) Duogynon treatment. Feel? Bloody hell. Fury. Didn't want any more panics like the previous three.' (This 'failure' was now a beloved fifteen-year-old son.)

Harry's summing up of his feelings, generally, was 'ANGRY . . . due to technical failure. And the conviction that men and wimmin [sic] should get things straight before they go bent. Who is using what? All in favour of the Swedish idea that as soon as a girl has her first period, stuff a device in just in case.'

Mike, a thirty-three-year-old Australian, had been responsible for three pregnancies, all outside marriage. A friendly, easy-to-like character working in the music business, he tried, with his first girlfriend in Australia, to perform the abortion himself.

'A man makes it clear to a woman that it's really her choice,' he said. 'Though I really was in love with my first girlfriend, I see now that I reacted to her rather badly. We got the abortion when she was four months pregnant: I think she never really recovered from it. It probably would have been a beautiful baby, too. I got swept along by the selfishness of my generation – this was the '60s. All the women around me were strong in advising me towards abortion. But she was a simple kind of girl and it was a damn shame. We did the abortion ourselves actually: we got the equipment at Ramsey's Surgical Supplies. Abortion was illegal in Australia at the time, though it was the usual hypocritical situation that the rich could manage it. Of course it was the end of the relationship. I always say I'm not against abortion – and I'm not – but the thought of what I did that time really shames me. The woman's health and happiness must come before the embryo, but it's not a pretty business.

'The second pregnancy made *me* a bit hurt. She was a very romantic girl, very influenced by mystical things – led her life according to the Tarot cards. She was using me for a stud, I found out. She moved away from Melbourne to Perth and joined a religious commune – Rajneesh, I think. But she produced this beautiful little girl which I must have given her. The third time, it was a Jamaican girlfriend here in England. Our relationship had virtually ended when she became pregnant. "You are having an abortion," I told her. "I am taking you down to the doctor straight away." She was very stubborn, however, and wouldn't go. Now she has this lovely little son. Motherhood has improved her social position and she's very happy. I now think black girls are suited to having babies, while intellectual white women are much too screwed up for it. I now think it is better to give babies to black girls; it's better for the uptight white feminists to have abortions. Why not breed from the ones more adapted to it? That's the law of evolution: adaptation.'

It is not unusual to find among men expressions of bravado and deliberately macho attitudes. Sometimes this is a front; sometimes it is simply the way the man expresses or organizes his emotions. There are many contemporary books now which emphasize this aspect of male behaviour as an emotional handicap. However, there are some women who like men to behave in this way. But although some men have a self-consciously tough or angry approach to abortion, it is also quite common to find a silent, more private response to the experience. The Englishman who said to me 'It is an unpleasant episode that you go through and forget about as best you can' may well have spoken for the majority. Crispin, who is in his mid-twenties, described his encounter with abortion as 'very unfunny indeed. It was the first time she had ever slept with anyone. It was very bad luck. I was really frightened. I said, "Well, at this point it's up to you – I'll support you and do the decent thing if you'd like that." But after finding out that she was pregnant, the whole affair just died. She hopped on a plane, went abroad and got rid of it. I felt riddled with guilt afterwards. I'd been head over heels in love with her, but afterwards it all just died. She didn't want to make love for months afterwards. Frankly, it's something I would rather just wipe out from my memory. It's made me wary. Up to then, I'd been the kind of person who wanted to give 100 per cent in a relationship, and expect 100 per cent back, but not any more.'

That an abortion experience can make men cautious is a point often raised by them, although it is uncertain how long this lasts. (A comon reaction to abortion among women is 'Never again sex!', but that too, of course, is never sustained.) One American study showed that 93 per cent of men questioned over abortion said they would do everything they could to prevent a recurrence. Yet at any given clinic, 30 per cent of the men were in fact repeaters.

'My girlfriend, aged twenty, had an abortion in 1970 at her insistence,' says one London chartered accountant. 'I was totally supportive, emotionally and part-financially. I was twenty-four. I was definitely the father. The emotional response from myself was entirely negative – i.e., get rid of the problem affecting our potential happiness. We continued together for a further six months. Emotional response zero was replaced by (a) pleasure that a correct decision was made; (b) pride that, at that time, I could father children; (c) knowledge of my own fertility prevents me forcing another woman to "prove" my manhood through pregnancy; (d) concern for contraception. My sole emotional hiccup was to discover that at three months the operation involved the removal of a fairly advanced foetus, and not merely the scraping away of a little mucous or tissue. The outcome would have been the same, however. I am now thirty-eight, unmarried and have no children. I remain curious but very careful of my motives.'

This controlled male approach seems characteristic. Arthur Shostak, the American sociologist, says that males typically approach abortion in an abstract and aloof way. What many women perceive as coldness is the standard male effort to control emotions.

Yet there are men who are desperately hurt, guilty and miserable about abortion. 'In early 1975, when I was twenty, I fell in love with a girl who was two years my senior,' writes Matthew, who lives in Birmingham. 'I was still living with my parents: she shared a house with two friends. I worked at a printing factory – she had gained an MA from the local polytechnic and had stayed on to work in an advertising agency. I mention these points to illustrate the difference in our background and experience, although we were both working-class. I had had relationships with girls before and wasn't a virgin when we met, but this was the first time I had been in love and it hit me like a mallet. Soon I was spending more time at her house than I was at my parents' home and in July 1975 we found that she was pregnant. I was happy about it and thought that with love and the support of our parents, which I was sure we'd get, we would be able to cope. She had recently been made redundant and was hoping to become a social worker because she had become disillusioned with advertising anyway. After a short amount of deliberation, she decided to have an abortion. It was she who was pregnant, it was her body, and she didn't want to sacrifice her career for the sake of bringing up a baby that would have a poor start in life.' Matthew argued that they could manage but his girlfriend was adamant. An acquaintance lent her the money for the abortion, which was done privately, and Matthew paid back in weekly instalments. After the abortion, the relationship deteriorated, and Matthew began to drink. His drinking worsened the relationship, and the inevitable happened. One night there was a quarrel and the abortion was used as ammunition. By the new year, they had split up.

Matthew met someone else; his former girlfriend pursued her career as a social worker, never married or had children. Matthew did marry and had three children. He sobered up and became a very devoted father. But he never quite got over the abortion. 'I still think of that abortion – nearly every day – and will do until the day I die. I have lit a candle in the church and prayed for the soul of my child and for forgiveness in consenting to its murder. This has brought me some peace. Hardly any attention has been paid to men who suffer as a result of abortion. It is not our masculinity that is threatened by abortion: it is a real feeling that we have done wrong.' Matthew is a Catholic, which will have played some part in his guilt feelings, though it seems to me that individual personality is what counts for most.

Peter Zelles, a health counsellor in Minneapolis who has helped more than 1,000 men through abortion experience, however, thinks that background culture is a strong influence. 'For a great many men, the abortion is distressing on multiple levels. Morally, they may find it in conflict with their familial values; this includes concern for their own sense of religious "rightness", as well as concern for the future of the pregnancy.'

A retired man from the East End of London describes

what happened to him, and how he resolved his feelings. 'I once fathered a baby by a woman I truly loved in what was the most beautiful experience I have ever had, and of which until that moment I did not think I was capable. I was in fact a soldier at the time and the experience occurred in another country and was so certain that immediately after the consummation the lady in question told me, though not in English, "You've give me a baby again." In the circumstances then prevailing I could not marry the lady but begged her to have the child, promising to see that it was provided for. She could not see it this way, and had a quick and easy legal abortion. I considered myself a pretty hard tough man after seven years wartime military service, but to my own astonishment the abortion broke me up, or broke my heart, whichever way you care to look at it, besides filling me with an appalling sense of futility and waste and denial of God's loving kindness and mercy. This feeling festered in me for many years, although I finally came to comprehend that, given true repentance, there are no limits to God's mercy and forgiveness. However, how to atone? I finally remembered Matthew Arnold's "Sohrab and Rustum" where the dying youth, slain by his father who wanted to drown himself in the Oxus, said that his father's atonement should be to do in his age the things that he (the son) would have done in his youth, had he lived. Since then I have truly felt that whatever soul I summoned from God has returned to me, not to haunt me but to help me, as I too strive to do in my age some of the things I should have done in my youth. I feel sure my experience is not unusual . . . Oscar Wilde, who was certainly no saint, nevertheless in the depths of his degradation stoutly maintained that God can make things as though they never were.'

Religious inclination certainly plays a formative role in the reactions of some men, but it seems to me that if the man feels little or nothing for the woman, abortion will not touch him deeply; if he cares for her, the abortion wounds him. It is as though the man's feelings for the child, or the potential child, are governed by his feelings for its mother. A man who wrote to me anonymously, and about whom I know nothing, put it very poignantly. 'I have twice experienced having pregnancies terminated for which I have been responsible. In a sense, I feel it is a relief to be able to write to someone about it. I have felt since a terrific sense of guilt and regret. The first abortion occurred with a woman with whom I lived and loved very much. It was her decision to have the abortion, my regret is that I didn't try to stop her. The most vivid part was when she came back from hospital producing milk and I had this awful feeling that it was my baby's milk and I felt sorry for the dead baby whose termination I had done so little to prevent. Needless to say, the relationship ended in appalling and painful circumstances. We felt we had been complicit in a crime. The second abortion occurred recently with a girl with whom I'd had only a casual relationship. There seem to have been no repercussions except that we no longer see each other and I was worried about the hardened attitude I felt. Surely abortion is unnatural and a convenient gesture to selfish materialism, but it's the individual choice and wholly the woman's decision.'

The other side of this coin, as Kristin Luker illustrates, is that pregnancy may be used as a test, consciously or unconsciously, by the woman to see if the man's reaction to fathering their child is positive. There are plenty of old wives' tales about women who trap men into marriage by conniving to 'get themselves pregnant' (as though pregnancy occurred by parthenogenesis and not through a voluntary act by both parties), but there is much mythologizing here. When a pregnancy does occur which is a surprise to the man (presumably because he expected the woman to have taken contraceptive precautions), it is not so much a question of entrapment as a testing of the relationship. After all, if a man reacts positively to a pregnancy and says 'Great! We may have money problems but we'll manage somehow', or 'Well, we would have had a baby sometime, anyhow, so why not now?' it is a vote of confidence in the future of the relationship. According to Luker, the woman may still go ahead and terminate the pregnancy (though it is less likely, if the man is welcoming to the child) but she has been reassured nevertheless by her partner's reaction.

Many men, truly, just do not know how to react to the news of a surprise pregnancy. They feel outside the whole experience. 'The reason men have no real or outward feelings on abortion is that very few men associate sex with babies,' writes the chartered accountant. 'Women have babies thrust upon them from infancy, plus the reinforcement of bodily development and periods; this leads women towards a sequential view of reproduction. Whereas women consciously choose infertility through contraception, men simply haven't got a clue. In my own case, I knew nothing about embryo development or the psychological aspects of pregnancy and abortion; merely that pregnancy could occur. I certainly did not want children. I firmly believe that men do not generally want children or heirs and children are seen as a product of a woman's body and her aspirations. Men have nothing to say – they cannot talk about abortion because it does not relate to them.'

That the idea of fatherhood is something which has to be taught to men is borne out by the experience of a man who consistently resisted his wife's pleas for a child – but had had his eyes opened afterwards.

'I was married for four years during which I found the idea of a baby or small child repulsive. I thought that I simply was not cut out to have or be with children. My wife, on the other hand, dearly wanted children. She cooed over her sisters' babies and over television adverts featuring "darling" little babies. This made me cringe inside and I continued to shy away from any involvement with other people's babies and kept putting off the idea of having children.

'Although I recognized my wife's desires and needs (she came from a broken home and was brought up with little love in several children's homes), I felt all the while that I was not part of her decision and determination to have children, especially when she threatened to stop taking the Pill without my knowing it.

'Our marriage broke up a year ago over a number of unresolved differences. I have now been living for the past nine months with my girlfriend who divorced two years ago and has a six-year-old daughter. Almost from the moment I met my girlfriend I felt I already loved her daughter. The bond between them is so great and so beautiful. Never had I seen such love from a mother who adores and cares intelligently for her child. I realize now that it was not that I disliked children but that I had been put down and excluded as a potential father. Gradually the daughter and I have been able to build a loving relationship. My girlfriend has shown me that she trusts me with her, while I am becoming a much loved and accepted stepfather. We have talked about having a child of our own, and I am still surprised but also happy to find that I am so taken with the idea. So much so that I know I would really want a child from such a beautiful mother, whose love is already reflected back to me through her daughter.'

One myth has it that men like to marry women who already have one child – since it proves the woman's fertility. Perhaps an existing child – who smiles, responds, talks and is human in a way that a foetus cannot yet be – teaches a man to respond to the idea of a child. According to Peter Zelles, men are not all that much interested in their fertility, as such. 'Many men experience a fleeting sense of satisfaction and pleasure that they are capable of reproduction,' he says, describing men's reactions to a pregnancy. 'But I emphasize that this is very temporary. Many young people – of both sexes – have a vague curiosity about their fertility; they wonder how necessary contraception really is since they may have gone a period of time unprotected without a pregnancy, leading many to believe they are infertile. A pregnancy, however unplanned, serves to allay this fear. But I don't believe that most men experience their fertility as intensely as most women.'

He suggests that basically this is because men don't have the responsibility for bearing children, and are not intimately involved with the gestational period. Though, in those cultures where fathering a child is greatly esteemed as a mark of virility, being able to have children obviously must be important to a man.

Women sometimes sense instinctively that men may find it hard to relate to babies and are thus more disposed not to look favourably on a pregnancy. They understand that men have to be 'taught' – by women and by experience – to love small infants. 'I have a relationship with a wonderful man who loves children but finds babies repulsive,' says a woman from Bristol. 'The truth is he is afraid of them; their helplessness makes him feel inadequate. Little boys were not allowed to touch the baby in the family in the not so distant past. But babies don't stay babies for long.'

'Five years ago I became pregnant, after wanting a baby for ten years, and already being the mother of a sixteen-year-old and a twelve-year-old,' says a mother from Essex. 'My husband had not wanted any more children and insisted I had an abortion, playing on my age of forty and my responsibility to my two lovely daughters. I had the abortion and was mentally shattered to such an extent my husband agreed to let me have another baby, and she was born one year after the abortion. He is absolutely besotted with her and constantly thanks God that he was allowed this chance, and to use his own words, thinks he must have been out of his mind to have contemplated the last abortion. Before, he did not care too much for babies and had never been all that keen on children, but he says he can really appreciate them now and realizes what a precious gift they are.'

Modern trends encourage men to participate more in fatherhood and to be present at the birth. 'The biological assumption implicit in strictly psychological studies of pregnant women has contributed to the neglect of men,' says a recent study on men as fathers. Perhaps greater socialization of men towards babies would make them more open and positive about pregnancy in general; and then again perhaps not. There is no consensus on the nature versus nurture arguments.

But there are certain cultural variables established.

Both Art Shostak, in his study of men and abortion, and Peter Zelles, working as a counsellor to men, have noticed that blacks, Hispanics and native Americans are more involved with abortion decisions than are white males, are more distressed by abortion and are closer to their partners *when the relationship is a going concern.* (Again, we must remind ourselves that Shostak and Zelles, by definition, never get to the men who just do a bunk at the mention of the word pregnancy, or refuse to be involved in counselling.) 'Many of these males seem to have a deeper desire to have children, and to "pass on" what they have learned,' says Peter Zelles. 'It has been suggested by some that black males may view abortion as a form of genocide. I wouldn't agree with such a generalization, but one-to-one contact with some of these men has that "flavour".' Even in those cases where abortion does take place, Shostak found that these men remained closer and more supportive of the women than white males.

In all partnerships, pregnancy may be a matter of manipulation of one partner by the other; and if the couple is fundamentally at odds, someone is going to get hurt. One elderly man, now living alone in Sussex, recalls an abortion as the major tragedy of his life. In her late thirties, his wife had become pregnant again. It wasn't planned, but he wanted her to have the baby. She, however, was adamant that with her two children already growing up, she did not wish to be thrust back into the throes of caring for a small child; she wanted to work and lead a more independent life. Against his deeply-felt wishes, she terminated the pregnancy. The marriage ended in divorce. The wife continued in her job and has led a busy and apparently prosperous life ever since. He sits alone, brooding over the child that might have been. She could have gone on with her life, he insists. He would have been happy to bring up the child himself. Here is a case where a man has been unlucky in not being able to fulfil what he so wanted – another chance at fatherhood. The relationship was clearly not strong enough to sustain the disagreement, and he was the loser.

In another case I encountered, a father of two children prevented his wife from having an abortion because they were living in a country where the husband's consent was obligatory. The wife insisted she did not want the child and tried hard to get an abortion, without success. When the child was born she changed her mind, became very attached to the baby, and left her husband, taking the children with her. The man had withheld his permission not, he claims, because he is authoritarian but because he was a believing Catholic at the time and felt it would be morally wrong. In the end he felt embittered that he had 'saved' his son's life – only to lose the child when his wife took him away. His opinions were dramatically reversed: he now rejects the Catholic view and supports abortion at any stage of pregnancy.

Peter Zelles firmly believes that the whole key to the issue is in the relationship.

> Unplanned pregnancy and abortion provide an excellent opportunity to recognize the couple as a system, and work within the ecological framework to assist both partners through a stressful and difficult experience. In most cases, however, just the opposite occurs; the woman alone is provided medical care and counselling without the involvement of her partner.
>
> Quite simply, the couple is not recognized as a couple, but as two unrelated individuals. Counselling is offered for the woman in the hope of lessening anxiety and producing some degree of change, but half the system is ignored.

What men most commonly experience in abortion, says Zelles, is this sense of powerlessness, of being that half of a system which is considered irrelevant. The majority of men interviewed by Art Shostak, for instance, said they would like to be present at the abortion, in the way that fathers are now commonly present at birth. (Whether this would be welcomed by women or not is another question. In Britain, some abortion counsellors are ambivalent about the presence of putative fathers in the clinic at all.

'Some men come along to be supportive,' said a counsellor at one of the London hospitals, 'but some come to make sure the woman has the abortion – in other words to keep up the pressure on her.' This is especially true if the man has shared the cost of the abortion. It is as though he wants to see his investment through.)

Zelles argues that concern for their partners is why most men come to the clinics.

> An area that I find is usually not considered by the general populace, however, relates to the feelings that men have for their partners who are going through this surgical procedure. The *first* question most men ask me is about the emotional and physical well-being of their partner; will there be emotional consequences, how can they help, is the abortion procedure dangerous, how often are there physical complications, will she still be able to get pregnant and carry a pregnancy to term, and so on and so on.
>
> Accompanying this concern is often an acutely uncomfortable feeling that they aren't doing enough to help, a feeling that no matter what they do they can't take away the discomfort and distress from her. This is not unlike a childbirth situation, where the male is grateful to his partner for enduring gestation and delivery. It is not considered appropriate, however, to directly express gratitude for an abortion, so many men struggle with how to let their partners know indirectly how they care, and appreciate the sacrifice made.
>
> If there is any aspect of abortion which is uniquely male, it is this detachment and powerlessness.

This indeed is the role-reversal alluded to at the beginning of this chapter. In abortion, women have power, and men have influence. Their influence is not, of course, invariable: women do go ahead with pregnancies against their partners' wishes; women do go ahead with abortions also against their partners' wishes. But, in the majority of day-to-day cases, the man's attitudes will be very important.

In the final analysis, of course, where pregnancy is concerned, the woman holds the cards. And there is widespread male acceptance of and acquiescence in that fact. Over and over again, men themselves make the point that she carries the baby, sustains it and delivers it; and motherhood is more binding in its early phases than fatherhood. But that men can be deeply affected by abortion is not in doubt.

'Re abortion and what I felt,' writes a man from Gloucester. 'Repugnance, horror, shame, embarrassment, sadness, sorrow. Wife and mother-in-law pleased; doctor very kind but I felt extremely foolish. Horror that a formed foetus was flushed down the toilet. Thirty years after still uncomfortable about it all.'

'I'm a bit drunk – it's the only way I can cope with thoughts about abortion,' writes an anonymous man. 'Twelve years on, here we are battling with the results of not one but two abortions. Talk about being fucked-up. Even now my wife will only admit to one of the abortions. She felt compelled to go through with the abortions because of her family and the hurt she might cause them. We were young, romantic and "in love". The Pill made her ill and condoms weren't romantic . . . we weren't married at the time. Today we are awaiting an appointment with a psychiatrist to try and sort out our heads. Oh, the regrets. And oh, the pain.'

4

ADOPTION – AN ALTERNATIVE TO ABORTION?

And a woman who held a babe against her bosom
said: Speak to us of Children
And he said:
Your children are not your children.
They are the sons and daughters of Life's longing for itself.
They come through you but not from you.
And though they are with you, yet they belong not to you. – Kahlil Gibran, *The Prophet*

Dr Shirley Bond is an anaesthetist with the abortion charity – PAS (Pregnancy Advisory Service). She is an experienced anaesthetist and takes pride in doing her job properly – seeing that women are comfortable when they present for abortion, helping them to relax, talking to them cheerfully if they are undergoing a local anaesthetic only (though this is not common practice in Britain) and being sure that they are clinically properly treated when they undergo a general anaesthetic. Dr Bond, who is married and a mother herself, sees abortion as a personal choice which seems to be beneficial for many women; she notices that the most usual reaction to abortion, by the woman, is relief that the operation can be carried out easily without major problems. Yet it troubles her that adoption is so seldom offered as an alternative to abortion when a pregnant woman says she does not want her child. 'I think the counselling for adoption is abysmal – it's virtually non-existent. Sometimes adoption is raised all right, but in such a negative way – "I don't suppose you want it adopted", kind of thing. Or "Have you thought about adoption?" And that is adoption counselling.'

Most of the pregnancy counselling, Dr Bond points out, is 'done by people who are very pro-abortion. Basically, it's geared to pro-abortion. I don't think there are enough people around who know about adoption, so women are put off the whole procedure. The social workers have always tried to persuade women to keep the baby: "You are its mother"; "The natural mother is the best for the child". I just think the whole climate of opinion about adoption is wrong in this country. It's negative.'

What moves Shirley Bond even more strongly on this subject is that public awareness of the shortage of babies is still lacking. Women who are presenting for abortion in their thirties may be told, as a precaution against future regrets, that this might be their last chance to have a child. And they will still sometimes say, 'Never mind – I can always adopt.' Even someone as well-informed as Billie-Jean King can speak lightly about adopting as though it were an easy personal option – and even think herself 'liberal' in that she would not object to a black or Vietnamese child. 'We're very liberal-minded people. Our baby doesn't have to be our own flesh and blood. Our child doesn't have to be white Anglo-Saxon Protestant. We could both love any baby – black, white, Vietnamese or whatever,' she said in 1983. In reality, inter-racial adoption is now frowned upon both in the US as well as the UK by the social-worker establishment, which has embraced the notion that the adoption of black or mixed-race children by white people is patronizing and detrimental to the child, denying the child its identity by subsuming it into white culture.

Shirley Bond ascribes some of the negative views of

adoption today to 'fashion': 'It is just not the modern thing to do. Adoption is not fashionable. Abortion is fashionable. You can sit and have a cup of tea with someone who will say they have had an abortion and no one thinks anything of it. But if a woman says she has placed her child for adoption, people are shocked. "What a terrible thing to do!" is the attitude.'

It is true that social practices go through the hoops of fashion as regularly as anything else: child-care itself has been subject to many swings of the pendulum since the seventeenth century – now breast, now bottle, now discipline, now permissiveness, now attachment to the mother, now separation, now closeness to the biological family, now social interaction and experience with peer groups, now nannies, now crèches. Adoption has also gone in and out of favour as a means of caring for children whose own parents could not, or would not, do so.

Before the industrialization of the nineteenth century, adoption and fostering was practised on a casual basis throughout Europe. The illegitimate children of the English nobility were accepted, sometimes with astonishing ease. Social historian Lawrence Stone tells us:

> The memoirs of famous courtesans like Harriette Wilson and Julia Johnstone provide plenty of evidence that there was a great deal of extra-marital sexual activity among many aristocratic husbands and some aristocratic wives. Harriette Wilson, for example, was the mistress of (among others) the Dukes of Wellington, Argyll and Beaufort, the Marquesses of Worcester, Anglesey, Bath and Hertford, Lord Craven, and many more of the lesser nobility. In these cases, illegitimate boys seem usually to have been well educated and to have suffered no social discrimination.

They were informally adopted into the household where they were born, or the one that could care for them. Lord Mulgrave remarked in the House of Lords in 1800: 'Bastardy is of little comparative consequence to the male children'; but girls had a harder time of it in England.

Only a small minority, remarks Stone, were as successful as the illegitimate daughter of Sir Edward Walpole, who in 1759 married the second Lord Waldegrave and, on his death, George III's brother, the Duke of Gloucester. In some other societies, however, illegitimate girls were not always repudiated. In China, a girl might be adopted as a future daughter-in-law; in Hindu law, too, adoption has traditionally been accepted for children of both sexes, though there have been prohibitions concerning caste.

Kinship adoption – taking in the children of a family member, or indeed of a family servant – was informally practised all over Europe, among the peasantry as among the landed classes. As mentioned earlier, agricultural societies have been more inclined to see children as an asset – an extra pair of hands if poor, an addition to the dynasty if better-off. In rural Austria, for instance, the children of unmarried servants were often made welcome during the de-populated nineteenth century. 'The property-owning farming population gladly keep the children of servants in the house; they care for them as so-called foster children, even when the mother leaves their service . . . For in the large households the children are not much of an expense and later give cheap and devoted service to the house,' Mitterauer and Sieder tell us. When it comes to marrying, too, 'the bridegroom will usually adopt illegitimate children, even when he is not the father'. In the early 1800s, illegitimacy in Austria stood at 11.2 per cent, in contrast to 5 per cent in England. By 1870, Austrian illegitimacy had risen to 27.8 per cent.

Curiously, the advent of labour-saving devices began to change attitudes towards extra children in the UK. The coming of the industrial revolution and the widespread move to the cities changed very radically the pattern of the family and the role of children. The Victorian age was also – in contrast to the more relaxed eighteenth century – a period of puritan morality. The great social scandals of the early and middle Victorian period included the spread of alcoholism, of prostitution, and the increased number of abandoned waifs and strays in the streets. The

Victorians believed that many of these social ills could be curbed by high moral principles, and noticed that the 'respectable' poor benefited from religious practice. The Methodists crusaded against prostitution and child abandonment by imposing sexual restraints. The taboo against illegitimacy became entrenched in the cities, and women who 'fell' were singled out for blame. This invoked the double-standard, for men got away with sexual licence while women paid the price.

Child abandonment also reached its height during the nineteenth century. In 1842 Lord Shaftesbury's Coal Mines Act forbade the employment of children under thirteen in the mines, and successive legislation covered the mills and other factories. Until that point, children were still something of an economic asset to their parents, as they had been in rural societies, because they worked. As humane concern for the conditions of children grew – greatly fuelled by the compassion of novelists like Dickens and Kingsley – so did, ironically enough, the abandonment of children. When Thomas Barnardo founded his home for waifs and strays in London in 1867, there were said to be 100,000 destitute children sleeping in the London streets.

Children were taken from homes like Barnardo's and sent to the colonies – principally Canada and Australia – where they were adopted by pioneering families who needed them for work. Many of the stories of these children are extremely poignant, as Gillian Wagner's history of Victorian emigrant children recounts. Yet the philanthropists who cared for them probably thought they were acting in the best interest of the child, and the Australian outback or Canadian prairie provided a better long-term opportunity for them than an English city institution or workhouse. Many of these children did prosper and make good. Abandoned children were not widely adopted in the home country partly, perhaps, because there was no great shortage of children in well-established families at that time: childless couples of the Victorian and Edwardian era had far more involvement with nieces, nephews and other kinfolk than they do today, and many a novel of the period tells of orphaned children going to live with distant relatives (not always happily, of course). David Copperfield had his aunt Betsy Trotter as a refuge, and there are many characters in George Eliot's novels who are brought up by relatives. Fanny Price in *Mansfield Park* is, of course, a classic example of a poor relation offloaded (in the end, happily) on cousins; finally her sister, too, is informally adopted by the same uncle and aunt. One of the most famous characters in English fiction, Heathcliff in *Wuthering Heights*, is not so much adopted as just picked off the street without further formality. In many of Dickens's novels, *Martin Chuzzlewit*, *Oliver Twist*, *Nicholas Nickleby* – children are just taken in by kindly folks.

Towards the end of the nineteenth century, we see a strengthening of prejudice against children born illegitimate, as is described in George Moore's novel *Esther Waters* (1894), in which a poor girl bears a child and struggles to raise it. 'She had sinned and the Lord had punished her for her sin.' Babies of such desolate young women were often put out to 'baby farmers' – couples who raised the children in exchange for money, but where neglect was commonplace and where the majority of the babies died.

Unmarried mothers who gave birth in the workhouse were often punished with direct hardship. 'Mothers, suffering the pangs of labour, were not permitted medical attention except in cases of dangerous emergency,' wrote Ian Anstruther in Angela Hamblin's *The Other Side of Adoption*. 'And once the ordeal was past, whether the baby lived or not, they had to put up with the inquisition with many sharp and frightening rebukes from the Workhouse Chaplain.' The stigma of illegitimacy was visited upon both mother and child, and there was a reluctance, in some quarters, to accept such children.

The 1890s may have been a time when concern for children flourished, but it also saw the rise of the powerful Eugenic Movement, which was greatly to influence humanitarian thought for the next forty years. The eugenic societies believed that characteristics were inherited and the children of 'paupers, criminals, alcoholics, epileptics and moral degenerates' would form a continuing moral underclass. The remedy suggested by the eugenics societies – which in Britain included liberal and left-wing thinkers (see page 190) – was the forcible sterilization of 'inadequate' girls. The eugenics societies' influences were not designed to make people feel more sympathetic towards illegitimate children, but probably had the effect of inhibiting those who might otherwise have felt moved to adopt, feeling that the 'degeneracy' of the parents would be visited on the offspring.

It was the First World War which changed everything. It brought more freedom for women and more tolerance of the single mother. Patriotic sentiments softened attitudes and a woman who slept with a soldier going off to battle was seen less as a fallen woman and more as a comforter of the man-at-arms. Crèches were suddenly opened in factories which would permit the unmarried mother to have her baby alongside her – since women's work was now seriously required for the war effort. In the aftermath of that war, the large number of 'war orphans' was regarded with compassion, and thus it was that in 1926 legislation for adoption was first enacted.

The movement was widespread throughout Europe, although laws differed very much from one country to another. In some continental countries, adopting parents had to be over fifty – Switzerland lowered the minimum age to thirty-five only in 1973. In the United States, adoption had been looked upon more favourably since Independence, though there, as in Europe, it was largely practised by the white ruling group. To this day, however, adoption is still not accepted in some societies: Islamic law has never favoured it, and it is a matter of shame in Japan. In Caribbean culture – both in the West Indies and among British and American blacks of Caribbean origin – the out-of-wedlock child is accepted by the family at large, so there is no necessity for adoption. Where the child is of mixed race there may be more problems.

During the middle years of the twentieth century, adoption became an acceptable means of alleviating childlessness among couples who could not have their own families. It also became a means of 'relieving' single mothers of the 'evidence' of their 'mistake'. By the 1950s, adoption was seen as a good solution to both problems, especially since the Second World War produced a boom in illegitimate births. In the post-war years, environment as a socializing influence had gained the upper hand over heredity (the eugenics societies had been dissolved, as the principles of eugenics became linked with the 'racial purity' ideas of the Nazis). Many papers were published which indicated that adopted children thrived; they were shown as developing equally well, intellectually and academically, as children born to natural parents in similar circumstances, though there was some evidence that adopted children were at a slight disadvantage in personal and social functioning. But the consensus of expert opinion was that by the age of eight, most adoptions were considered successful.

Adopting parents were, in the 1940s, '50s and early '60s, seen as kindly, altruistic people who took on a disadvantaged child. There was a growing number of babies available for adoption as the 'permissive society' gradually gained ground. Numbers reached a climax in 1967, with 25,000 adoptions in England and Wales. That year the Abortion Act was passed. And the supply of babies immediately began to decrease.

Dr Shirley Bond refers to 'fashions' in adoption, and it is true that the adoption fashion of the 1950s and early '60s left one vital person very much out of the picture – the natural mother. In many, many cases, natural mothers were literally forced to yield their babies. Sometimes this was done in circumstances we would now consider unbearably cruel: women can remember young mothers in mother-and-baby homes actually having their babies torn from their arms.

Sylvia was the youngest in a Jewish family in London. Her father was a taxi-driver. She was seventeen and her boyfriend twenty-three when she became pregnant in 1958. 'We were going to be married, but my boyfriend disappeared. My parents tried for an abortion and I went to see a doctor in Harley Street. I was five months pregnant by then. And I really hadn't known I was pregnant – it just hadn't occurred to me. Looking back, I remember feeling that it just didn't seem real. It was a dreadful thing to happen in those days. You kept it quiet and you didn't let anyone know. The doctor decided that I should have a caesarian, because it would be less traumatic than going into labour, and better if I didn't see the baby. Nobody knew I was pregnant in the family. I remember wearing a girdle to hide it. My brother had emigrated to Canada, and my sister only learned about it recently – I wrote and told her. It was like that then – it wasn't respectable.'

When the time came for the baby to be born, the caesarian was duly performed. 'I remember coming around from the anaesthetic and I was crying and I was apparently saying "Don't put me in prison, don't put me in prison" because I felt so guilty. And the doctor was saying, yes, fine, you've got a lovely little boy. I had to sign certificates and so on. As far as I am aware it was all done through this doctor in Harley Street – he was Jewish too and very kind. It was as if there was no alternative; this was what they had decided. It was so unreal to me that I went along with it.' But Sylvia had one physical lifelong reminder – the caesarian scar. 'About six months afterwards I had adhesions which were rather nasty – and then had more surgery to get those out. I was scarred physically as well as psychologically. I knew I was different – I couldn't wear a bikini.'

Nearly twenty-six years after her son was born, when I talked to Sylvia, she uttered the words that so many natural mothers whose babies were taken for adoption repeat. 'Not a day goes by but I think of him. I don't know where he is, I don't know what he does, he might not still be alive, he might be married. I'd like him to know that I'm there if he needs me. He was adopted in London and was adopted by a Jewish couple, because it was arranged privately. They were reasonably well-off. I would love to see him from a distance. I used to walk around imagining that I'd bump into him, in London, in Harrods or somewhere. A lot of wealthy Jewish people shop at Harrods. You know, you get boys in nice school uniforms, in Harrods, at private schools. I'd look at them and think . . . would one of them be him? I look at actors on television and wonder.'

Sylvia subsequently married but never succeeded in having another child.

Many, many women lived through similar experiences. Sylvia's parents at least had the means to make private arrangements and she was never subjected to a public ward in a hospital or to a mother-and-baby home.

'I was twenty years old before I had a boyfriend,' wrote a woman from Northern Ireland in *Jigsaw* magazine, a now defunct publication which helped natural mothers and adopted children. 'I was very gullible and naive when a tall, handsome Canadian invited me out. He deserted me when I became pregnant and went back to Canada. My family disowned me. I was a maid in a boarding school and was given five minutes to pack my possessions and get out when the matron found out.

'As I was homeless and penniless I was really destitute. I had to humiliate myself and go to the police station and ask if they could help me in my plight. As my pregnancy was not noticeable I was found a job as a maid and arrangements were made for me to go into an unmarried mothers' home in Belfast when I was seven months pregnant. I cringe when I remember how we were all treated like criminals.

'One's first-born is a very special baby. There is that awful fear and dread of the unknown, especially the labour. Olivia was born on a Friday and I shall never forget that day. When I was admitted to the hospital several of the staff made derogatory and insulting remarks; one in particular took pleasure in frightening me and assured me that I would be yelling in labour. After the birth I just sobbed and sobbed.

'I begged them to let me keep her but the matron in the unmarried mothers' home put pressure on me to sign the papers. I tried to foster Olivia but when she was four months old she was adopted. I can describe in detail every item of clothing I dressed her in that terrible day. It was the most poignant, heartbreaking moment in my life when she was taken out of my arms for the last time. Adoption is worse than losing a baby in death. I later lost a three-week baby girl and a premature baby boy. It's heartbreaking, but one has to accept it.'

As another woman, whose son was born in 1953 in Dorset says, 'It always seems to have been assumed that the mother has no real feelings, having disposed of a rather dreadful burden with the "minimum of fuss and bother" and no one involved really wishes to know how she feels.'

And that, indeed, is how many women remember adoption experiences: a situation that they were forced into, which had no alternative. A Catholic social worker, recollecting dealing with unmarried mothers in 1962, describes it as being 'like a production line, quite honestly. We were doing two or three hundred adoptions a year [in that agency]. We had pages and pages of babies. Although other social workers from our agency had interviewed the mothers before the birth, we in child-care didn't see the girls until after the babies were born, and even then, because we would be seeing eight, nine, ten girls in a day, there just wasn't time for counselling as such. I find it horrible now, but in those days we didn't because we knew the alternative for the child was being brought up in a children's home.

'The mothers who asked for adoption had no accommodation and in any case did not want their families to know anything about the child. About one-third of the mothers who came to our agency for help had their babies adopted. The others either took them home, were allowed to keep the children with them in their living-in domestic jobs, or placed them in residential nurseries. Seeing forty-eight babies in cots with no individual love seemed far worse than visiting them in adoptive homes – many mothers felt the same, or were persuaded to do so.'

Yet not all the natural mothers reacted in the way I have described. Others went back to their single lives with relief. The same social worker now has the happier task of bringing natural mothers and their grown-up children together (since 1975, adoptees can obtain their original birth certificate and after counselling can sometimes trace their biological mothers). And she says: 'I am amazed at how well some of the mothers have coped.'

Adoption, in the 1980s, has changed beyond all recognition. First, as already mentioned, the numbers have dropped quite dramatically: in 1967 there were 25,000 adoptions in England and Wales; in 1983, there were just 1,400. The Catholic Crusade of Rescue were doing up to 300 adoptions annually in the early 1960s; today, they may do about thirty-six to forty. In the London Borough of Hammersmith, the adoption officer receives about 400 requests for babies each year from would-be adopters; about four new-born babies are placed in a year. There are thus 100 couples for every baby who becomes available for adoption. Many adoption societies have now closed their books for small babies, and adoption experts generally are keen to get across to the general public that there are virtually no babies available. Tony Hall, Director of the British Agencies for Fostering and Adoption (BAAF), says that the real interest has now shifted from small babies to older children, handicapped children and hard-to-place children.

Obviously, the principal reason for the fall in the number of babies is the passing of the Abortion Act. More easily available contraception also plays some part, but contraception alone seldom eliminates 'unplanned' pregnancy.

The second reason for the decline in the number of adoptable babies is that the social climate has altered so dramatically towards the single mother that many more unmarried girls are now keeping their babies. In a tangled sort of way, this is also linked with abortion; if a young woman decides positively against abortion, it indicates that she wants to have the child and thus to keep it.

With the wider availability of contraception, the legalization of abortion and the trend of single mothers to retain their children, the fashion has indeed moved against adoption, and since the middle 1970s has become well and truly entrenched. Young social workers in particular, who, from the 1970s onwards, tended to be of a more radical and feminist cast of mind, recoiled against the trauma of adoption, and the inevitable pain and grief that the natural mother felt in parting with her child. Adopting parents were subjected to assessment of a more and more searching type, and were often found to be wanting. The feminist view gained ground that adoption was about poor girls giving up their babies to rich, middle-class white couples. 'Essentially adoption in nuclear family societies is a way of taking babies and children from powerless women and giving them to heterosexual middle-class couples; from black to white and from single to married,' wrote Caroline Leinster in *Spare Rib* magazine. And with kinder social welfare laws, under which single mothers could be housed by the local authority and qualify for more allowances and benefits, the financial situation was also eased for the natural mother.

In crude terms, the 'market' altered. Adopting had been a 'buyer's market' when there were 'pages and pages' of babies. It is now a 'seller's market' – with fewer and fewer babies and the natural mother gaining more choice, more alternatives. Vast numbers of women, when faced with an unwanted pregnancy, actually only considered two alternatives: abortion or having and keeping the child. By the 1980s, adoption was seen by many as a third alternative for women who presented too late for abortion, or who came from more traditional cultures – Irish, Spanish, Maltese, Asian, where old-fashioned values sometimes still prevail, and the single mother is not always accepted. However, it is common in many Western societies today that the single mother *is* more accepted. Even in Spain, for instance, there has been a very noticeable change in such attitudes – with the exception of middle-class families in large cities where 'respectability' and family honour are still matters of the utmost importance. In such milieus, an abortion in London (often a late one) or a very secret adoption are still the courses chosen.

Partly in response to this change in attitude towards the single mother, the approach of the adoption agencies has changed too. Because the numbers are so reduced, social workers can now usually offer much more time, more counselling and more care to young women contemplating an adoption placement. They have shifted from offering practical help to insisting on overall care. The law which enables adopted children to obtain their birth certificates probably subtly altered attitudes to adoption, too. The natural mother may now feel that the break is not necessarily for ever. Adopted children were not always told they were adopted. Since 1958, there have been guidelines advising that adopting parents must tell children the truth. The whole trend has been towards more honesty.

By the middle of the 1970s, some agencies had introduced another innovation: introducing the natural mother to the adopting parents (obviously, only when she agreed to it). Photographs of the natural mother are sometimes provided for the child and the mother may leave a letter or a memento for the child so that the child could properly understand that he or she was not being adopted because he was not 'wanted' but because the natural mother had decided to give him the chance of a 'better' life.

Many of the old mother-and-baby homes have now closed down or changed completely. Before the 1970s, these were institutions where the pregnant girl would go six weeks before the birth of her child, and theoretically emerge six weeks afterwards, when the child would be placed for adoption: sometimes they stayed longer, caring for their children until an adopter was found. Today, the more usual practice is that the woman has her baby in a hospital, and the baby either goes directly from the hospital to prospective adopters, or goes to a foster-home while the mother decides if she wishes to go through with the adoption. (Organizations like Life, Lifeline and Let Live also have flats and houses where expectant young women can stay whether they are proceeding with adoption or intend to keep the baby. Such organizations can also arrange for a young woman – and it is often the younger ones who need it – to stay with a host family during the pregnancy and, if necessary, afterwards.) There is great anxiety not to press the mother in one direction or the other, but to let her reach her own decision through counselling and support. That, of course, is the ideal, but we do not live in an ideal world, and mothers can find themselves under subtle pressure of one kind or another. Nurses in maternity hospitals can make casual – and hurtful – remarks such as 'How could you give away such a lovely baby?'; West Indian nurses in particular, who come from a culture where illegitimate babies are easily accepted, may be shocked that a mother is considering adoption. 'Sometimes hospital staff make an adoption feel like a rejection,' says the adoption officer of one London local authority. 'The girls who think it through and are very well-intentioned about adoption are obviously very hurt and feel very misunderstood when people say this kind of thing. They are making an altruistic decision in the best interests of their child and society does not always support them in this.'

Whereas, formerly, mothers never received counselling before the birth of the child, and seldom very much afterwards, it is now agreed that the earlier counselling can start the better for the mother. Adoption is something which does need to be thought through, and the longer the better. If the counselling is good, it makes all the difference in the world. 'She was more like a friend than a social worker,' says Jane, a twenty-year-old mother from Lancashire who placed her son for adoption fourteen years ago. Jane was referring to the social worker who supported her right through the crisis, helped her to make her own decision, and helped her to come to terms with her decision.

Jane's case was an interesting one, and, as she puts it, 'it turned out for the best'. She was fifteen when she became pregnant, by her boyfriend, and their son was born just two weeks after her sixteenth birthday. She was the youngest in her own family, and although her parents were very kind about the baby (after the initial shock and, yes, disappointment), Jane herself felt that she would probably not be able to cope with a young baby as a schoolgirl mother. Moreover, her own mother was not in very good health, so she made enquiries about adoption. Helped through the process by an understanding social worker, she decided to place her son, Steven, for adoption. 'He was adopted when he was six weeks old. I met his new parents, their love for Steven and their gratitude to me was overwhelming. They asked me if they might change his name to Michael James. I told them that he was their child now.'

Of course Jane went through a period of mourning – which is always necessary after an adoption (and sometimes after an abortion too) – but she had to return to school, and besides, her mother's health was worsening. In fact, the illness was terminal and the mother died eighteen months later. Jane very much wanted to help nurse her mother through this last illness, and looking back, she knows that it would have much more difficult with a baby.

Two years later, Jane married her boyfriend, and three years after that they had a daughter, and subsequently another. 'As the years passed, I find it difficult to have regrets about my actions,' Jane writes. 'Had I had an abortion Steven would not have had a chance of life, and his new mum and dad would not have that beautiful child. If I had kept him there's every chance that my relationship with his father would have broken down under the pressure of trying to be a wife and mother at such a young age – besides the fact of my mother's illness. (I was the only daughter, having four brothers who would have found it difficult to tend to Mum as she had had a colostomy and required very personal attention.)' Like every mother who places a child for adoption, Jane has never forgotten her first baby. 'Steven is in my mind every day, and I sincerely hope that when he is eighteen he will seek me and his father out. Both of his sisters know about him and they too would love to meet him.' Jane adds that she is not anti-abortion; it is just that 'abortion is not reversible'. With adoption, the child lives, brings happiness to others, and there is always the hope that when he reaches eighteen, there will be a reunion.

Jane, in fact, did not go through any real depression when the baby was adopted – perhaps because she is a remarkable person herself, and also because she was supported by her family and the social worker. When her daughters were born, she reflected more on 'the pain I'd caused my own mother – though there was never a cross word from her . . . my dad was shocked at first – though afterwards he was great. My husband – then my boyfriend – at the time was more embarrassed than anything else.' Like Sylvia, like many women who remember being pregnant as a teenager, she remembers, too, how 'unrealistic' it all was at first; she said nothing to anyone about the pregnancy until it began to show. It was in fact her music teacher who first noticed, remarking that her voice had altered – a hormonal change that occasionally occurs in pregnancy.

So much depends, in adoption, on the reasons for adoption and on the kind of support that the natural mother gets. 'I had my son adopted simply to save my parents' good name,' says a woman from Hampshire who gave birth to a boy in 1954. She too has since married and had two children but 'hardly a week goes by when I don't think about the son I have lost and the deep personal sorrow this brings to me'. To feel pressurized into adoption for reasons of social respectability – and not to have any family support or surrounding social support – causes pain which may remain unresolved for many years. It is a negative experience for the mother when it is done under pressure, in secret, in isolation, without thinking through the process and without being helped through the mourning stage. The only way that adoption can be a positive alternative to abortion is when it is carried through with maximum support for the mother, and a freely-made decision on her part that it is for the best.

Some women choose adoption because they are too late for abortion, and some because they are opposed to abortion – even when they cannot keep the baby themselves. Debby Sanders is the founder of a small supportive organization called Women for Life. She has been put fully to the test of her principles. Divorced, with two sons, she became pregnant some years ago by a man who claimed that he was sterile. Presenting at a London hospital, she was asked straight away if she wanted a termination. 'I was single and hadn't planned to get pregnant – but I wasn't showing any signs of distress. On subsequent visits to the hospital, the same doctor ridiculed me for not having an abortion. I think the idea that anybody could actually have an unwanted child, and go ahead and put it up for adoption is by some people considered inhuman – whereas abortion would have been acceptable. But abortion didn't enter my head; whatever my predicament, the baby has rights too.'

Debby was, naturally, depressed about the situation, but she deliberately put herself in a frame of mind that she thought might be helpful: she knew she wanted to protect the baby's life and to bring him safely to delivery, but she tried not to identify with him as 'her' baby. The pregnancy was healthy, and she went into hospital determined to be detached from personal feelings about the child. She had come to dislike the father at this point, resentful of his deception. She told her existing children that the baby was going to be adopted, and they accepted this.

'And then the surprising thing was that when the baby was born – I imagined that because I really disliked the father that the baby would be really ugly and repellent to me. But he wasn't. He was absolutely beautiful. I was surprised that he was so lovely, and he looked so like the other boys. I never had the slightest change of mind about the adoption, but still, he was lovely.'

When she came out of hospital, Debby did have one very bad day. 'I always get post-natal depression for a very short time. And when I came out of hospital, I visualized these little fingers locked together and I thought "I'll never see that again". And I cried for hours, solidly. But it was a healthy thing – it was positive. Then the following day I went into the adoption office for the hand-over time. The baby had been kept in hospital overnight, and then we all met in the office and I was able to meet the baby's parents. They were lovely people. At any stage either party can change their mind. If I hadn't liked the look of them I would have been able to say "You are not having my baby". You don't have to meet, but if both parties want it, you can. I think it's valuable. For me it was absolutely right, because then it meant that the baby wasn't going into a sort of limbo – the baby was going to two people. You aren't given surnames, or where the people live.

'They were Jewish. That was fine – obviously, I felt human rights would figure very strongly in their make-up. I told them that I wanted the baby to be brought up in the knowledge of being adopted and I wanted him to be brought up pro-life. I was also able to say that when the baby is older you can say that I did love him, and it wasn't a possessive or selfish love, and that he wasn't to worry about me – but on the other hand I didn't want him to think that I was neglecting him – pushing him away. I do wish people would stop thinking about adoption as something inhuman. A few of the mothers in hospital said "How on earth could you do that? Why didn't you have a termination?" They were very judgemental. And I was very upset at the time, but I realize why now. I think they obviously loved their own children and identified with them, but it would be acceptable if I had had a termination because then nothing would be seen. I think they could kid themselves that there was nothing there, but if it's a real baby you're dealing with something different. The unborn baby is seen as inhuman; the born baby is seen as a full human being. It is a form of discrimination against human life just because it is not seen.'

Debby was told at every step, 'You may change your mind, and if you do, that's fine.' This was very important. 'I've known other people where they've been pressurized into having babies adopted, and suffered very much. I think people should be helped to go through the pregnancy, and then they must reach their own decision. Not alone – they need help.'

Debby's life has not been without its suffering, and for

all her positive attitudes and her unswerving commitment to the unborn child which sustained her through the aftermath of the adoption, she still often thinks of her little boy. When I wrote an article about Debby's experiences in the *Sunday Telegraph*, we got a message from the adoptive parents of her son to say that he was doing wonderfully and they valued him beyond rubies; this gave Debby a real moment of happiness. The child has still remained in her heart.

'If the mother can just hold on to that idea – that she has done her best for her child,' says Jean Thompson, an experienced local authority adoption officer, 'this will help her to get through the grieving times.' Miss Thompson reckons that on average it takes a woman a year to work through the bereavement of adoption.

It is, of course, all very well saying that every mother should have the choice of keeping her baby – and that our welfare laws should be structured to support the young single mother in this way. Of course every mother should have the opportunity of keeping her baby – yet there may arise a conflict between the feelings of the mother and the best interests of the child. In the adoption business, the child always comes first – this indeed is part of the shift of attitudes about adoption which took place in the 1960s. In former times, adoption was oriented towards the adopting parents; now adoption is focused on the child's best interests, and the adopting parents come third in the list of an adoption officer's priorities. (First, the interests of the child; second, the interests of the natural mother; third the interests of the adopting parents.) In any case, there are just far too many adopting parents, and the ways and means of choosing them have become stricter over the years.

In Britain, a couple wishing to adopt a baby must be over twenty-one years of age; the man must be under forty and the woman under thirty-five. When I asked Tony Hall, the director of the BAAF, why it was that a woman could not adopt over the age of thirty-five, although in normal circumstances women can become natural mothers well past that age, he replied: 'It is simply a rationing system. It is one way to reduce the numbers.' The couple must also be financially stable, have a good marriage but not be too involved with one another (one couple was turned down in England in 1983 because they were '*too* happily married, which would not give a child a realistic perception of relationships'). They must be energetic but relaxed, responsible but not over-anxious, they should have a wholesome desire for a child but not a neurotic longing (couples obsessed with getting a child are almost automatically turned down – so if you long to adopt a baby, don't show it too much). They should have a real understanding of the nature of adoption and a loving respect for the natural mother and the sacrifice she has made. Adoption officers today hold up their hands in horror at stories of adopting mothers blackening the name of the natural mother. 'She was not a good woman,' or 'She didn't much like children,' was what adopted children were told about their natural mothers in the past. Adopting parents are chosen much more carefully today. In addition to virtues of character, they should not be more than seven pounds overweight and should not smoke; neither should they have any hereditary illnesses.

The natural mother is in control as far as the adoption is concerned and can, if she wishes, make quite idiosyncratic stipulations about the adopting parents. Claudia Brady, an Irish girl, gave birth to twins in 1977 and waited a year for the right adoptive parents. She wanted a professional couple who were musical and liked to go walking together. She found them.

Claudia's case is exceptional because she is an exceptional person: very intelligent, curious, highly-tuned and spiritual – 'an unchurched Christian', she calls herself. She was nursing in the west of England when she became pregnant. The putative father was a friend, but not a boyfriend: a concerned, warm-hearted man, a professional social worker. Claudia had been on the Pill – she was aged twenty-four at the time – but had come off it for a while. Abortion was suggested, of course – indeed, offered on a plate. Claudia thought about it. It was very convenient. Quite early on in the pregnancy, she learned it would be twins. Any notion she had had of keeping the child herself went out of the window: she knew she was not in a position to keep two babies. 'And yet I had a sense of awe about nature and whatever lies beyond nature: this was very much to the fore during this period. Also I knew there were women around me who would help, who would befriend me, who would just be there when I needed them.' The father of the twins was happy for her to continue the pregnancy – he did not oppose Claudia's feelings, yet he did not particularly want to be involved, either. Neither of them wanted marriage, and were quite without rancour on that point. She felt strong enough to go ahead, strong and affirmative about her pregnancy. She also had an extremely good social worker, but her strongest counsellor was 'my inner voice, God, whatever you like to call it'.

The twins were born early – a boy and a girl – and were put in intensive care. Claudia visited them there, and when the little boy was quite poorly, sat with them while they were christened. He pulled through. ('The baptism was a healing.') Claudia's father came over from Ireland to see the babies and was sweet, kind and loving about it all.

Grief there was, certainly, over that adoption. For a year they were in a foster-home while waiting for adoption. She would visit them, come away and cry and cry. But eventually the right parents were found, and the babies went to them.

Claudia is exceptional because she has a spiritual dimension to her life which few people possess. 'I could not have carried through – done it without that spiritual help. I'm not strong in myself – I don't know where it came from, but it transformed the situation into something very positive. Even though I was the loser in a way I thought – there is sacrifice; and there is also resurrection. You come through pain and find a sense of renewal.' Sometimes she wonders what the twins are like now, but doesn't worry because she knows, really, that everything is all right. 'I feel we are never quite separated,' she says of her children. Perhaps one day they will contact her –

but whether they do or not, the spiritual link is still there.

Claudia went back to her nursing after the babies were born and qualified. Since then she has changed direction, gone to college to study theology, and become particularly drawn to Oriental religions which teach the value of 'letting go', of not clinging on to things as personal possessions.

Claudia had the insight to realize that, because of her circumstances, it was in the best interests of the children that they should be adopted. And that, quite rightly, is the key phrase in child-care today: 'The best interest of the child.' Often the best interest of the child and the woman's right to choose are in direct conflict. 'Sometimes our job is very difficult,' says an adoption social worker who places babies. 'You must never pressurize the mother in any way, just support her in whatever decision she makes herself. Yet in your heart of hearts, you know that it would so often be better for the child if he were to go to an adopting family than to stay with a teenage mother, who might be single and living alone in a council flat. But you still have to support the mother's decision, whatever it is.'

It is well-established that adoption is not regarded favourably by women today; in one survey (quoted in *Single and Pregnant* by Sally MacIntyre) of thirty-six pregnant and unmarried young women, only *one* woman said she would choose adoption, and eighteen dismissed adoption immediately as intolerable; abortion, single parenting or getting married were, overwhelmingly, the preferred choices. Indeed, adoption has a poor image throughout society as a last-ditch option for a child who has absolutely no other way of being cared for.

However, there is no doubt that some children would do better if adopted from the start. There are 96,000 children in care in Britain and the majority of them will never be reunited with their natural parents. It certainly would have been in the best interests of many of these children if they had been adopted as babies, for it is well-established that growing up in care often perpetuates the whole cycle of deprivation and is a very unsatisfactory basis for the forming of personal relationships. Many of these youngsters might have been adopted at birth if society had had a more positive attitude to adoption; if it supported women through the adoption process, and if people could learn that adoption is a loving choice, an altruistic choice that a mother may make in the best interests of her child – and not a gesture of abandonment.

What does happen quite frequently is that a young mother will want to keep her child – as, naturally, nearly every mother would want to. She will be housed by the local authority and will qualify for a single parent's allowance. So there she is in her flat with her baby. And she does her best for her baby. But babies grow into toddlers; they become demanding. The mother is lonely. Perhaps a boyfriend moves in who may himself be young and have little regard for the child. And it is here that problems may start. The child disrupts their lives. This is the profile of the child 'at risk' of abuse or battering. If the child does become battered, it gets taken into care; perhaps it will be fostered with a hope that the family can be 'rehabilitated'. Perhaps the family cannot be rehabilitated – so the child is adopted at the age of two, three, four. The child can be successfully adopted at that age, but it has already gone through a certain amount of disturbance which would not have occurred if the baby had been adopted at birth.

This situation cannot be helped directly; whatever the circumstances of the mother, she must have a totally free choice as to whether she keeps her baby or relinquishes it. Sometimes we have to try something out before we know we cannot do it, and sometimes young mothers can learn only by experience that they cannot, in their present situation, cope with a child. But there is a new trend now of trying to make young mothers aware that it is all right if they do want to place the child for adoption as a toddler; it is never too late to come back to the adoption officer or agency and say that she has changed her mind. No one will ever reproach her for this. Indeed, a mother who comes back with a two-year-old saying that she has decided that she cannot mother the child as much as she would want to, or that she is afraid of battering the child, is often admired for her insight and wisdom. The mother who is afraid to face up to these possibilities may herself be at risk, and her child may be at more risk.

The growing trend for fostering and adopting older children (and handicapped children) is partly because there are so few babies, and partly because there are so many older children who need homes, which in turn is partly because they weren't adopted as babies. Fashions in adoption may change again – for fashions in ideas are always on the move. In the future the law may be further amended, too, so that natural mothers can trace their children who were adopted years previously (at present children can trace their mothers, but the mother may not trace the child). Mothers may be able to feel they can place a baby for adoption in the hope that they will be reunited in the future. More flexibility in social attitudes to child-care would help adoption gain a better image and become a useful option for mothers.

It is obvious that adoption is seldom problem-free, and people who grow up in an adopted family sometimes feel there is a missing link in their lives (although this is probably now diminishing with the more open attitude of adopting parents, and the rights of the adopted child to know of his biological parents). 'I was an adopted child,' wrote a mother of four from Swanley in Kent. 'My own home now is happy, stable and the children well-adjusted. I think a natural mother who has her baby – rather than aborting it – though she isn't in a position to bring it up herself, is acting out of love.'

'I am twenty-eight, happily married with a daughter of eleven and a son of eleven months,' wrote a schoolteacher from Devon. 'I was adopted, and I take the positive view that *someone* wanted me, even if the woman whose womb carried me didn't.'

Some experienced workers in this field believe that there will be less adoption in the future, as there will be an ever-diminishing number of babies as contraception and abortion become universally available. Tony Hall, probably the most authoritative voice in the British adoption world, certainly believes that the 'baby market' for adoption is almost at an end – the number of babies will simply continue to fall. But the demand for babies, in the developed world, is acute; it has rightly been called a 'baby famine'. In West Germany the average family is now down to 0.7 children. Infertility has always been with us, and although in some cases it can be helped more today with drug treatment and surgery, besides IVF, some infertility is actually caused by new developments – from the IUD, occasionally from prolonged use of the Pill, from venereal infections, and, ironically, from abortion itself. Some women who have early abortions do not succeed in getting pregnant later, and apply to adopt.

This demand will at some stage become irresistible. In America the surrogate mother is already part of the response to the baby famine, as is the growing trade in babies from the Third World. Surrogacy has been banned in Britain, but it will still go on illegally. It has been going on for years – particularly within extended families – with no one knowing about it. In contrast to natural mothers who become pregnant by accident and yield their babies for adoption with a real sense of pain, surrogate mothers actively want to have a baby for another couple with the intention of handing it over. They have been criticized as greedy and materialistic, since they are – in the States – paid for the pregnancy, but research on the women who do it has revealed a more complex picture. They do it from a mixture of motives; some like being pregnant; some like the notion of the gift relationship involved; and some, significantly, want to compensate for an earlier abortion or miscarriage which has left them with a feeling of 'unfinished business'. Surrogate mothers who go through a pregnancy for another couple speak of the gratifying experience of making the commissioning couple so happy.

Not in the child's best interest? Perhaps. But is abortion in a child's best interest?

Of course, some people who argue for abortion think that you cannot compare creating life with destroying it:

'If you kill a foetus, nothing happens, there is no child.' But if you bring a child into being 'You might produce an unhappy individual. The responsibility is of a different kind' (from *Saving Life and Causing Death* by Jonathan Glover). This is the utilitarian view which has so predominated our whole evaluation of life in recent years: everything must be avoided that might produce 'unhappiness'. But that is not how life is. 'As soon as there is life, there is danger,' said Balzac, and the true appreciation of life lies in understanding that inherent risk. There is always danger in life, always a risk of unhappiness, and the best-laid plans have never successfully avoided difficulties or dangers. Yet the fact remains that most people are glad they are alive: the evidence is overwhelming that whatever is living wants to live.

The real truth is that people will go on having babies, by hook or by crook. Many of these children grow up in care and in unsatisfactory situations for themselves because our society is so squeamish about adoption; we are so keen never to suggest to a woman who cannot cope but who does not want to kill that there are 100 families crying out for her baby, and that far from creating 'unhappiness', adoption is a loving choice very often in the best interests of the child. Yes, it is hard, but the hardship varies according to many other contingencies; according to the support available; according to the individual woman herself; according to social approval or disapproval; according to accepted custom and practice. In *The Myth of Motherhood*, the feminist writer Elisabeth Badinter puts forward the theory that motherhood is learned, not innate, and that if social conditions are favourable, women can as easily forget about their children as care for them. A third of Parisian women in the eighteenth century sent their children to be wet-nursed with hardly a backward glance, although most babies thus treated actually died. Mothers can take or leave their children, were Badinter's implications.

It is not an argument I necessarily agree with, because I do not believe that people are simply constructed by 'society', but I do know that people are infinitely variable, infinitely resilient, and very receptive to social ideas and pressures. It follows that adoption *could* be viewed more positively – and flexibly – than it is today.

5

MEDICAL AND GENETIC ABORTION

'People want "quality babies" and are prepared to be selective and reject the imperfect.' – Dermot McDonald, *Ethical Issues in Reproductive Medicine*

'The consequence of selective abortion is to eliminate individuals with particular genes or chromosomal abnormalities.' – Harry Harris, *Prenatal Diagnosis and Selective Abortion*

When we speak about abortion today, we are usually referring to 'social' abortion, that is, those undertaken because the woman, or the couple, do not want or feel they cannot cope with a child at this particular time. There may be pressing circumstances, such as housing difficulties or shortage of money, but, in general, a social abortion is one which is carried out on a healthy woman who has no *medical* need to be relieved of a pregnancy. (It was formerly called 'criminal' abortion.)

Only 2 per cent of all abortions are carried out for what I call here 'medical' and 'genetic' reasons. Not everyone is happy with these terms so I shall define them for the purposes of this book. A 'medical' abortion is one which is carried out because the mother's health is in danger and an abortion may save her life. I do not include in this category abortions carried out on psychiatric grounds as this is a grey area, and 'mental health' is no longer seen as a true medical qualification for abortion. Medical abortion relates to physical illness: cancer, serious heart defects, serious chest illnesses. This form of abortion is sometimes called 'therapeutic' abortion, but I decline to use this form since abortion is not a therapy. Medically, it may be a last-ditch effort to save a woman's life, but it is not a therapy in the dictionary sense of having a 'curative power'.

A 'genetic' abortion is also an imprecise term. What I am speaking of here is abortion because the foetus is found to be defective. Now sometimes this is for 'genetic' reasons – an inherited abnormality – but sometimes the foetus is abnormal for other reasons, such as infection. There is no satisfactory term to describe abortion in the case of the abnormal foetus: in America it is known as 'elective' abortion, and in Britain 'selective' abortion. So although 'genetic' abortion is an imprecise term, I will nevertheless use it to refer to abortion of the abnormal foetus because it is at least through the science of genetics that we have learned most about abnormalities in the unborn. Sometimes genetic abortion is also referred to as medical abortion, but it seems to me to be important to distinguish between abortion undertaken in the hope of saving or prolonging the mother's life (where the baby is perfectly normal), and abortion undertaken to destroy the abnormal foetus (although the mother is essentially healthy and in no danger of dying).

To confuse matters further, medical textbooks of the past have had different interpretations of the word abortion itself. Sometimes it meant miscarriage (as it still does in an agricultural context: a cow who has an abortion is a cow which has miscarried). But here abortion did not mean miscarriage, it meant medical abortion – an operation to save the life of the mother by sacrificing the child. Of course, there was more call for medical abortion in the past when pregnancy was much more dangerous than it is now. In the 1930s, it was seventy times more dangerous for an American woman to have a baby than it is today: the rate of maternal death stood at 700 per 100,000. Causes of death included infection (250 out of the 700), toxaemia (180), haemorrhage (70), clots to the lung or leg, cancer, TB, and deaths from anaesthesia. Today the rate is 10 maternal deaths (11 in England) for every 100,000 live births.

Chronic illness could be an indication for medical abortion, and tuberculosis was an obvious case in point. Many medical textbooks of the 1920s referred to the controversy over whether a woman with TB should be aborted. As often happens, medical opinion was divided. Some argued that abortion would prolong the woman's life; others countered that the sacrifice of the child was not worth the three extra years (on average) that would be added to the woman's life. But the question did not weigh very heavily with doctors, who were more accustomed to the procedure of destroying a fully-formed baby than perhaps doctors are today; until the Second World War, doctors carried around with them a nasty instrument called a cranial saw. In the case of obstructed labour, they had the option of literally sawing off the head of the baby to save the mother's life. It was known as the 'Destructive Operation', and when it had to be done it had to be done. Of course, some refused to do the operation and some women refused to undergo it.

TB is now no longer an indication for medical abortion because today it is curable. There are other dangerous chronic conditions which would once have been a reason for medical abortion, such as cardiac disease, hypertensive heart disease, diabetes and kidney troubles. These conditions can now usually be managed in pregnancy. Indeed, a woman who received a heart transplant, Betsy Smith of San Diego, California, subsequently gave birth to a child. (She died about a year later but her death was not connected with the pregnancy, which had been managed very successfully.)

The great decline in maternal mortality – of women dying as a consequence of pregnancy and childbirth – began in the 1940s. Indeed, in 1944, an optimistic medical paper was read at the New York Obstetrical Society in which gynaecologists ventured the opinion that abortion would soon be 'a thing of the past'. They were, of course, focusing on medical abortion. Social abortion – or criminal abortion, as they would have regarded it – simply did not figure. What actually happened, of course, was that medical reasons for abortion declined rapidly at the same time as the demand for social abortion rose.

There is another interesting difference in medical attitudes past and present. The essays and books of the 1920s and '30s discussed grounds for medical abortion purely on the basis of what the *doctor* thought best. Discussions over whether women with TB should be aborted or not hardly ever took the woman's feelings into consideration. This conforms to the common medical attitude towards mothers in the past. As Ann Oakley points out in her book *The Captured Womb*, doctors in general (who have usually been men) have tended to look on women's bodies as de-personalized anatomies to be 'managed', and not as part of a sentient and intelligent human being whose wishes deserve consideration. It is thanks to the feminist campaigns that women's bodies are beginning to be treated with the dignity that is proper to a person, and thanks to the abortion-on-demand slogan 'It's a woman's right to choose' that doctors are now generally more sensitive to the patient's choice. When medical abortion is recommended today, the woman's own feelings are much more likely to be considered. Cancer remains the outstanding example of an indication for medical abortion: if the woman has cancer and is pregnant, in many cases medical abortion gives her a better chance of survival. 'However,' says Mr Christopher B-Lynch, a gynaecologist with a practice in Harley Street and a National Health consultancy as well, 'the woman's own feelings must always be the first priority. We must put the facts before her, and she must choose.' Given the facts, and the true prognosis, the woman will choose more freely, he observes.

One of his patients was a woman of thirty-five with cancer of the cervix and pregnant. She was eight weeks pregnant and abortion would have been simple and uncomplicated at that stage. However, she had only recently been married (for the second time) and was desperately keen to continue the pregnancy. She told the consultant that she would have the baby 'even if it killed her'. He was personally doubtful about her decision because he would have preferred to start treatment for the cancer immediately – a procedure which would harm, and probably destroy, the baby. However, he bowed to the woman's choice, but suggested a compromise: he would induce the baby at the earliest stage at which he considered it would have a good chance of surviving, and then begin the treatment. She agreed.

The pregnancy continued until thirty-two weeks (forty is the norm) and the baby was then induced. The baby was fine at caesarian delivery, and a radical hysterectomy (removal of the womb) was performed at the same time. Two years afterwards, both mother and baby were doing very well indeed. The mother was very happy with her child, and there had been no recurrence of the cancer. The woman was as healthy as she would have been if she had chosen termination, but she also had the baby.

The problem with these cases is that nobody can be sure how they will turn out. An afflicted woman may choose termination to prolong her life (often for the sake of her existing children), and despite the termination she may still die. She may choose to continue the pregnancy, give birth, and also die. She may choose termination and life. She may choose to have the baby – and still live.

Perhaps the most difficult cases are those where both the pregnancy and the cancer are advanced. There have been several outstanding cases where a moribund woman (a woman with very little chance of personal survival) has chosen to continue the pregnancy, altruistically deciding that it is better to save one life than neither.

Mrs Sheryl Skirton, a nurse from Bristol, was diagnosed with cancer of the liver during a routine pregnancy check-up. She was thirty weeks pregnant. The cancer was advanced; the pregnancy was already viable. She decided not to have the baby induced, but to let it have its chance, and she also refused all drugs which might be bad for it. A few weeks later, she gave birth to a son weighing 2lb 10oz. Despite his low birth-weight, he survived. Several days after the birth, Mrs Skirton died. She already had one child, which might have been a consideration for providing a sibling. There was no way her life could have been meaningfully prolonged, for by the time the cancer was discovered she was, in truth, already doomed. But it was heroic of her, all the same, to wish to give life to her second child.

There have been other cases where moribund mothers have asked to be put on to life-support machines should they fall into a coma – so that the baby can be brought through the final stages of pregnancy.

In the west of England, a twenty-six-year-old woman, married with one child, presented with what the cancer specialist described as a 'very advanced tumour on her breast'. She was twenty weeks pregnant – just half-way through the gestation of a much-wanted child – but her condition was very serious and required immediate surgery and radiotherapy. The latter would definitely affect the baby. On the other hand, the baby could probably be saved by deferring treatment for the mother. I talked to the cancer specialist in this case. He was in the classic dilemma that so seldom occurs nowadays: mother or baby? The doctor put the facts before the woman and her husband. After much deliberation, the couple chose abortion – they already had one child. The woman knew her own chances of survival were not good, but she did not want to leave her husband with a young baby in the event of her death. The pregnancy was terminated – obviously traumatic, since it was done by inducing labour. Treatment for the cancer was commenced immediately, but the woman died two years later.

No one can make definitive statements about the progress of any disease, including cancer. In the case of a mother in Surrey, cancer of the breast was diagnosed at sixteen weeks pregnancy. The woman had two children already but chose to continue the pregnancy. The birth was normal but, despite surgery and radiotherapy, the woman died when the baby was one year old. The young husband was left with three children to care for, in difficult circumstances. Afterwards people said: 'If only she had had an abortion, perhaps she would have lived.' But we simply do not know.

A useful comparison can be made with the Republic of Ireland which, in a way, is a unique laboratory for the study of maternal health. Abortion is absolutely forbidden. The unborn child is, by Constitutional Amendment in 1983, a citizen of the Republic and the state is pledged to the protection of the foetus. In a mother-or-baby decision, the ethic advanced is that doctors should strive equally for both lives. This is, in fact, the doctrinal Catholic position, and would not be accepted in non-Catholic countries or, indeed, in many other Catholic countries today. However, it does mean that maternal health can be studied more conclusively in the Republic of Ireland than elsewhere, and it is possible to examine objectively if good standards of maternal health can be maintained without recourse to abortion.

In fact, as everywhere else in the developed world, maternal deaths have steadily decreased in the Republic of Ireland in recent years.

Maternal Deaths per 100,000 Live and Still Births

	Republic of Ireland	Northern Ireland	England and Wales	Scotland
1962	43	30	36	39
1968	36	27	24	15
1976	16	11	13	15
1980	7	7	11	14

As the above table shows, in 1962, there were 43 maternal deaths per 100,000 live and still births in the Republic, in comparison with a figure of 30 per 100,000 in Northern Ireland (where abortion is permitted for medical reasons), 39 in Scotland (medical abortion permitted) and 36 in England and Wales (abortion available medically and sometimes socially). In 1968, after the Abortion Act in Britain (which liberalized social grounds) the figures stood thus: Republic of Ireland, 36; Northern Ireland, 27; England and Wales, 24; Scotland, 15. By 1976, things had greatly improved, and by 1980, the Republic of Ireland's maternal deaths were comparing favourably with those in neighbouring countries with abortion laws.

Thus we can see that maternal health can, today, be maintained by good medicine without recourse to abortion. It is the opinion of many Irish doctors that *contraception* is medically necessary to protect the health of older women and women suffering from illnesses where a pregnancy is inadvisable.

After examining twenty-one maternal deaths (out of 75,317 births) at the National Maternity Hospital in Dublin, Dr John Murphy and his colleague Dr Kieran O'Driscoll concluded that eighteen of these deaths were medically unavoidable (they included deaths by traffic accident and drowning, pulmonary embolisms, cancer diagnosed late in pregnancy, infection before and after delivery, and cerebral-vascular accident). Three cases remained arguable, Dr Murphy thought. One woman died from an asthmatic attack. In Britain, she might well have been offered an abortion early in pregnancy as she was a known asthmatic although she was well until twenty weeks in the pregnancy. She died when twenty-seven weeks pregnant and so did the child. A late abortion would not have saved her – any operation would have hastened her death. The doctors could have done a caesarian to save the child, but declined for fear of making the mother worse. Another woman had an eclamptic fit. This woman might have been offered an abortion in Britain because she was forty-three years old, but early in pregnancy she did not seem dangerously at risk. Her blood pressure was 'moderately high', but it never went over 140/90, which is considered manageable. She was admitted to hospital at thirty-seven weeks pregnancy, had labour induced, had an eclamptic fit and never woke up. The baby was delivered by caesarian section and was healthy. In the third case, the woman's life would certainly have been saved by an early abortion. She was a person with an unusual congenital heart defect called

Eisenmenger's syndrome. She was advised not to become pregnant at all. As a doctor's wife and a doctor's daughter the risks were fully known to her and she deliberately chose to become pregnant. With Eisenmenger's syndrome the heart shunts are inverted and a person in this condition is delicate, pregnant or not. When pregnant, there is a reported 50:50 chance of survival. In this case, the woman embarked on the pregnancy, collapsed at thirty-five weeks and died. The child survived. At around the same time, another woman at the same hospital with the same heart defect made the same gamble – and survived to become a mother.

In the treatment of pregnant women with cancer, the policy in the Republic of Ireland, according to Dr Murphy, is to treat the woman as a patient and 'the baby must take its chances'. This is not necessarily how it is done in countries where abortion is available. In Britain, the woman will be offered an abortion before treatment begins. If the 'baby takes its chances', it may abort spontaneously with some cancer treatments, or it may be affected by scattered radiation. Babies born in such circumstances may develop leukaemia, have heart defects or microcephaly. The problem of the pregnant woman with cancer is by definition an unusual one, because women in their child-bearing years are not characteristically a cancer-prone group. But where it occurs it will continue to be a serious dilemma because doctors just do not know whether they are sacrificing a child to save the mother, or sacrificing the mother to save a child. As a general rule a woman who is too ill to continue a pregnancy is, today, quite seriously ill. And even some medical abortions now are partly done for 'social' reasons – not necessarily to save the life of the mother, as she is moribund anyway, but to save the 'quality of life' of those she leaves behind. In fact, figures for 'medical' abortion cannot really be successfully compiled in most countries today because an abortion done on medical grounds often includes social reasons.

'We can manage nearly all pregnancies today, medically,' says Dr David Paintin, of St Mary's Paddington. 'That is, if the woman wants to continue it. Of course, if a woman with a chronic condition such as heart disease or diabetes wants a termination, she will immediately qualify on medical grounds. But if she really wants the baby, we can usually bring her through it.'

What is widely called 'genetic' abortion is something which touches the lives of many more people today. Each pregnant woman who is offered pre-natal screening knows she may be faced with the dilemma of a 'genetic' abortion. Again, I must reiterate that the term is imprecise because, as it has been pointed out to me, abortion cannot be inherited, and some indications for these abortions are not for genetic reasons – as in the case of rubella, for instance. (This is where the mother contracts German measles early in the pregnancy and the chances are that the baby will have been affected. Abortion is usually offered in such circumstances because the baby may be born handicapped – though not invariably.)

Pre-natal testing for abnormalities takes several different forms. There is, first, *ultrasound*. Originally developed by a French physicist, Paul Langevin, for the detection of enemy submarines, this technique of measuring sound waves whose echoes can be projected on to a screen was pioneered for pregnancy by Professor Ian Donald in Glasgow in the late 1950s. (He originally employed the technique to observe cancers, and it is still used in cancer diagnosis.) Ultrasound in pregnancy is fairly routine and has many uses. It can diagnose multiple births early in the pregnancy – perhaps as early as six to eight weeks' gestation. It can measure the date of the pregnancy accurately, and is often used, too, in routine abortion. Indeed, the competent abortionist always uses ultrasound for later abortions (– so I was told by an experienced abortion doctor). It can help predict some miscarriages. It can discover what is known as a 'missed abortion' (where the foetus has died, but not yet aborted spontaneously). It can diagnose ectopic pregnancy and verify a placenta pravia (where the placenta is suspected of blocking the baby's exit). It can detect abnormalities such as anencephaly (a gross malformation of the head, where the baby actually has no brain), hydrocephaly (water on the brain – a treatable condition in many cases), diaphragmatic hernia (a protrusion into the chest of stomach-gut) and, perhaps most important, spina bifida, the neural tube defect whereby the arches at the back of the spine are incomplete and varying degrees of handicap occur as a consequence.

Secondly, there is *amniocentesis*. 'Amnio', as women call it colloquially, is a more invasive test than ultrasound and is not routinely offered in Britain to women under thirty-five years of age, though it is becoming more usual to offer it to all pregnant women in America. Some hospitals offer amniocentesis with a view to information, so an abortion would not necessarily follow if the test showed something was the matter with the baby. Other hospitals want agreement to abortion automatically. Some people believe that amniocentesis ought to be offered to all women. However, it would not be 'cost-effective' within the National Health Service to do so, (a private amniocentesis costs about £250). Statistically, women are not considered to be 'at risk' of having a Down's syndrome child – the most common chromosomal abnormality – under the age of thirty-five – some would say under the age of thirty-seven. It is not a pleasant procedure – a needle is penetrated through the abdominal wall and into the uterus – and it can create a great deal of anxiety, for young women in most cases needless anxiety.

There are no tests which *guarantee* a healthy or a normal baby, but amniocentesis indicates when there is a chromosomal abnormality, the most common cause of which is Down's syndrome (or mongolism, as it is erroneously called). In 1966, Dr Mark Steele and Dr Roy Breg first reported successful culturing of cells taken from the amniotic fluid (the 'waters' surrounding the baby) and getting chromosome studies from these cells. In 1968 Down's syndrome was diagnosed for the first time in the uterus using this method. Since then the practice has grown. It is carried out at about sixteen to eighteen weeks' pregnancy because before that time there is not enough amniotic fluid for the needle to draw out from the womb. The cells from the amniotic fluid are cultured – which takes about two weeks, but possibly more if there are difficulties growing the cells. Many, many women say that those few weeks waiting for the results of an amniocentesis are the longest weeks in any pregnancy. The test simply shows whether the baby has a normal chromosome pattern.

The risk of miscarriage with amniocentesis is very low, about one in 200, but it is difficult to measure this because women miscarry when nothing has been done, and doctors differ. Professor Peter Huntingford puts the risk at one miscarriage for every 100 to 200 tests. However, if miscarriage does follow amniocentesis, the woman may feel worse about it, and may blame the test. Amniocentesis should always be preceded by ultrasound.

Amniocentesis tests are often offered on the understanding that if there is an indication that the baby is affected, the woman will agree to an abortion. It is seldom that a woman refuses an abortion when abnormality has been diagnosed: at London's University College Hospital (UCH) one of several leading teaching hospitals where amniocentesis has been done since 1971, only two women are known to have refused an abortion in these circumstances, and in one of these cases the woman arranged for her Down's syndrome child to be put into care when it was born. Small wonder that doctors sometimes argue that to give birth to a handicapped child is to impose a 'burden on society'. Dr Harry Harris wrote in *Prenatal Diagnosis and Selective Abortion*, a textbook that is still an authority on the subject of these abortions,

> In traditional societies, the doctors should only be concerned with the welfare of their patients. But in these changing social times, some may take a wider view of their responsibilities. They may, for example, consider that the family, even if they are not inclined to the idea, should be pressed to take advantage of the opportunity for the social good . . . it is socially

desirable to minimize as far as possible the amount of ill health in the community.

Now that the state pays the bills, the state has a vested interest in minimizing the damage.

Yet, in truth, few women have to be pressed. 'Most people are absolutely rabid about one point,' says a leading genetic specialist and counsellor. 'They do not want a handicapped child.' There is probably more demand for pre-natal testing than there is supply, and it is likely that demand will continue to grow. Opinion polls indicate too that the majority of people are overwhelmingly in favour of aborting the defective foetus; and according to Michael Tooley, there is much support for infanticide of the new-born handicapped, too. Many people who are anti-abortion in other circumstances would agree with abortion of the abnormal foetus.

However, a minority of women choose not to present for pre-natal testing because they do not want to know if there is anything wrong with the child. One consultant gynaecologist in Cumbria puts this at around 15 per cent of pregnant women to whom such testing would normally be available. One Catholic woman in Lincolnshire, for example, does not go to her doctor when pregnant, until it is too late for such tests. 'I'll accept what I am sent,' is her very deliberate attitude (she is in her early thirties with four healthy children).

Other tests which may be done pre-natally include the *alpho-feto-protein* (AFP) test: this is a test of the mother's blood to establish the level of AFP being produced by the developing foetus. It is done at about seventeen weeks. It can indicate a suspected neural tube defect in the baby, as well as certain other congenital abnormalities, notably of the gastrointestinal area. A high level of AFP would normally be followed by ultrasound and amniocentesis.

Sex-linked tests: some hereditary diseases are passed through the mother to male children only. The sex of the baby is known by growing its cells obtained by amniocentesis. Thus sex-linked tests are done by amniocentesis.

Foetoscopy and chorionic villus sampling: foetoscopy is

the inspection of the foetus and placenta through the uterine wall with a foetoscope, to allow direct visualization of the unborn child and its support system. It is now seldom done simply to look at the foetus, but it may be used as a method to obtain foetal blood.

Chorionic villus sampling – formerly known as trophoblast sampling – is a test done very early (at eight to eleven weeks). It is also an invasive technique – the most common method is by the insertion of a flexible catheter via the cervix – and it is considered most useful when there is a high risk of a detectable abnormality such as thalassaemia where the risk is one in four. It can also be used for the exclusion of chromosome abnormalities in older women. It is not useful, however, for neural tube defects (spina bifida) and it carries a higher risk than amniocentesis. However, it may be used more in the future, when it is perfected.

Radiography, though frequently mentioned in textbooks, has now been technically superseded by ultrasound.

Measurement of blood antibodies in the maternal bloodstream may be done to discover whether the woman is infected with rubella (German measles) or not. There is, alas, no test to indicate whether the embryo or foetus has been affected by the mother contracting German measles, so it is calculated on the basis of numerical odds. If the infection is contracted in the first month of pregnancy, the statistical chances of the child being born deaf, blind or having another form of disablement such as a heart defect or perhaps mental retardation are about 50 to 60 per cent. In the second month of pregnancy, this drops to about 25 per cent risk; in the third month, about 7 per cent. There is also a continuing risk of spontaneous miscarriage. The connection between rubella and foetal malformations was not suspected until 1940 and not fully established until 1965. It is to be hoped that this is a diminishing problem because young girls are now routinely given a vaccination against rubella, preferably at about the age of ten. Of course there are always individuals who fall through the net, and very occasionally immunization itself fails. There have also been cases where adult women have not been sufficiently strongly warned not to become pregnant for at least three months after immunization. 'I was married a few days after my rubella injection,' a teacher from Wigan in Lancashire wrote. 'And happily set about starting the family I wanted. It was almost in the same sentence that my GP told me I was pregnant – and that my baby had a 30 per cent risk of being deformed in some way. Either blind, deaf, mentally retarded, or would have a hole in the heart . . . the doctor advised me, over and over again, that I should have an abortion.' The woman refused on religious grounds, and through a difficult pregnancy stubbornly clung to the belief that the baby would be all right. Indeed, her daughter was born healthy and normal. In this case, the GP was not correct in advising termination: according to *The Lancet*, it is advisable not to begin a pregnancy until three months after rubella immunization, but it is not an indication for termination. In tests in the United States, out of 730 women who had received rubella injections in the three months before or after conception, no child was born with congenital rubella syndrome defects as a consequence. However, some doctors, and some people, would rather pursue a policy of 'better safe than sorry' with regard to handicap.

Those who champion pre-natal testing generally call it a great advance for women and for parents. Those who oppose it call it a 'search and destroy' mission. As indicated, the people who oppose abortion of the handicapped foetus are in the minority. However, there are ethical problems associated with this form of abortion and they should not be ignored. Handicapped people may feel offended that their kind are singled out for pre-natal elimination. One of the most interesting expansions in the Society for the Protection of Unborn Children (SPUC) in recent years has been a 'Handicap Division', wherein the disabled argue that they, too, have a right to life, and a right not to have their quality of life judged by others.

Alison Davis, who heads this group in SPUC, has been

told by doctors that she would be better off dead – because she has spina bifida. Parents in the Down's Children Association are often hurt by the callous dismissal of Down's syndrome children as vegetables only fit for the abortionist's incinerator. Nabil Sheban, a fairly severely disabled actor born with brittle bones who spent all his childhood in hospital, was rejected by his family, and lives in a wheelchair, is a firm opponent of abortion for the defective foetus. 'Those who choose to abort the handicapped are making judgements about *my* life,' he says. 'I would like to make my own judgements about that. I have a right to choose, too.' The disabled point out that anyone can become handicapped through accident or illness at any time, and from my own observation I would say it is more difficult to adapt to disablement in adult life than to be born so. Nabil Sheban spent a couple of years trying to cheer up a friend who was struck with multiple sclerosis in his twenties, but in the end this friend committed suicide. Nabil Sheban has never even considered suicide.

There is some evidence that clinical depression is more likely to follow a genetic abortion than a social one. 'Genetic terminations,' said a paper published in the *British Medical Journal* (BMJ) on 21 February 1985, 'end planned, or at least wanted pregnancies. They are also preceded by a period of intense anxiety accompanying the process of pre-natal diagnosis at a time when foetal movements are often already apparent. The surgical techniques in genetic terminations are more radical, and the abrupt end of a pregnancy is obvious to friends and relatives.' Actually some women keep the news of their pregnancy secret until the tests have taken place and the baby 'cleared' (as much as it is possible to be) of defects to avoid embarrassment of 'explaining away' a terminated pregnancy. But in the small group of women interviewed for the BMJ after genetic abortion, all the patients showed signs of emotional strain. 'It is reasonable to conclude that the small numbers of women undergoing termination of a planned or wanted pregnancy after pre-natal diagnosis constitute a high-risk group, vulnerable to depression and social disruption. Considerable care is necessary before, during and after the event if they are to cope emotionally and socially with this experience.'

Yet not all women go through emotional strain, depression or disturbance. Writing in the *Observer*, Ruth Brandon described feelings of relief after an abortion for a Down's syndrome baby. In her late thirties, she had an amniocentesis test and it proved positive. 'I elected to have an abortion,' she wrote. 'What I had in mind was a swift routine operation during which I should be mercifully unconscious.' But of course by the time the test can be done – sixteen weeks and after – and the cells cultured, it is too late for a simple surgical abortion and 'what must be undergone is an induced birth', she explained.

> Any merely physical ordeal, though, is as nothing compared to the psychological trauma of this situation. Clearly, it is very difficult for hospital staff, or indeed anyone, to gauge the best psychological approach to adopt towards the ex-mother. I was treated with enormous kindness . . . and for this I am deeply grateful. But what struck me was that everyone expected me to go to pieces. 'You can expect to have quite a reaction after this,' said one doctor. The obstetrician repeatedly told me how well I was taking it. Friends have since asked me, in awestruck tones, how I could bear to undergo it all. Yet this situation, though sad, is not terminally depressing in the way that having the child undoubtedly would have been. Indeed, because one is having an abortion for such an excellent reason, it is probably less depressing than many abortions performed for other reasons.

Ruth Brandon experienced no clinical depression, and was simply glad she later had a normal, healthy daughter. Her strongest emotion afterwards was a sense of resentment against anyone who would have denied her the chance of abortion. 'What I cannot tolerate is the thought that there are people who would have wished to prevent me acting as I did. When I look at the normal, healthy baby whom I had sixteen months later, and think that, instead of her, these people would, if they could, have condemned me to have an avoidably handicapped child, my blood runs cold.' This point of view would undoubtedly be shared by many women. None the less, the article elicited letters from parents of Down's syndrome children who pointed out that their handicapped child was a joy to them.

Down's children are, as a matter of description, often very loving and sweet. It is perhaps later on, in adulthood, when their parents are no longer there to care for them, that life becomes more problematic for them.

That Mrs Brandon was in her late thirties is significant concerning Down's syndrome. For a woman aged twenty to twenty-four, the statistical risk of having a Down's syndrome child is one in 1,550. Between twenty-five and twenty-nine, the risk is one in 1,050 live births. From thirty to thirty-four, the risk is one in 700. And at aged thirty-five, it increases to one in 350. At thirty-six, it is one in 300. At thirty-seven, one in 225. At thirty-eight, one in 175. At thirty-nine, one in 150, and at forty, one in 100. Aged forty-one, one in 85; forty-two, one in 65; forty-three, one in 50; forty-four, one in 40. And forty-five plus, one in 25.

Down's syndrome occurs because of a chromosomal abnormality, and, like much else in the field of foetology, it was not discovered until recently. Professor Jerome Lejeune, the French geneticist, discovered the reason for this condition (which had first been systematically observed by the British physician, John Langdon Haydown Down in 1866, and which thus carries his name). The cause is an extra chromosome. People normally have twenty-three pairs of chromosomes, adding up to forty-six; the Down's syndrome individual has forty-seven. There are 6 million Down's syndrome people in the world and they have been termed 'mongols' because of their round, flattish faces and slanted eyes (but the phrase is considered opprobious to ethnic Mongols). The condition also occurs with primates: chimpanzees can be born with the condition and, interestingly, the chimp mother does not reject such young. Down's children remain handicapped for life and are always mentally retarded, though there is a wide variation in the range of IQs and abilities, and they are much more educable than was thought possible in the past.

In 95 per cent of cases, Down's syndrome is directly linked with the age of the mother. But in about 5 per cent of cases, the chromosomal abnormality arises from what is known as a translocation in an ancestor, usually inherited through the mother, though occasionally through the father. There is also some speculation, as yet anecdotal only, that genetic mutations may be taking place as a consequence of environmental factors such as radiation fall-out, chemicals and drugs. There has been a puzzling increase in the number of Down's babies born to mothers in the Sellafield (Windscale) area, where there is a nuclear reactor. In her book, *The Bitter Pill*, the endocrinologist Dr Ellen Grant claims that the contraceptive Pill may be implicated in causing Down's syndrome because of its ageing effect on the ovaries. This is not accepted by experts as hard evidence of the deleterious effect of the Pill, though perhaps it should be researched in future.

There are other chromosomal abnormalities in the same group as Down's syndrome which are detected by amniocentesis, though they are much more unusual. In Down's, the extra chromosome is No. 21 (in French, the defect is known as *Trisomie 21*). In the rarer *Patau's* syndrome, the extra chromosome is No. 13; in *Edwards'* syndrome the extra is No. 18. Both these are very severe disabilities and the babies seldom survive more than a few months.

Within this grouping, there are also sex-linked chromosome abnormalities, such as *Klinefelters* syndrome 47XXY. These are apparently normal males, but sterile. They may vary from a man with some breast enlargement and poor beard growth to a man so apparently normal that diagnosis is made only by investigation into male infertility. There is about a 10 per cent risk of mental retardation.

The *XYY* males are also frequently undiagnosed,

though some have been found in prisons for violent offenders and are noticeable for their great height. There has, in fact, been a television thriller, 'The XYY Man' about an ex-villain trying to go straight but plagued by an extra male chromosome. XYY men probably have normal fertility but there may be a reduction in IQ when compared with the rest of their families. In this case, the abnormality is not related to maternal age – the Y chromosomes come from the father.

With *Turner's* syndrome, the person is female in appearance but short (less than five feet in height) and almost always infertile with lack of breast development and absent periods. Intelligence is usually normal, but there may be difficulty with numerical concepts.

All these chromosomal disorders, whether autosomal ('of itself') or sex-linked chromosomal, are detected through amniocentesis. *Neural tube* defects are also picked up by such testing, though, as mentioned, AFP blood tests will occasionally initially indicate that there is a suspicion of such a problem. (If the AFP level is raised, there is about a one in twenty chance that the foetus is affected by this.)

Neural tube defects include spina bifida, anencephaly, and hydrocephaly. About 50 per cent miscarry spontaneously, and the degree of disability varies in those who survive. Anencephaly is lethal – the baby never survives beyond a few hours after birth. Hydrocephaly is the accumulation of fluid in the brain causing enlargement of the head; unless it is corrected immediately, mental retardation, convulsions or death will follow. But it can be lived with. Sometimes it occurs in association with spina bifida itself, but it may be present as the only abnormality. Spina bifida occurs from the failure of spinal bones and membranes to close properly, thus exposing the spinal nerve. Surgery is necessary soon after birth and the individual with spina bifida will usually suffer from paralysis of the legs and from renal complications. However, it is quite wrong to write off spina bifida babies as hopeless cases.

'I was born a spina bifida person and I'm very glad I was

allowed to live,' says Olive Snell of Clevedon in Avon – and she was born in 1912. 'I had good, caring parents and I never heard them grumble over the task of having to look after me. They were always very proud of anything I achieved. I think that disabled people are far better citizens than a great many able-bodied people. A disabled person can often help an able-bodied person to face life when they have some ordeal to face. I'm still glad to be alive – and I'm seventy-two.' There is no evidence that spina bifida is linked with maternal age: indeed, 95 per cent of neural tube defects are the first in the family, when a woman is not likely to be in the older age-group. If a couple have had one spina bifida baby, there is an increased risk of about 3 to 4 per cent of having a second child affected.

More people with spina bifida are surviving today and have reached the age when they can have children themselves. If a parent – whether a father or a mother, the risk being the same – has spina bifida, their chance of having a child with the condition is about one in thirty. And women with spina bifida (or those whose husbands are affected) are now presenting themselves for pre-natal diagnosis, with a view to abortion if the baby is affected. This indicates that some handicapped people would themselves use selective abortion to avoid a disabled son or daughter. However, neural tube defects can occur at random to completely healthy couples. A total of 95 per cent of births with a neural tube defect are to families in which there is no history of such problems. After a couple have had one affected child, the risk is in the order of 3–4 per cent of having another. The cause of these defects is not known.

Genetically inherited disorders are, obviously, disorders which are usually already present somewhere in the family, and some can be detected pre-natally. They range from the inconsequential (colour blindness) to the tragic (cystic fibrosis). Huntington's chorea, achonodroplasia (a form of dwarfism), Tay-Sachs disease (more common in Ashkenazi Jews, but occasionally present in other groups), sickle-cell anaemia (which affects one black child in 500) are examples of genetically inherited disorders. They are usually present in the medical family history.

X-linked disorders, that is disorders linked with the sex of the baby, such as haemophilia and Duchenne's dystrophy, are also genetically inherited. In both these last cases, the woman is the carrier, but the disorder affects only males. An amniocentesis can tell the sex of the baby and the couple can then decide on an abortion if the child is a male. Pre-natal testing cannot yet diagnose all genetically inherited disorders by any means. Huntington's chorea cannot be diagnosed in the womb. Neither yet can cystic fibrosis – although it soon will be – muscular dystrophy and other enzyme deficiencies. With time and research it is likely that it will be possible in the future to spot all these in the womb.

People with genetically inherited disorders are today advised to take genetic counselling, where the odds and chances of having a handicapped child can be quite carefully calculated. This is a controversial area because ethics and sensitivities vary here. Take, for example, sickle-cell anaemia, which varies in severity. Some black people are touchy about suggestions that they should be subjected to screening for it in pregnancy. I have come across one family – the father a doctor, the mother a university graduate – where there were seven children despite Huntington's chorea being in the maternal family background. Huntington's chorea is a crippling disease, but rather odd in that it does not strike until middle life – characteristically in the late thirties and early forties. The mother was already beginning to be affected by Huntington's during her last pregnancy. Out of the seven children, it is likely that some of them will be affected. This was judged by certain friends and neighbours to be downright irresponsible. Psychologists might ascribe the deliberate choice of a large family to 'genetic over-compensation' – an instinctive urge to have more children because some are likely to be handicapped. A man with Huntington's chorea in his family told Miriam Stoppard on one of her television programmes devoted to the disease: 'Better a short life and a happy one than none at all. Better take the chance to live well until you are forty!' This was his reason for going ahead fearlessly and having children.

Other individuals, seeing the suffering that disability can cause, feel quite the opposite. They feel that people with inherited genetic disorders should refrain from having children. 'I do not think that genetic engineering is the answer for disabled people,' says Stella Morris, a woman who developed muscular dystrophy in adult life. 'I rather feel that it is better not to have children at all (if possible to adopt) than to start a life and then terminate it because it is not perfect. I have two children of my own and will suggest to them that they might consider not having children on the grounds that they may carry the genes for muscular dystrophy. Had I known that I would develop muscular dystrophy before carrying two children of my own, I would not have embarked on pregnancy.' It is apparently not uncommon for a mother to advise childlessness to her own children in this situation. Genetic specialists believe that proper research and counselling to establish the true risk is a better option.

Mrs Morris's view has, however, been occasionally voiced by geneticists, notably Dr Hermann Muller of Berkeley, California, who claimed that it was more socially altruistic for couples with hereditary disease in the family to refrain from child-bearing for the sake of the 'gene pool'. While individuals with hereditary disabilities may screen out a defective foetus, their healthy children nevertheless will carry the recessive genes, which will then be 'put back' into the common 'gene pool'. Modern genetic counsellors, however, dismiss this view, and say that the increase of deleterious genes in society generally would be very small.

Today, in any case, there is as much anxiety about defects arising from some environmental and socially transmitted problems. Defects in the foetus for *multi-factorial reasons* fall into this category. These are defects which do not arise from a chromosomal abnormality nor an inherited genetic disorder, but come from a series of different agencies: X-rays, chemical agents, drugs, possibly radiation fall-out, alcohol abuse, even cigarette smoking, which is known to produce smaller babies. A cleft palate is an example of what is now a minor birth defect which comes from multifactorial causes. It is seldom diagnosed pre-natally, and can be found on ultrasound only if it is specifically looked for. It is today a repairable malformation and generally regarded as not worth pre-natal diagnosis – though perhaps some women would wish to be prepared for such a problem.

A classic example of birth defects by outside agents is, of course, thalidomide, which produced malformations of the limbs in thousands of babies. In fact, the thalidomide scandal gave the final push to the abortion law reform lobby in the 1960s, see page 196). Interestingly, the thalidomide people who were born turned out to be as capable and as happy as any other group of people. Marjorie Wallace, who conducted the *Sunday Times* campaigns to win compensation for thalidomide victims, has personally interviewed over 100 thalidomide people and says: 'They represent the full range of perfectly normal personalities, and are not unhappier than any other random group of 100 fully able-bodied people.'

Today, new problems are arising which replace some of the difficulties we have vanquished. There is likely to be more worry about the hazards of acquired immune deficiency syndrome (AIDS) being transmitted to the child in the womb than about rare genetic disorders.

And there are, indeed, some very rare *metabolic disorders* which may also sometimes be diagnosed in pregnancy. Metabolic disorders are caused by a deficiency of a specific enzyme. Sometimes the enzyme is known, and if so pre-natal diagnosis may be possible on foetal cells. Screening is not really practicable as these disorders are so very rare, with names as recondite as *metachromatic leucodystrophy* and *propionic acidaemia*, but it may be possible to check that the parents are carriers of the disorders in question. The 'brittle bones' disorder suffered by Nabil Sheban, properly called *osteogenesis imperfecta*, is a metabolic disorder; he also has a sister with the same disability (and two siblings who are unaffected). With brittle bones, a baby's bones keep breaking, and, of course, as the child is in pain, it cries a great deal until the diagnosis is made. Also the legs do not grow properly. Thus, if there is a known metabolic disorder in the family, again it is worth seeking careful genetic counselling advice.

In greater knowledge is greater sorrow – some would agree with this warning from the Book of Ecclesiastes. In the past, people did not spend so much time thinking about the defects that a baby could be born with. Even I feel, nowadays, that if I had known what could go wrong when I was having children in the 1970s, I should have been much more apprehensive about pregnancy. I was, perhaps, of the last generation to have children before pre-natal testing became widely used or spoken of. In 1974, I knew no one who had undergone amniocentesis, even among women having their babies in their late thirties. By 1985, everyone I knew who became pregnant was aware of the amount of tests available. For instance, in 1966 there were just 574 known disorders which were genetically linked. By 1978, this figure had risen to 1,364 disorders known. By the early 1980s, it had risen to over 4,000. There has been a real explosion in knowledge about these problems.

My mother-in-law, born in 1900, casting her memory back to the 1920s and 1930s when her contemporaries were having children, tells me that it simply did not occur to women to worry about having an abnormal child. 'It rarely entered our heads,' she recalls. First, no pre-natal tests were available. Secondly, handicapped children died quickly after birth more often than they do today. And thirdly, it is sometimes the case that in larger families one handicapped child didn't seem to matter as much as it might today.

Recently a woman was sitting in a café watching the world go by during the weeks of waiting for the result of an amniocentesis test, and saw a family of six children come in. 'There were five golden-headed beauties, and one mongol child,' she noticed. 'The five golden-heads made a fuss of the defective child, and somehow it all seemed OK. I also thought that the parents could feel "look we have produced five beauties, so don't judge us by the one that is not perfect".' It seems to me that this gut reaction is very natural, and if you have only two children, or perhaps only one child, there is greater pressure for that child to be perfect than if there are several more. Christopher Lasch makes this point in his book, *The Culture of Narcissism*: with a family of five or six, parents could 'afford', emotionally, to be charitable about the one or two who went astray – the black sheep who went off to foreign parts, the homosexual eccentric, the son who liked to dress in ladies' clothes, the one who took to drink and couldn't hold a job. This was part of people's traditional attitude to life; you win some, you lose some, and there is always a risk. 'Planning' one's life – or one's children – has changed all that. Now we expect things to be better, and as we plan to have only one or two children, we expect those two little targets to carry out all our expectations to a higher standard. There is more pressure on parents, and more pressure on children to be perfect.

In the past, of course, there was also shame and mortification over an abnormal birth – much depended on the individual and the society. The village idiot might have been affectionately regarded in some places (in Ireland, the mentally defective were called *Daoine le Dia*, God's people), but in other societies cruelty and disgust punished the child born different.

There have been many stories of children locked in attics and secret places because they seemed 'monsters' to others. The late Sir Iain Moncrieffe of that Ilk, the Scottish genealogist, recounts a rather typical story of this kind. The first son of Lord Glamis is said to have been born, early in the nineteenth century, 'in a hideous form with a massive body, covered with matted black hair, tiny arms and legs and a head sunk deep into his barrel chest'. Such a creature was not judged worthy to inherit the title of the Earl of Strathmore and was kept in a secret room in the castle which is the setting for Macbeth (and, incidentally, where Queen Elizabeth the Queen Mother was born). He was exercised at night on the roof and only four men at any one time were allowed to know of his existence – the Earl, the family lawyer, the agent to the estate, and the eldest normal son, who was shown the rightful Earl, his brother 'the monster', on his twenty-first birthday. This unfortunate creature, who apparently lived to be very old, was hidden from public view all his life.

Our attitudes to the handicapped are often ambivalent. Nabil Sheban's mother, from a remote Cypriot village, regarded his birth as a punishment from God. She was absolutely distraught when a second baby was born with the same defect. Both babies were abandoned and Nabil himself was rescued by English Methodists. Yet there are other stories where mothers have derived a special joy from having a handicapped child. 'I have two healthy, lively, "normal" children aged twelve and nine and a Down's syndrome daughter who arrived somewhat unexpectedly three and a half years later,' wrote Mrs Esther Langrish of Leamington Spa. 'The fact of her handicap has brought out understanding, sensitivity and caring in our older children, in many friends and in ourselves. Because the paediatrician had painted such a gloomy picture of her potential, her progress to date through the stages of development has been exciting in a way that that of a "normal" child would not have been . . . I have become greatly aware that the concept "normal" is hardly meaningful. We have greatly enjoyed the work we have done with Kathryn and are reaping the benefits already.'

Perhaps there is, for some people, an 'acceptable level' of handicap; perhaps we can understand and accept handicap better when we come to know it more. It is certain that one of the first emotions on meeting a handicapped person is fear. A nephew of mine recently told me he was bringing a friend to stay for a few days. It was mentioned to me, casually, that this friend had 'never grown properly'. In fact, the young man – he is eighteen – suffered from dwarfism. At first, this made me very nervous, embarrassed, apprehensive, and indeed I rather wished that this was something I didn't have to cope with. When I met the lad, and talked to him, my feelings very gradually changed from apprehension to a sudden sensation of tenderness.

It seems perfectly understandable that any woman faced with the news that the child she is carrying is abnormal or disabled would immediately wish to choose abortion. Listen to Anne Filer, a mother of four living on the south coast of England. She was surprised to find, at the age of thirty-eight, that she was pregnant once again. Surprised because she had been fitted with an IUD, and the contraceptive had obviously failed. She could have had the IUD removed, which would have had the effect of aborting the pregnancy, but she felt this would be wrong. 'Our four children bring me untold joy and pleasure and I really felt that this unplanned bonus was a gift from God not to be done away with as lightly as that.' They have a large house and enough money for another child. The pregnancy would have to take its chance, and would be loved and welcomed.

All went well at the beginning, but amniocentesis was recommended because of Anne's age. This was the late 1970s, and she was not familiar with the process because it had not been carried out in her earlier pregnancies. As it happened, the obstetrical registrar who was to conduct the test was not particularly kind or helpful, and thrusting a form into her hands explained that the test bore certain dangers, including the danger of miscarriage. She was uncertain whether or not to proceed with amniocentesis. At around sixteen weeks' gestation, she could feel the baby kicking and she felt quite healthy generally. Still, in the end, she decided it was sensible and signed the forms. Amniocentesis was carried out. Three weeks passed. Her next appointment was with her obstetrician when she was about twenty weeks pregnant. 'It was a hot, sunny afternoon and I spent the hours before my 4.30 p.m. appointment happily buying cool, cotton sundresses to fit my expanding frame. When the consultant invited me into his office instead of showing me into the examination room, I felt no alarm, only excitement that today I would know the sex of the baby. His words turned the heat of the sun-filled room to ice. I only understood the gist of what he was saying: that there was something wrong with the baby and that he felt the pregnancy should be terminated. I couldn't take it all in. My mother was waiting outside and I asked him to repeat what he had told me to her.'

Anne Filer was told that the baby had a chromosomal abnormality. 'The baby would be born looking like a girl, but would certainly be sterile and would not develop properly as a girl at puberty. She would never have periods, probably not develop breasts and might grow body and facial hair. In addition there was a great chance that she would be mentally handicapped to some degree. He had discussed my case with the geneticist who had carried out the test, who happened to be a woman, and she had no doubt that the pregnancy must be terminated.' The baby, she was told, would be a freak, an XXY child, with an extra female chromosome. Her only reaction at that time was one of quiet reason and disbelief.

All the time she was hoping that there might have been some error, some wrong diagnosis. But she was assured by the consultant that it could not be so. The consultant 'made me understand that, having had the test in the first place, there was really nothing to consider. I finally agreed that the pregnancy had to be terminated and asked him to take me into hospital as soon as possible, give me an anaesthetic and get it over with as quickly as possible. It was only then that I learned that I had to have an induced labour . . . I wanted to speak to another woman who had experienced the same thing, but he knew no one, so rarely does this occur in our town. He was very sympathetic and made me an appointment to report to the hospital ten days hence. I left his room, burst into tears, and wept uncontrollably for the rest of the evening, feeling all the while my baby kicking and turning inside me.'

Anne Filer felt the need to speak to someone about this – it is the sort of case where a support group of women who have been through something similar might have been of help. Moreover, it is nowadays unusual for a woman to be kept waiting for an abortion for as long as ten days in these circumstances. Genetic and medical abortions are regarded as emergencies and are done as quickly as possible after diagnosis and consent. Everyone was kind to Mrs Filer and agreed that there really wasn't any choice but to terminate. Yet 'everyone seemed to think that, having had the amniocentesis, I should have been prepared. I could not imagine that we had produced a defective child. I felt that, as it was my decision to terminate, I was about to participate in a murder. I thought that, in some ways, things would turn out all right if only we left them alone. I thought and thought and thought, until I felt as if my head would burst.' When it was all finally over, she 'felt nothing but relief'. The nurses were extremely kind – something women often worry about – and her husband remained with her through labour and delivery. Still, looking back seven years later she still feels that women should have full counselling and advice in this 'heart-searching experience'. She was frightened of all sorts of things, including that the baby would cry. There wasn't enough information placed before her at that time. Historically, of course, we are talking of the very early days of pre-natal testing.

It is a complex issue. Although amniocentesis tests in particular are accepted, more and more, as part of pregnancy, most people probably have not thought through the difficulties, medical, ethical and emotional, of a genetic abortion. We are really only at the beginning of pre-natal screening as a developed science, and the future will see a great expansion in its possibilities. It is likely that testing will soon become available earlier in pregnancy so that the harrowing later abortions will be replaced by earlier simpler ones where the woman is anaesthetized.

Pre-natal testing has reduced the number of disabled and abnormal babies at birth. In the west of Scotland, for example, the rate of anencephalic and spina bifida live births and still births declined from 4.3 per 1,000 in 1976 to 1.7 in 1981. On the other hand, the overall number of handicapped children per head of the population is the same as it was in 1920: one child in fifty. This is almost certainly because handicapped children who are born are surviving for longer. Some people claim that environmental factors could create new disabilities – it is a theme strongly pursued by anti-nuclear campaigners. It is certainly true that the early human foetus is extremely vulnerable. There was a time, up to the 1950s, when doctors believed that the placenta was a barrier and a protection for the baby, and that drugs and outside elements did not cross the placenta. This is no longer the case and in pregnancy today women are scarcely recommended to take an aspirin.

Very careful, sensitive and well-informed counselling is required for any woman at risk of conceiving or carrying or terminating a pregnancy diagnosed as being abnormal. A lot more understanding and a lot more support is required. Some of the decisions women are called upon to make can be pretty horrendous, after all. For something like Duchenne's dystrophy, for instance, amniocentesis simply reveals the sex of the child. If the child is a girl, there is no problem. If it is a boy, there is a 50 per cent chance that it will be affected by the illness. But there is a 50 per cent chance that he will not be. The mother will never know, either, whether she has aborted a healthy baby, for the onset of Duchenne's dystrophy – described by a specialist as 'a stinker' – does not begin until the child is about five or six. Though the condition is rare, the problem is an appalling one, and there is suffering whichever way one turns.

Sensitivity to the feelings of the born handicapped is also something which needs to be developed a lot more. Casual public discussions about aborting a defective foetus are nearly always hurtful to someone. Rex Brinkworth, the founder of the Down's Children's Association, has devoted enormous energies to his own Down's daughter since she was born. As a teacher of handicapped and educationally sub-normal children he, with his wife, has been able to help Françoise a great deal, and by the age of nineteen she had accomplished much. One day she saw a television programme about 'genetic abortions'. It was explained by the presenter that mothers could now be tested for Down's syndrome and could have an abortion if the foetus was affected. 'Does this mean they kill Down's babies?' Françoise asked her father. She watched as Rex Brinkworth tried to explain about pre-natal testing. 'They would have killed me, though,' she concluded. 'Will they try to kill me now?'

6

WHAT HAPPENS AT AN ABORTION

'First of all, many women want to know exactly what happens at an abortion – but no one tells them.' – Lynn Reed

'Abortion is the expulsion or removal of the products of conception from the uterus before the 28th week of pregnancy, this being the time when the foetus is generally considered to be viable. The methods vary greatly. – *Abortion: Classification & Techniques*

'I believe the choice to have or not to have a child should be left to the individual woman. But I also think a woman must be made fully aware that what is at stake is not a clump of inert cells but the beginnings of human life. If a doctor can spend several minutes explaining how he plans to remove a superfluous organ such as an appendix, shouldn't he be willing to give this kind of decision extra time?' – Dr Thomas Verney, *The Secret Life of the Unborn Child*

FIRST TRIMESTER ABORTION BY THE SUCTION METHOD

It was a sunny Monday morning when I went to a semi-detached house in a suburb of north London which had been converted into the Whitehouse clinic, run by

Marie Stopes House, named after the pioneer in birth control. About thirteen abortions are carried out here in an average day's session. Women make appointments by telephoning the Marie Stopes centre and arranging an interview. On most days patients start arriving at 8 a.m. But Mondays and Thursdays are afternoon sessions, so on these days the women turn up soon after midday.

The women came in one by one. Some were alone. Some kissed men goodbye at the gate. Some had boyfriends or husbands who remained with them in the reception area. A young girl of fifteen was accompanied by her mother – the mother was herself young, tanned, attractive and altogether calm.

This clinic deals in early abortions, usually in the first trimester of pregnancy (up to fourteen weeks, counting from the first day of the last menstrual period), though they have performed abortions up to eighteen weeks. Most of the women waiting did not look pregnant.

In the waiting room, the air was still. Some women looked sombre and few seemed disposed to talk, even to those accompanying them. One woman fiddled nervously with a paper clip; a young American girl resolutely got on with her reading – *Papillon*, the story of a prisoner. An Irish woman perused *Cosmopolitan* magazine which announced an article on the front cover entitled 'That First Baby Won't Wait Forever'. An intellectual-looking couple, man and woman, nearing middle age, sat together looking undisturbed, the woman relaxed, the man carrying a copy of Proust. A pretty Scottish girl, tiny in stature, sat on the edge of her chair wearing brightly plumed punkish hair.

'We get all kinds of women here, from the very young teenager to the mum in her forties,' said Liz Deaves, the thirty-three-year-old administrator of Marie Stopes, a beautiful young woman who has had abortion experience herself, and therefore feels she understands. 'When they arrive they are often nervous, hungry – since they have been told not to eat since midnight – and they may not have slept very well. And they are pregnant. Of course they often feel rotten. By the evening, everything has changed. You can feel the tension disappearing as they sit up in bed and chat with one another. Sometimes boyfriends bring champagne and there is an atmosphere of celebration.'

In the waiting room, Liz (or the receptionist of the day) takes each patient's papers in turn, and organizes the payment. An abortion is legal in Britain if two medical practitioners certify that the pregnant woman's existing children or her own physical or mental health would be at greater risk if the pregnancy continued than if it were terminated; that is to say, if it is safer to terminate the pregnancy than to continue it. As it is always safer to terminate a pregnancy in the first trimester than to continue it, in practice all pregnant women qualify under the 1967 law for an abortion. An individual doctor may refuse an abortion to an individual patient, either on grounds of conscience or because in his or her judgement the woman's mental or physical health does not justify an abortion; yet all pregnant women can justifiably claim grounds for abortion under the Act. Few women in Britain are obstructed from getting an abortion, though some are delayed by administrative inefficiency in the National Health Service. About half of all abortions in Britain are performed on the NHS, and about half are done privately in a clinic like this one, in one of the abortion charities, or through a private arrangement with a doctor. Some women fear they might be delayed in the NHS, some do not wish to involve their own general practitioner and some feel that abortion is not an illness and would prefer to by-pass the health service.

The total cost of an overnight stay and a termination of pregnancy up to thirteen weeks at Marie Stopes is £160; from fourteen to fifteen weeks the price is £195; from sixteen to eighteen weeks it is £215 (1986 prices). After eighteen weeks pregnancies are referred through private arrangements. The medical examination and the medical papers are arranged at Marie Stopes House in Whitfield Street, in central London. The clinic accepts Access or Barclaycard, but decided against American Express because the billing system does not allow for staggered payments. If a woman has difficulty paying, a credit scheme can be arranged. As the patients paid, I recalled the observation of an American woman that it was the only operation in the world for which you pay in advance.

Just before two o'clock in the afternoon, the surgeon, a beautiful young Indian woman, wearing a filmy, canary-coloured sari and bangles around her ankles, arrived. There is a rota of doctors, most of whom work in other fields of gynaecology and family planning as well, since it is considered repetitious and medically unrewarding to do abortions all the time.

While the operating theatre was being set up, the women waited in semi-detached wards – some have private rooms. They can elect to have a local anaesthetic, or a general anaesthetic. Most prefer a full anaesthetic.

The operating theatre was similar, in the eyes of a lay-person, to any other. In the theatre was the surgeon, now in white coat and cap, the anaesthetist, the theatre sister and the nurses.

Each patient walked into the theatre wearing a nightie and plastic sterile slippers. (The anaesthetic is fast-acting, and wears off quickly too, so it is best to be conscious until the last minute.) Some women came in calmly. Some were anxious. A stout girl shook with tears while climbing up on the operating table. The anaesthetist soothed each one, smoothing their brows as he injected into their arm, covering their faces with the oxygen mask. The patient becomes unconscious almost immediately.

As soon as the patient was unconscious, her legs were lifted into stirrups and the surgeon set to work. First, the genital area was washed with sterile gauze, held at the end of a surgical tongs. A spectrum was passed into the vagina to expose the cervix, which was grasped with a forceps. A series of sterilized dilators – short steel rods – were introduced to open up the cervix (the neck of the womb). A tube was passed through the cervix and into the uterus. Then a machine was switched on which sounds like a vacuum-cleaner and works on the same principle. The vacuum aspirator, connected with the tube, very quickly drew out the foetal material from the uterus, passing it down through the tube and into a bottle. The products of conception, with perhaps a pint or less of blood, flowed into the bottle fitted on to the vacuum pump, and these were then emptied through a sieve down the sink of the tiny sluice kitchen. There was very little to look at – just clusters of blood, and what would be (if seen through a microscope) human cells. Up to ten weeks of pregnancy, the foetus is unformed to the ordinary eye. By the eleventh or twelfth week, the early human outlines can be seen – for instance, a woman miscarrying spontaneously will pass a foetus which is recognizable as an early human form at this time. But with modern techniques of suction abortion, this is very quickly shredded and reduced to indiscriminate matter.

The women were wheeled out within minutes, and very soon brought back to consciousness. Some were quiet and slept for a while. Some were in pain. Some wept. The intellectual whose boyfriend was reading Proust cried like a child. Her notes said she was thirty-seven, an age when women often feel their last chance of motherhood is passing. The punk-haired young Scottish girl was soon sitting up having a cup of tea and a cigarette. A cheerful London woman joined her and they talked philosophically. 'Well, I mean, nowadays, you've got to consider having a baby, haven't you?' said the Londoner. 'I'm not proud to be here, mind, but with my other two so young and what with having a job, we felt we couldn't manage another.'

In a sunny garden room I talked to Joyce, aged twenty-two, and Carol, thirty-two, both of whom said they became pregnant while taking the Pill. The most common reaction after an abortion is relief at the removal of the problem; the relief can quite often be euphoric. Both said with smiles that they were very happy.

If there is another reaction – loss, sadness, misgiving – it comes later. 'Obviously there are women who do regret their decision,' says Liz Deaves. 'We know that from the number of women who apply to us for reversals of sterilization. If people regret sterilization, with all the counselling that involves, they must regret abortions too.

But it is their decision.' They have considered post-abortion therapy at Stopes, but cannot see how it could be done practicably. The BPAS says that after exhaustive efforts to offer post-abortion counselling it has found there is very little demand for it.

For many women, an abortion is something to put behind them and forget. But even if they do want to reflect upon the experience afterwards, it is possible that they would wish to do so in a different context, and with different people. Returning to the scene of the operation might not be an altogether attractive proposition. Women are instructed to return for a physical check-up six weeks afterwards, and many opt out of that.

In the evening, the women had supper, read, talked and slept. They left the clinic early next morning.

SECOND TRIMESTER ABORTION BY THE SURGICAL METHOD

The difference between an early abortion – that is, before twelve to fourteen weeks – and a later abortion is so marked that Malcolm Potts, the birth control specialist, has suggested that the two operations should have a different name. An early abortion is extremely safe for the woman when carried out under skilled medical supervision. As mentioned earlier there is a small risk of infection and some risk of haemorrhage; there is also a slight risk of miscarriage in subsequent pregnancies. But it is considered to be statistically insignificant, and the operation is not regarded by any expert as being traumatic.

At about twelve weeks' gestation, a gradual but perceptible change happens, both in the womb and in the foetus itself. At eight weeks a foetus weighs about one gramme; at ten weeks, about 5 grammes; at twelve weeks about 25 grammes. Then the rate quickens rapidly: between twelve and fourteen weeks, the foetus doubles in weight to about 50 grammes, and from this stage onwards, the observer can see a very small but perceptible human form being evacuated in the process of the abortion.

Thus, the techniques of abortion alter between the first trimester and the second trimester. By the time the pregnancy has entered the second term, the foetus has become too well-formed to use the suction tube. Abortion has to be done either by prostaglandin induction or by surgical evacuation of the uterus. Prostaglandin induction effectively means inducing labour, so that the womb contracts and expels the foetus. Surgical techniques are less usual, and need greater skill; the advantage is that the woman is totally anaesthetized and knows nothing of the events.

At the Samaritan Hospital for Women in London's Euston Road, a Friday-afternoon abortion session is held on the third floor. This is where Dr David Paintin conducts his weekly caseload of later pregnancy terminations.

Dr Paintin is a neat, bespectacled man who has been associated with the Abortion Law Reform Association since the 1960s. He is committed to legal abortion as a proper medical procedure, and indeed believes it can be good medicine. He is liked by nurses, considered gentle and kind by the hospital counsellors, and is a truthful man who is ready to share his experience and knowledge. He comes from a Methodist background, and indeed, in appearance could be a clergyman – bringing to the subject of abortion an earnest sense of moral righteousness. That is, in doing abortions properly Dr Paintin clearly believes he is doing the right thing.

On the afternoon that I visited the Samaritan Hospital, Dr Paintin was to operate on eight women, ranging from a thirty-three-year-old woman with a repeat pregnancy (she had just been aborted eight weeks previously) to a twenty-three-year-old girl twenty-two weeks pregnant, whose boyfriend had changed his mind about wanting the baby. All were social abortions.

The atmosphere in the operating theatre was clean, busy and professional. Several young male doctors, gowned for the theatre, were standing around when I entered, talking cheerfully about the cricket score. There was no hint, here, of life-and-death drama – it was just another day, another hospital theatre session. The sister in charge, a friendly Chinese nurse, greeted me and asked if I wanted a coffee. Although she was busy, she attended to me with efficiency. She took me to a small office and provided me with a sterile gown, shoes, cap and surgical mask.

Operations commenced at two o'clock. A student nurse prepared the instruments in an obstetric theatre like any other, with an operating table in the centre and a large set of lights overhanging it. The place gleamed with technical apparatus, everything labelled, sterilized and properly wrapped.

Sister Lee explained to me as she prepared the theatre that part of her job is to be reassuring to the younger, less experienced nurses. 'Nobody likes doing abortions,' she said. 'The later abortions can be especially distressing. I was brought up as a Christian, and of course it's upsetting to me. But in medicine you learn to do what is necessary in the best way, and Mr Paintin is wonderful and has explained to us that we are doing the best in difficult circumstances.'

The student nurse said, while she was working, that she had had an abortion herself, which sometimes made it more difficult for her, recalling a sad experience. But working in the abortion theatre was just a short stint in her training and, besides, you learn a certain scientific detachment. Catholics and some others with a conscientious objection can refuse to assist in abortions, but it does mean they gain less medical experience and this can count against them. It is better, from a professional standpoint, to participate.

On the National Health Service, fewer abortions are done in a single session than in the private clinics. This is partly because the private clinics are more cost-conscious and must have an 'economy of scale' to be financially viable. Twenty abortions in a session in the private sector are not unusual because of this need for productivity. In the NHS, moreover, the doctor teaches as he goes along, which will slow down the procedure. For many reasons the NHS can never be as efficient as the private sector.

The earlier abortions are always performed first. This is because the early ones are likely to be the least complicated and the least likely to hold up the others.

At St Mary's (for the Samaritan Hospital comes under the general umbrella of St Mary's Paddington) the average age of patients for abortion is twenty-four. About 60 per cent are unmarried women – higher than the national average, which is roughly half married women, half single. At the Samaritan, the high prevalence of single women reflects this neighbourhood in central London.

The first patient was wheeled in on a trolly already anaesthetized. (Patients may request a local anaesthetic but few do.) She was eight weeks pregnant with the repeat pregnancy, and had requested the insertion of an interuterine coil after the termination. Around the patient stood the anaesthetist, the sister, the student nurse, Dr Paintin and his registrar – a young doctor. A sluice nurse also went in and out, and later, another young registrar was present. The young doctors were there to gain abortion practice.

The first patient was straightforward. The perineum was washed with a disinfectant called Cetavlon. A speculum was placed at the base of the vaginal entrance, and Dr Paintin began to dilate the cervix. Then he inserted the tube and the abortion was done by suction evacuation. It was over quite quickly and what remained in the bottle at the base of the suction pipe was a small amount of blood and the remains of the foetus, which cannot be seen with the naked eye. The IUD was inserted and the patient was wheeled out. The foetal material was washed down the sluice and all the instruments disappeared to be sterilized. A fresh pack was opened for each patient to minimize infection risks.

The second patient was wheeled in. She was a young woman of twenty-two, the mother of one child. She was fourteen weeks pregnant. Dr Paintin inserted the dilators as before, using slightly thicker ones. The size of the dilators – sometimes called cannulas – accords with the number of weeks of the pregnancy: thus 8 mm for an eight-week pregnancy, 10 mm for a ten-week and so on. When he drew out the material with the forceps, he found very little in the way of foetal remains. He concluded that in this case, the foetus had been abnormal and had perished naturally. The woman would have miscarried. Medically, this is called a 'missed abortion'. He remarked that this knowledge will probably be of some consolation to her – a genuine abortion did not take place since the foetus had already died.

The third patient was aged sixteen, and again was fourteen weeks pregnant. This time it was a normal foetus. When the uterus was evacuated into the small bowl under the operating table, the contents were again examined. Here the remains of a very small body, about the size of a new-born kitten, could be seen. It is tiny indeed, but its form is unmistakable.

The fourth and fifth cases were also young girls, aged sixteen and fifteen respectively. They had been admitted overnight and had had a catheter – a small tube inserted through the cervix – the night before. The catheter contains sterile water and the presence of a small balloon near the tip of the catheter softens the cervix, preparing it to open. (The presence of anything in the cervix will stimulate the woman's own endogenous prostaglandin production at the site of a 'foreign body'. Abortions were induced by placing herbs or pastes in the vaginal passage in ancient times, though without modern precautions it is a dangerous zone for infections.) In addition, a prostaglandin pessary is sometimes added to help the softening process. In very young girls, the cervix is not as elastic as in older women or as in a woman who has given birth. Also, after fourteen weeks' pregnancy, the cervix is injected, on the operating table, with adrenalin to lessen the blood loss.

There are other substances which can be used to help the softening-up of the cervix. A small, tube-sized object called a laminaria tent is sometimes inserted prior to uterine evacuation. Placed in the cervical canal up to four hours before the operation, it swells and produces an opening effect on the cervix. They are seldom used in pregnancies of less than twelve weeks' duration, except in a case where the girl is so young and the cervix so tightly closed that they are deemed necessary. Antibiotics are usually used with laminaria tents, since they can cause or encourage infection. As the substance in question is derived from seaweed, its pedigree probably is ancient. Methods of sterilizing it have improved and it can be gamma-irradiated, thereby minimizing infection risk.

The sixth patient was a woman of twenty-three who had one child. Dr Paintin looked at her notes. The counsellor had seen her – as with all the other cases – and described her as a thoughtful, caring young woman. 'She felt pleased to be pregnant and the idea of abortion is repugnant to her – but she feels she could not cope with another child,' the counsellor had written. The patient comes from a family of three girls and her parents were divorced when she was a small child herself. 'In so many of these cases, there is a bad family background,' David Paintin explains. 'A shotgun marriage of the parents, poor relationships in the family, divorce.' A woman who presents for abortion will not be judged, but sometimes her parents, her family background, will be.

The seventh patient was eighteen weeks pregnant. The foetus now will weigh about 200 grammes. This abortion took longer, and the registrar performed it – for he has to learn to do these things. It seemed that this had now become a much more bloody operation: amniotic fluid gushed out first. When the registrar introduced the forceps, the first thing that he grasped was the umbilical cord, which is very thick and tough with its blood vessels. The foetus was gradually removed in bits, its human form more recognizable than ever. The girl was aged sixteen.

The last patient was aged twenty-three, blonde, tanned and pretty and visibly pregnant. She was just two weeks away from the twenty-four-week deadline now regarded as the threshold of viability. Two more weeks and she would not have been given an abortion on the NHS, though a few private clinics are willing to go later. Her pregnancy was diagnosed late because of break-through bleeding during the pregnancy, wrongly interpreted as a menstrual period. She was unmarried and lived with her mother, who was described in the patient's notes as a 'busy career woman who seems very preoccupied with her own life'. (Woe betide the abortion patient whose mother is a busy career woman! By implication, the daughter had been overlooked.) The patient's boyfriend, described in notes as 'P.F.' (putative father) had reacted to the pregnancy by saying that he felt his virility flattered but he wanted the abortion just the same. The young woman had sought advice from friends, but all the advice given was conflicting. She did not have a steady job, but had worked as a croupier, and in the antiques business.

Sister Lee said softly it was going to be tough going. The procedure began. About half a litre of amniotic fluid flowed from the woman's body as the dilators were inserted. The cord was extracted – the last life-line of the foetus. Dr Paintin did this abortion. The forceps went into the uterus, quite roughly this time. Fluid and blood continued to fall into the bowl underneath the table. After some vigorous action he started to extract the foetus. First came an arm, perfectly formed, a tiny, baby's hand, fingers curled. A limb was extracted. Then two limbs lay in the bowl. Dr Paintin worked away and pieces of the trunk emerged. The intestines, brain tissue, liver, lungs came away. Last of all – the most difficult part – was the cranium. The skin was torn, and there was not much more than a skull. After all the parts had come away, the suction was inserted, and the uterus cleanly evacuated. With later abortions like this one, the remains are not taken to the sluice, but incinerated. Sometimes, foetal parts are taken to a laboratory to be used for tissue culture. The woman's perineum was cleaned. Her stomach was flat again.

The last patient was wheeled to a nearby recovery room. She would sleep for some time.

With great swiftness, everything was cleared away. We went into the surgeon's changing room and Sister Lee served us tea. Here, as in so many other places, the men did the significant work, the women assisted and served.

The men did not seem to mind doing the abortions and showed no signs of distress. The women seemed more sensitive to the situation. Overall, there was a very perceptible atmosphere of relief that the day's work was done. The sense of relief was so strong that Dr Paintin and I talked light-heartedly, gossiped a little, made a joke.

I left the hospital, passing the ward where the women were drowsily recovering. Their faces were pale. The last patient slept deeply, her hand clutching the blanket like the hand of a small child.

LATE ABORTION BY PROSTAGLANDIN INDUCTION

There are other methods used for women facing late abortions. One is hysterotomy, which is similar to a caesarean section; the patient is fully anaesthetized and an incision made in the lower abdomen. (This would take place after the sixteenth week of pregnancy.) As with a caesarean birth, this leaves a scar and now is infrequently performed, except in cases of medical urgency – cancer in the woman, for instance.

The other is the induction of immature labour by prostaglandin (a natural substance in the body which acts to produce contractions in the uterus at the end of a full-term pregnancy). Prostaglandin chemicals are drugs which act in a similar manner and trigger-off labour, causing the woman to expel the foetus. With prostaglandin abortion, a solution of urea, or of hypertonic saline, may be introduced into the uterus, with the object of causing foetal death. Saline solution is widely preferred in the United States, where it has caused much controversy. Anti-abortionists describe it simply as a salt poisoning of the baby, involving suffering and pain in its death-throes. This remains disputed. But many doctors in the UK are wary of saline because of its poisonous properties and consequent risk to the woman. Prostaglandin abortion is generally contra-indicated for women with asthmatic or bronchial disorders, or those prone to kidney or liver disease, or to epilepsy.

Prostaglandin abortion is also a more distressful experience for the woman. The procedure takes between twelve and thirty-six hours to complete. The woman endures the contractions and pains of labour, and delivers at the end of it, what she may perceive (if she actually sees it, which she may do) as a dead baby. Obviously, the operation must be performed by an experienced doctor who is careful that the urea or prostaglandin is not erroneously injected into the maternal vascular system or abdominal cavity. And a curettage (D&C) is required afterwards, to clear out any retained products.

Prostaglandin is still the method used for most late abortions. It is probably safer, still, than a surgical method. The main advantage is that the patient dilates her own cervix, gradually, over a period of many hours – rather than having it dilated forcibly over a period of a few minutes. Prostaglandin simulates normal labour, and is thus sometimes seen as being more 'natural'. And some women, apparently, prefer to experience abortion – dimly, because consciousness is lowered with drugs – than to sleep through it.

From a laboratory viewpoint, the delivery of a foetus intact is more useful than a dismembered foetus. Better research can be done on a foetus which is in one piece and, if it happens to be abnormal, more can be learned from it when it is delivered whole.

At the London Private Hospital, situated in the centre of London near Oxford Circus, late abortions are carried out by the prostaglandin method, although the hospital also does earlier abortions too. The London Private offers a range of abortion procedures.

'Up to twelve or thirteen weeks,' said its chief medical director, Harley Street gynaecologist Dr Alan Rogers, 'I do aspiration and curettage. After thirteen weeks I do whatever is appropriate: usually from fourteen to sixteen weeks it is a curettage – dilatation and evacuation. Seventeen to eighteen weeks – it's a prostaglandin. Sometimes I will do an evacuation up to eighteen weeks.

Sometimes I'll do a prostaglandin as low as sixteen weeks. It depends on the patient – on the "physicalness" of it, really. It depends on what her cervix is like, on whether she wants more children . . .' If the patient does want children at a future date, the question of the cervix is relevant because stretching the cervix can produce problems later, often a predilection to miscarry. Mr Rogers is not as convinced that the cervix returns to normal easily if a dilatation and evacuation are done much past sixteen weeks. Others might disagree: but this is his experience.

As everywhere in the independent sector, the price of an abortion here varies according to the duration of the pregnancy. A day-care termination at under twelve weeks' gestation is £145. An overnight stay at under fourteen weeks is £155. At under sixteen weeks the cost is £180. Sixteen to nineteen weeks, it is £210. Under twenty-two weeks, it is £290. And twenty-two to twenty-four weeks – £325. These are 1986 prices. The group accomplishes about 400 abortions a week, and the telephone line is always busy.

Mr Maitland Cook, a well-mannered and elegantly dressed man who is the overall non-medical director of the London Private Nursing Homes group (and whose secretary is a Roman Catholic who goes to Mass each day) told me that his organization has close working relations with the French Family Planning Association, with the Italian and Spanish birth control organizations, and with the Well Woman Centre in Dublin, which refers Irish women for abortion in Britain. Abortion is legal in France and Italy, but more restricted than in Britain; forbidden in Southern Ireland; and only just starting – for medical reasons only – in Spain. There had been an 'explosion' in the market of Spanish women coming to London for abortions, he noted. In 1968, just eleven Spanish women came to Britain for abortions. By 1982, that number had risen to over 19,000.

Women also come to London from Northern Ireland for abortions, as abortion is not available for social reasons in the province. All over the developed world, abortion has increased and, with it, the abortion business.

Mr Cook was also very pleased to say that the Marsden Hospital in London – the well-known cancer hospital – used many of their aborted foetuses for cancer research. The foetuses were refrigerated and collected on a weekly basis by the Marsden van. He emphasized how pleased he was about this because it was nice to think of foetal material being put to constructive use. Women were not usually told that their foetuses were being used in this way, since talking to women about this kind of thing when they were coming for an abortion might be distressing.

At the London Private, a woman may be referred by the doctor she has already seen in her own country, or in Britain itself. Or she may have made an appointment independently – the clinic advertises in women's magazines. If the client telephones for an appointment, she will be given one about two days later. Counselling will be offered, but is seldom requested or desired, according to the hospital authorities. Lengthy talks about their private lives are not welcomed by most of the patients who come here; it is a practical matter they want dealt with as competently as possible.

Attending the London Private for a late abortion, the patient is admitted on a Monday afternoon. She will be seen by a doctor and an ultrasound picture will be taken of her pregnancy to determine dates.

I arrived at the London Private, as an observer, on a Monday afternoon. The building was smart-looking, and a bright chandelier hung in the hall; as did an impressive oil reproduction of Queen Elizabeth II, as though the place boasted the royal seal of approval. I had tea with Maitland Cook, who was preoccupied for a few moments about his son's studies at a private school.

Presently, Dr Rogers arrived. He is a lanky, chirpy Welshman in his early forties – confident, experienced, upbeat, talkative. Some patients have found him very helpful, ready to chat away to them and sort out feelings when that is what they want – for some patients will have seen him previously at his Harley Street rooms. He has specialized in abortion and sterilization, as well as contraception, since the 1960s. His experience makes him assured; abortion may be, in most cases, a technically simple operation, but you can run into unusual cases. There was the case of the woman who had a double vagina; and the woman who had two wombs and had conceived a baby in each, thus requiring a double abortion. A less experienced doctor might have missed that. Less experienced doctors have missed twins, too, aborting one foetus and mistakenly leaving the other untouched.

Dr Rogers presently took me up to the fourth floor of the clinic, where nine women were waiting in small rooms off a central ward to have their abortions induced by prostaglandin. All were more than eighteen weeks pregnant; one young student was just on twenty-four weeks. All were healthy and normal and Alan Rogers did not expect any complications.

The atmosphere on the fourth floor was subdued. It was just after 5.30 on a warm, bright afternoon. Dr Rogers's first patient was a Spanish woman, aged twenty-two, and eighteen weeks pregnant. As he entered her little room, she was weeping silently. He spoke consolingly to her, stroking her arm comfortingly, using a few everyday words of Spanish. 'This young woman didn't realize how far the pregnancy had gone, I think,' he said. Her stomach was exposed and it was noticeably that of a pregnant woman. Iodine was rubbed on to the lower part of the abdomen, and an 18-gauge needle used to puncture the amniotic sac; then a catheter was introduced into the wall of the belly; this extracts the amniotic fluid. Then a mixture of prostaglandin and urea was introduced via the same tubing. The urea, Mr Rogers explained, kills the baby, though no one knows how long it takes to die. The woman continued to cry. 'She is crying because she is afraid,' he went on. He was very understanding. The young woman was in a foreign country, she did not speak English, she was alone, and she was about to undergo a late termination of a pregnancy – later than she thought. It was natural to cry.

Prostaglandin treatment may be given either intravenously (by a drip), or orally, or, as here, by intra-amniotic method. The latter is considered to be highly successful in the second trimester of pregnancy.

Dr Rogers examined the ultrasound photograph of the pregnancy, and was satisfied with his diagnosis. He referred critically to a recent case at Luton in Bedfordshire where a doctor had been accused of complicity in murder because he aborted a woman who was thirty-three weeks pregnant on the supposition that the pregnancy was only at twenty-four weeks. He shook his head at the *unprofessionalism* of it.

Dr Rogers, assisted by the sister, settled the patient who was somewhat calmed by his reassurances, and left the room. She now had to wait for her contractions. He moved on to the next patient, Margaret, a fifteen-year-old schoolgirl from Belfast. Her pregnancy was at twenty-two weeks. This was not unusual. Very young girls often do not recognize or acknowledge a pregnancy until it is well advanced. Margaret was a Protestant who looked about twelve years old and said that she had been afraid to tell her mother. When she did break the news, the mother hurriedly brought her to London on the boat. The journey to London had been a fraught one; they lost their luggage and Margaret's mother was staying in a cheap lodging house in Hammersmith – all the money they could get together had to go for the abortion. Margaret seemed more perturbed by the lost luggage than by the abortion itself. 'The problem is,' she said, as Dr Rogers injected, 'I haven't got a change of jeans, now. I'll have to go back home in the clothes I came in. Do you think I could have them washed, here, in the meantime?' Alas, the hospital didn't run a laundry service. She lay in bed, worrying about her clothes. What about the boyfriend, I asked Margaret when I went in to talk to her. 'He has been very good, like,' she replied. 'He even offered to pay half the price of the abortion, though he's on the dole.'

The third patient was French, and was seventeen weeks pregnant according to her own reckoning. The scan showed nineteen weeks. She was a student, blonde, extremely pretty. She was reading a novel when Dr Rogers arrived, and resumed her book when he left her.

The fourth patient was a Yugoslav girl who spoke only Serbo-Croat. The fifth and sixth were both French. The seventh was a French-Algerian girl, a student aged twenty-one. She was also in tears when Alan Rogers arrived at her bedside. She was, he said, 'a good twenty-three weeks' – which meant she was into the twenty-fourth week. She was very tense and he tried to calm her. He was good at giving reassurance. She nodded, weeping. As the amniotic fluid was extracted, her bulging stomach slackened.

The last two patients were Spanish. One was smiling and confident, a little giggly, a little flirtatious. The other was an older woman – thirty-seven, the mother of two children. She was weeping. Pictures of her school-age daughters were by her bed. She was twenty weeks pregnant, married to an older man, and did not feel able to cope with any more children.

By 6.40 the doctor's round was over. All the women had had the injection which would trigger labour. It could take four hours, eight, twelve – the last would be delivered well into the next morning; sixteen hours in labour and, as one woman remarked, nothing to show at the end of it. Relief, perhaps, but that was not what she meant.

For a short time the ward was quiet. But within a couple of hours most of the women were experiencing some contractions. Dr Rogers had left for the night, and the women were tended by a midwife and a nursing sister. There were, of course, other medical personnel in the hospital, and a doctor sleeps within the building, but for the most part the nurses do what has to be done during this night of ghost childbirth. The chief midwife wore a badge from the Royal College of Midwives. She was a stern, stout woman, capable and experienced. She pointed to an incubator and to resuscitation machinery which was kept on hand just in case a baby was born alive. 'Any chance of a baby surviving and I would see to it straight away that it was given intensive care,' she said firmly. She was keen to impress on me that abortion was not what she was trained for; her real skills were midwifery. None of the nurses was easy about my presence on the ward. In contrast to my experience in the NHS hospital, where everyone seemed keen for me to learn as much as possible and to observe in what good conditions and with what accomplished skills abortion was performed, the personnel in this private clinic regarded me as a snooper. I felt, in a sense, an intruder though later I was to be of some assistance to one patient. But the nurses' sense of unease stemmed from something deeper than the inconvenience of having an outsider about. 'Nurses who work in abortion clinics often don't have a high sense of professional self-esteem,' Alan Rogers had said to me. 'It's not the sort of thing you brag about. "What do you do?" "Oh, I work at an abortion clinic." Sometimes I have to give them a little pep talk. You'll often find that after doing, say, twenty abortions, nurses can feel quite dejected. You have to help them along, tell them that they have made twenty women very happy that day.' The sister on the ward reflected this sense of misgiving. 'I remember this hospital when we cured people,' she said, for at one stage, the London Private had concentrated on arthritic illness.

By nine o'clock in the evening, low moans could be heard from most of the small rooms, moans in the rhythmic pattern of the onset of labour. Women were, in turn, panting and sometimes calling out in pain.

I went to the bedside of Marie-Claire, one of the French women. She was an attractive girl, aged just twenty. She seemed to welcome conversation. She was unmarried, living with her boyfriend, and already the mother of one child to whom she gave birth at the age of seventeen. She was living in a Parisian suburb, and desperately wanted to 'improve' herself with 'studies'. She worked as a clerk in a publishing house, but her dream was to become an advocate. Her father left her mother when she was a young child. She had been more or less alone since she was a teenager. She was a soft, emotional person. 'The baby was moving when the doctor injected the needle,' she whispered. From the moment the needle went in, the movements had stopped. 'I feel like a murderer.' Tears fell. I asked her what I could do for her. 'Just stay with me,' she said. She asked my age – the same as her mother's. 'If you can stay with me I will feel that my mother is with me.' Her mother was far away in the provinces of France. She remarried – to a man unsympathetic to Marie-Claire – had two more children, and divorced again. Marie-Claire was to some extent reconciled with her mother when her first baby was born, but life had still been difficult – struggling to get an apartment, to get her little boy into nursery school, to work and study. Her boyfriend was kindly, and it was a steady relationship: he had come to London with her, and had brought the little boy too. Marie-Claire had been on the mini-Pill and had forgotten it 'just once'. Breakthrough bleeding had occurred and she didn't recognize the pregnancy. She had found obstructions with doctors in France, where abortion is relatively easy to get in the early stages of pregnancy, but difficult after the first trimester.

In speaking to women about unwanted pregnancies, I have been surprised by how often the Pill is reported to fail, how often sheaths are said to tear, and how frequently women seem to conceive while wearing an IUD. I have also been surprised by the non-recognition of pregnancy symptoms. A menstrual period delayed by three or four days is often a cause for instant attention, and yet among women presenting for abortion, it can seem that many of them, the younger ones especially, do not recognize the symptoms of pregnancy for several months. Of course, individuals vary greatly; it has been known for some women to give birth without having realized they were pregnant in the first place. The bodies of some women change radically straight away; others have few signs in the early months. And among young women in particular there is a phenomenon known as 'non-acknowledgement': the thought is so appalling that they put it out of their conscious mind and simply hope it will go away. Practised experts, however, are sometimes more sceptical. 'Women say a lot of these things,' Alan Rogers told me. 'They say they've used the Pill or that they've had periods all along. You have to take some of these statements with a pinch of salt.'

The Spanish woman with two children seemed advanced in her labour by nine o'clock. The young Ulster girl was crying, with the puzzlement of a child in unexpected pain. Pain-killers were administered by the nursing staff when the need became acute. Because Marie-Claire and the Spanish woman were already mothers, the nurses thought that it was likely they would deliver first.

At about 11.45, the nurses started to fuss around the Algerian-French student. She was panting as though in the final stages of labour and crying out. The nurses got her out of bed and moved her to a commode. She was terribly pale and in great distress. She sat on the commode, eyes closed as though in a dream. She was straining, in the final stages. 'Push,' the nurses told her. 'Push, push, push!' She spoke no English, but obeyed. Screaming hard, suddenly, she pushed down with an almighty urge, and a plopping sound was heard in the basin of the commode. The foetus had come out. A terrible relief crossed her face, the nurses eased her off the commode, covering it quickly. They helped her back to the bed, having guided her to put a sanitary pad in place: she must do it herself to minimize infection. She fell into bed, exhausted, and was soon asleep. The commode and its contents were removed. The nurses did not examine the foetus straight away, but after the woman had been settled, they wheeled it off to the sluice room. I asked to see the foetus, in its twenty-fourth week of development. 'No way,' said the midwife, forbiddingly. 'I've had enough young nurses fainting on me at the sight of a late abortion without you creating a nuisance by passing out.'

At midnight the women laboured on, all in different stages. Marie-Claire seemed near to delivery, and felt as though she might vomit – nausea, vomiting or diarrhoea are side-effects with prostaglandin abortions. She thought, in her pain, of the infant life. '*He* must be suffering too,' she reflected. Then she asked, 'Will the nurses arrange it so that I don't see the baby?' Yes, they will, I told her. 'I feel as though I've failed at everything,' Marie-Claire reflected, in the shallow stages of her labour. 'I think badly of myself . . .' She asked me to mop her brow, and was touchingly grateful when I did.

Soon after 1 a.m. the nurses told me that it was time I left. They were soon going to be very busy, and it was not convenient to have me under their feet. I explained to Marie-Claire that they wished me to go, and she smiled wanly. 'Will you come by and see me tomorrow?' she asked. I said that I would.

The women delivered through the dawn; the last abortion took place at 10.15 a.m. on Tuesday. During the course of the morning, each woman was taken to the operating theatre for a final curettage called an ERPC (evacuation of retained products of conception). They generally check out of the hospital the following day, on Wednesday morning.

I called in on the Tuesday evening to visit Marie-Claire, as promised. Her boyfriend was there and her small son. She was still pale, but seemed recovered. Most of the women on the ward seemed back to normal, though some wore a curiously chastened expression. The feeling was of the calm after the storm. Marie-Claire chatted to me, her small son played around, and her boyfriend Philippe made friendly conversation about how agreeable, how helpful everyone in England had been. She had delivered quite soon after I had left – around 2 a.m. But she had been alone at the end because the nurses were so busy. She saw the foetus, and was left with it for several minutes. It had been a boy.

'The moment I saw it, I regretted everything,' she said. Now she was going to put the experience behind her. We talked some more about London and Paris and the generalities of life. We had a strange conversation about the population in France coming to a halt. 'The French are ceasing to have children,' said Philippe. 'In France, only immigrants have children now. When we are old, there will be no young people to look after us. It's a disaster.' Such reflections on one's personal past and on the communal future are the very cornerstone of much abortion experience.

I said farewell to the young couple, and Marie-Claire asked for my address. She has written to me every month since then.

ENDOMETRIAL ASPIRATION

It is not just the act of having an abortion that is significant, wrote Christine Burley, a mother of three living in Surrey. 'The *way* is important.' As there is a gentle, positive and natural way of giving birth, so there should be a gentle and positive way of having an abortion. 'I searched for a gentle way to abortion,' Christine wrote to Lynn Reed in response to her *Daily Mail* article. 'Eventually I found it after a great deal of researching and then I sought to obtain it. I spoke to many doctors, consultants, nurses, hospitals and pregnancy referral clinics, both NHS and private throughout the south east. Every time I was met with a total blank or negative response. Many had not even heard of what I wanted. I was asking for termination of pregnancy by endometrial aspiration. It involves the gentle syringing of the contents of the uterus, without the need for vacuum pumps, dilation of the cervix, anaesthesia or pain-killers. Eventually I did find a London-based NHS hospital offering endometrial aspiration. The small unit is manned by a wonderful, empathetic lady doctor who has gathered a marvellous supportive and sympathetic team. I rang on Wednesday; on the Friday I attended for a consultation and examination, and on the Tuesday following I went in for the termination. The actual procedure took less than ten minutes; I had no drugs, although offered valium and a pain-killer. For me, it was less painful than having a coil inserted and even women who haven't had children can accommodate the small, flexible tube without any lasting discomfort. I was aware of a "coming away" feeling (like someone's hand gently resting on yours and then being removed) at the climax of the termination. Mild cramp, less than for a bad period, and rather floppy legs were the only feelings that lasted; and those had gone after half an hour.

'I had previously asked to see the contents of my womb and was shown a small specimen jar of about 25ml. I found this a very necessary moment to reflect and momentarily mourn, even though I was and am convinced that the path I took was the right one. Too often, this essential grieving is brushed under the carpet and the anxieties, depression and sometimes illness which can come later can be extremely difficult to extirpate.'

The 'wonderful, sympathetic lady doctor' was Dr Roslyn Stephens of the National Temperance Hospital in Hampstead Road, London. She does two abortion sessions a week using the method described by Christine Burley. This form of abortion – sometimes, wrongly, called 'menstrual extraction' – must be done very early on in the pregnancy, within twenty-one days of when the last menstrual period is due. Seven weeks pregnancy is the outside boundary for endometrial aspiration. Dr Timothy Black of the Marie Stopes clinic reports that this technique is now used widely in many other countries. He accepts the terminology 'menstrual extraction' because people feel it sounds 'nicer' than abortion. Dr Stephens's clinic is one of the few places in Britain where abortion is done in this way; the women who come here are, by virtue of the swiftness of their reaction and the speed with which they have organized the operation, generally highly motivated. In the field of abortion, the sooner the woman has an abortion, the less likely she is to be ambivalent about it – there are exceptions to this rule, but it is a sufficiently fair generalization none the less. Most of Dr Stephens's clients are referred by their GPs or a family planning clinic.

On the day that I went to observe, there were to be just two patients. One was an American girl in her late twenties, married to an Englishman, and the other was a Russian, whose husband was now in the Middle East, though most patients are in fact British. The atmosphere was tranquil, cosy and intimate. There was a waiting and consulting floor, then a floor with the operating theatre and a rest room where the patients lie down for a couple of hours after the termination.

In the theatre was Dr Stephens, her assistant Mikki, a glamorous, middle-aged woman working there on a part-time basis, and a nurse. The American girl was wheeled in first. She was calm and controlled, but possibly a little nervous underneath. The conversation was friendly and inconsequential as Dr Stephens prepared to do the operation. Holding the vaginal entrance open with a speculum, the perineal area was made sterile with an antiseptic. The patient had no general anaesthetic, but an injection of Lignocaine was inserted into the cervix in order to numb the area. Because it was so early no significant dilatation of the cervix was required. Dr Stephens explained to the patient what she was doing. 'Do you do yoga?' asked Mikki, who stood by the woman's head, and whose function was to calm, soothe and stroke the patient. 'No, at times like this I wish I had,' the young woman replied, smiling. She was called Leslie and she came from Boston.

Dr Stephens then inserted a large plastic syringe gradually and drew out the contents – about 30mm of blood, foetal tissue and placenta. It was so little it fitted in a small dish the size of a ramekin.

Leslie explained that she had only just started to feel 'pregnant', but she made up her mind three weeks ago because she was certain she did not want to continue. She had just recently been married, and on the first night of the honeymoon she found she had left her diaphragm at home. She was very pleased to have 'caught it in time', she said. This experience was so different from an earlier abortion under general anaesthetic. 'This one, you know you are only six weeks, you know the foetus is only tiny – it's not developed yet,' Leslie said.

It was very simple, and was soon over. Leslie was wheeled out on a trolly, back to the rest ward. When she had gone, Dr Stephens examined the contents in the sluice. Nothing could be seen of the embryo, but the doctor extracted a tiny, white, frond-like substance which floated in water in a small plastic container no larger than a mustard pot. This was the placenta. It waved in the water, like a miniature palm tree. 'It's beautiful, isn't it?' said Dr Stephens, holding it up to the light. Though the embryo was unrecognizable at this stage, the placenta was already a complete life-support system.

The second patient entered in a happy mood. The American woman was small-boned and fastidious-looking; the Russian was large and hirsute. She said she was giggling from the effect of the valium, but this was short-lived. During the brief operation she felt pain and moaned. Mikki soothed her and Dr Stephens was upset. 'I hate it when I cause a woman pain,' she said afterwards.

Lydia, the Russian, was a post-graduate student, and a recent émigrée from the USSR. She had had three abortions in the Soviet Union. 'You think I'm bad to have three – I know women in Moscow who've had thirty-three,' she said later. She described her marriage as nice and sweet but mostly asexual. It was just this one time, she went to see her husband in the Middle East, and somehow, intercourse happened. 'All this sex comes from the devil,' she said afterwards. 'Human beings should think about their souls.' Contraception is not necessary for her, she says, since she plans never to have sex again. (A sincerely-expressed feeling, and not so very unusual after an abortion; but seldom entirely realistic.)

This experience she just wanted to put in the past, but beside her experience in Russia, it was nothing. 'In the Soviet Union, abortion is a lot of trouble and worry, though nobody considers it a sin. But they are horrible to women – "Stop shouting, stop crying, nobody forced you here," they yell when you go to have an abortion. "What did you think about when you went to bed with your man? So quit complaining now."'

Leslie, the young Bostonian, was – as she had been in the theatre – much more controlled, very together, a smiling, well-organized kind of person. She was a secretary, her husband a lawyer; they had a nice but small flat, they were saving for a house; they wanted to plan their children – if they decided to have any at all – not rush into unprepared parenthood. She was pleased she had had the termination: it had been simple, quick, it didn't hurt, and it was a relief to get it done so early in the pregnancy. Her husband had said he would go along with whatever she wished. But when she chose abortion, he was highly relieved just the same.

Leslie said she might consider having a child later on. She wasn't sure. Actually, she would quite like to adopt a baby rather than have one of her own. That would be her preferred choice. In this, however, the right to choose is greatly diminishing. Partly because of abortion, there are virtually no babies to adopt.

The techniques of abortion are altering and developing all the time. Abortion became legal in most countries in the Western world (and all, save Albania, in the Communist world) in the aftermath of the Second World War, partly because of increased demand for it. But medical technology also played an important part. It has been known since ancient times that dilatation of the cervix could be brought about by inserting into it substances which would act as an irritant – such as asparagus steeped in alcohol, or dried compressed seaweed. But the important technical breakthrough came in 1958, when the Chinese doctors Wu and Wu showed the effectiveness of vacuum aspiration. By the late 1950s and early 1960s, vacuum aspiration was being used in Japan, Russia and Eastern Europe. In 1967, the woman gynaecologist who is credited with pioneering abortion techniques in Britain, Dorothy Kerslake, began to use suction termination and, from this period onwards, abortion has moved into the area of high medical technology.

As abortion became legalized – and it was perhaps not altogether a surprise that the legalization of abortion coincided with its technical simplification – better equipment came on the market, and as more doctors performed abortions, more experience was gained. It is almost certain that, medically, the techniques will go on developing, and within a few decades some of the methods used in the 1980s may come to seem crude and primitive. An abortion pill is now under trial – a drug which will stop the pregnancy at any stage in its development, not dissimilar to the present post-coital pill. Pregnancy testing itself is being perfected each year, and it is now technically possible to determine whether a woman is pregnant before she misses her first period. Over-the-counter pregnancy tests are available in pharmacies which give a highly accurate indication of pregnancy within the first days of a missed period. Only a decade ago, women had to wait weeks.

The feminist goal of taking abortion out of the hands of doctors and back into the power of women themselves is theoretically already in sight. Indeed, when Christine Burley was researching a method of endometrial aspiration, she came across a group of feminists who were doing just this. Using the techniques of endometrial aspiration, they had equipped themselves with the Rocket Syringe (the instrument used by Dr Stephens) and were performing early abortions secretly. Rocket Syringes cost £2.50 each, and they were bought by this group from well-known medical suppliers. They were performing abortions for women at a cost of £22 each, which indicates that it can be a very inexpensive operation. Abortion by unskilled practitioners has always been condemned for its dangers; but modern antibiotics and medical treatment can usually save a woman's life even if infection or haemorrhage occurred.

Safe, easy-to-get and early abortion has been the goal of those who have campaigned for abortion. The technology is now available, and most women in the countries where abortion has been legalized can now get one; even where it has not be legalized, it is either performed under the guise of 'menstrual extraction' or 'D&C'. Alternatively, a thriving industry exists in which women travel from one country to another for the operation, as with the Spanish traffic to London. Within the National Health Service, it is true that there are delays and obstructions: there are delays and obstructions, too, for the treatment of kidney disease or hip replacements – nationalized industries are notoriously vulnerable to bureaucracy and a patronizing attitude towards the public. But abortion, it is true, has the extra difficulty of the ethical dimension. Some nurses and doctors just do not want to perform abortions, and unless there is a coercive policy towards the medical profession, it would be impossible – under present arrangements – to iron out all regional differences. However, abortion is actually relatively cheap in the private sector – costing less than a week's average wage – and as it is constantly stressed that it is an optional operation (the whole notion of 'choice' means that it is optional) – if it must exist then the private sector seems to organize it very efficiently.

'One day very soon,' says Dr Timothy Black of Marie Stopes, 'women will have their abortions, perfectly happily, in the morning, go out to lunch and spend the afternoon shopping. It will be as simple as having a cup of coffee.' Technically, yes. But the human problems will remain always.

7

A SHORT HISTORY OF MODERN ABORTION

'Abortion must be the key to a new world for women, not a bulwark for things as they are . . . Abortion should not be either a perquisite of the legal wife only, nor merely a last remedy against illegitimacy. It should be available for any woman, without insolent inquisitions, nor ruinous financial charges, nor tangles of red tape. For our bodies are our own.' – Stella Browne, 1915.

'The principle which the Western world has accepted in theory, although it has certainly not always lived up to in practice, is that, apart from self-defence against aggressors, human life may not be taken. Innocent human life is sacred.' – Norman St John Stevas, *The Right to Life*, 1963

In the era following the Second World War, there was a worldwide trend to liberalize abortion. At least sixty countries have made abortion legal or easier to get since 1945. Britain's legislation, in 1967, was very influential.

Abortion freedom started in Russia in the revolutionary period, in 1920. Marriage and 'bourgeois morality' were at the time theoretically abolished, but this was reversed by Stalin in 1935. Nearly all dictators have been pronatalist – at least for their own people. Mussolini forbade both abortion and contraception, although Dennis Mack Smith, his biographer, tells us that one conception in three was aborted in Italy during the Mussolini years. Hitler, too, was emphatically against abortion and birth control for German women, but he was ardently in favour of all birth-restricting practices for non-Aryan peoples. 'It could only suit us if girls and women in Slav countries had as many abortions as possible,' he said in his famous Table Talks. 'Active trade in contraceptives ought to be actually encouraged in the Eastern territories, as we could not have the slightest interest in increasing the non-German population.'

Abortion was also briefly legalized in Catalonia, in Spain, in 1936, again alongside the abolition of bourgeois marriage. This was during the period of revolutionary government there. Franco, of course, reversed these measures, but they had not been altogether popular even with revolutionary women, who complained that their daughters were being turned into concubines.

A Yugoslav law of 1929 also permitted abortion to protect the health of the woman, and a somewhat maverick law in Argentina in 1921 permitted abortion for rape, or the 'violation of an idiot or insane woman'.

The Second World War was a huge source of social change, in this, as in other things. A hidden sexual revolution took place during that war. However, one of the first countries to legalize abortion after the war was not moved by notions of individual liberation but by pressure of population. The expansion of Japan's population was considered insupportable, and abortion was legalized there in 1948. Exposure to radiation after the atom bombs were dropped on Hiroshima and Nagasaki also raised awareness of the problems of the defective foetus, for a horror of foetal damage always increases public sympathy for abortion. (The thalidomide tragedy of the early 1960s, for example, was probably the decisive factor which won public opinion over to abortion law reform, see page 196.)

War always has far-reaching psychological effects. Many who went through the brutalizing experiences of wartime are not inclined to be sentimental about foetal life. When they see babies suffer unspeakably, they are more likely to think unborn life better off terminated than brought into a horrible world. Concentration camp survivors, with the exception of those with a strong religious faith, tend also to be pro-abortion.

East Germany legalized abortion in 1947 – partly because a lot of women were reported dying of illegal abortion. Curiously, however, legalization did not stop the back-street trade in the GDR – in fact, it increased. In 1950, the authorities decided that the abortion experiment was a failure and rescinded the original liberalization. It is very likely, however, that the de-population which had occurred in Germany during the war was also an influence in rescinding. Unlike other members of the Warsaw Pact, the GDR was not to return to free abortion until the mid-1960s.

The Soviet Union legalized abortion again in 1956. The truth was that the operation was continuing to be practised, legal or not. When in 1981 I asked a young Moscow woman why it was that Russian women still had so many abortions – the average for city-dwellers is said to be between six and ten abortions per woman – she replied, a little embarrassed: 'It is just the old-fashioned way of doing things that still goes on.'

The USSR's satellites followed suit: by 1960, Poland, Czechoslovakia (which had also copied Russia in 1920, later revoking the law), Bulgaria, Hungary and Romania had legalized abortion. China had passed its law in 1957. Only Albania has retained laws forbidding abortion – again, the motive being to increase population, a source of irritation to the neighbouring Yugoslavs.

Abortion, by and large, was, and remains, more acceptable in atheistic systems. Stella Browne, the British feminist who first publicly aired the subject of abortion as a matter of desirable choice in *The Malthusian* magazine in 1915, was herself a communist and had been influenced by the German socialists and communists who had argued for abortion as early as 1897.

However, what was really crucial in the changing

attitude to abortion in the post-war period was not ideology but technology. It is said that abortion has been practised in all societies and at all times but, in truth, until at least the 1880s, it was a very dangerous operation. The reason doctors campaigned so virulently against it in the nineteenth century was because of its manifest hazards to the woman, and only partly because of an increasing awareness of the humanity of the foetus. Instruments introduced into the cervix may well abort a pregnancy, but they may also perforate another delicate or vital organ and introduce infection. The knitting needle or the crochet hook which were favourite objects used to disturb a pregnancy, could so easily cause internal damage or even kill a woman. It was estimated in one American study of 1880 that one-third of patients at that time undergoing any serious surgery died as a consequence (James Mohr, *Abortion in America*).

Anaesthetics were first used in 1846. In 1867, Lister published his work on antiseptics. In the 1880s, the gynaecologist Hegar produced the Hegar dilator. This was to prove the key surgical instrument in abortion, and is indeed still in use today. It could open the cervix under antiseptic and anaesthetic conditions and abort the pregnancy with quite new degrees of accuracy. In the late nineteenth century, the 'dry-cupping of the interior of the uterus' was used to evacuate the womb: having dilated the cervix, a catheter was introduced, with a syringe at its extremity. In the 1920s, the Russian Bykov injected irritants into the womb to provoke abortion. And while skilled doctors, from the turn of the century onwards, could perform abortions with some success (Lillie Langtry, and at least one of Lloyd George's mistresses, Frances Stevenson, were successfully aborted on several occasions), the techniques remained dangerous in the hands of those who did not know what they were doing. Scraping out the soft interior of the uterus remained, until the 1950s, a tricky business. It was only with the invention of the vacuum aspirator by Wu and Wu in China in 1958, that abortion finally changed for ever. This simple instrument made early abortion easy, safe and accessible.

In the minority of cases where infections still arose post-abortion, antibiotics were now at hand to control them. The change in the medical status of abortion – from being a dangerous and criminal operation to a high-tech and safe one – was not due to campaigns, to morality, to women's rights: it was largely due, quite simply, to technology.

At the beginning of the nineteenth century, there was hardly any legislation concerning abortion. It was generally thought that there was a difference between the 'quickened' and the 'unquickened' foetus ('quickening' being the moment when the mother feels the child move in the womb, usually around fourteen to sixteen weeks). The traditional forms of abortion had been infanticide and abandonment: when Pope Innocent III opened the hospital of Santo Spirito in Rome at the end of the twelfth century, it was in response to the number of babies being flung into the Tiber. In 1527, we hear of a priest complaining that 'the latrines resound to the cries of children who have been plunged into them'. In Dublin in 1775–6, a foundling hospital admitted 10,272 abandoned babies, of whom just forty-five survived. Many intelligent people accepted infanticide; the utilitarians Jeremy Bentham and his colleagues Godwin and Francis Place felt that even if it was regrettable, death was preferable to a life of poverty and crime. Malthus, the first modern advocate of population control, promulgated the closing down of foundling hospitals on the grounds that they only encouraged babies to live, and indeed encouraged promiscuity.

After the Enlightenment the view gradually gained ground that the foetus was alive from the moment of conception. Britain's first law against abortion went on the statute books in 1803. The Ellenborough Act, as it was called, distinguished between the 'quickened' and the 'unquickened' foetus, as had traditional practice. Before quickening, abortion was deemed punishable with a fine or transportation up to fourteen years. After quickening, abortion could be punishable by death. But, of course, it hardly ever was. Public opinion took a more lenient view and, anyway, when abortion was successful, there was no complainant. Abortion cases usually came to light only when the woman died, and even here abortionists were sometimes let off easily. Infant life was still not *that* highly valued in nineteenth-century Britain. One classic case was that of a Nottingham couple charged with the deaths of several babies who had been in their care – they had starved them to death. They were each fined ten shillings and sixpence (52½p). On the same day and in the same court, a man convicted of trespassing in search of game was fined two guineas, *four times* as much. Property was and sometimes still is regarded as being much more important than human life.

Nevertheless, the medical view was gradually moving towards an appreciation of foetal life, just as the enlightened social view moved towards more concern for babies and young children. The beginnings of modern ante-natal care, of examining the foetus in the uterus, can perhaps be dated from 1818 when a surgeon in Geneva, François Mayor, first heard the foetal heart-beat in a woman five months pregnant – at least for the first *recorded* time. By the 1830s, doctors were beginning to apply the stethoscope to the stomachs of pregnant women. The superstitions and practices of many midwives were starting to be cast aside at this time – the practice of bleeding pregnant women, for example, or the theory of 'maternal impressions' whereby if a pregnant woman was frightened by a cat she would give birth to a baby who looked like a cat. And thus it was that the 1839 Offences Against the Person Act made abortion at *any* stage of a pregnancy equally wrong. The medical profession undoubtedly played an influential role in changing attitudes. In 1832, one medical paper had called upon 'an enlightened legislature' to outlaw all abortion and to close the gap previously allowed by common law, which had tolerated abortion in the early stages. In 1861, a further Offences Against the Person Act ratified the earlier legislation and made abortion at any stage, or to supply or procure poisons or instruments knowingly for the purpose of abortion, a felony punishable by three years' imprisonment. This Act is still theoretically on the statute books.

The trend was broadly the same all over the 'developed' world. Of course, British law also applied to the British Empire. France and Belgium both introduced prohibitions against abortion in 1810. In America, Connecticut passed an abortion law in 1821 and the legislation then spread from state to state. Portugal made abortion illegal in 1854, Iceland in 1869, Holland in 1886. The German Reich forbade abortion in 1871, following on the Prussian Penal Code law of 1851. Swedish legislation was altered in 1864 to reduce the penalty for abortion – which was death – to imprisonment for six years. This might count as a liberalization of Swedish law, if it hadn't been for the fact that the penalty was formerly so extremely harsh. (In the twentieth century, however, Sweden played a leading role in discussing abortion in Parliament, and indeed in legislation.) And in 1869, the Vatican moved to tighten its stance on abortion, declaring it, for the first time, absolutely forbidden deliberately to destroy the unborn child. This caused no great commotion at the time since it was the accepted, even the progressive view. In America, the feminist Elizabeth Cady Stanton declared abortion to be a horror and a degradation upon women.

However, although abortion and infanticide were forbidden, both continued to exist. Indeed, the fact that legislation was spreading to tighten up abortion practice is an indication that it was on the increase.

The numbers of unwanted and abandoned children were also on the increase as the nineteenth century wore on. This had many causes: the great population shifts from country to city, the well-meaning legislation which gradually forbade the employment of children, thus turning offspring into economic liabilities rather than assets, industrial poverty and so on. For example, between 1819 and 1823 some 151 infants were found abandoned on the London streets, Sauer tells us. In one year, 1870, reports Walvin, 276 babies were found dead in London. There was much public concern about abandoned children, and children who were killed. One letter to *The Times* in the 1860s asking for suggestions about halting this scandal of infanticide elicited 1,000 replies. When Dr Barnardo founded his children's homes in London in 1867, there were said to be up to 100,000 urchins living rough in the London streets, quite often abandoned from an early age by their parents.

In the 1860s the Society for the Protection of Infant Life was set up, led by doctors, charitable women and Members of Parliament. This organization campaigned for the care of unwanted and abandoned infants, collecting funds for foundling hospitals, for nurseries and even for a maternal allowance for poor mothers. (This was vetoed by rate-payers because it would be 'too expensive' and would only 'encourage bad morals'; fathers should be made to take responsibility for their children.) In consequence of this campaign, however, the Infant Life Preservation Act was passed in 1872 which required the registration of babies and those who were in charge of them. The Act was considered weak and ineffective because 'baby-farming' – often a highly neglectful form of child-minding – continued, and infants continued to die. George Moore's famous novel of the 1890s, *Esther Waters*, drew attention to the plight of the single, unmarried girl trying to care for her infant. Here baby-farmers are seen as caretakers who half-deliberately do away with their charges, sometimes even as a favour to the natural mothers.

> You girls is all alike: yer thinks of nothing but yer babies for the first few weeks, then yer tires of them . . . and then yer wishes they 'ad never been born, or yer wishes they had died afore they knew they were alive [says the baby-farmer, Mrs Spires, when Esther comes to visit her baby, who is not thriving]. I don't say I'm not often sorry for them, poor little dears, but they takes less notice than you'd think for, and they're better out of the way, and that's a fact; it saves a lot of trouble hereafter. I often do think that to neglect them, to let them go off quiet, that I be their best friend; not wilful neglect, yer know, but what is a woman to do with ten

or a dozen, and I often 'as as many? I am sure they'd thank me for it.

Despite legislation, abortion also continued in a clandestine form. In 1846, the development of an abortion trade in Nottingham was noted, says Sauer in *Population Studies* No. 32, and in 1853, *The Lancet* first reported on the existence of professional abortionists who advertised their trade through leaflets in London. 'None but the ignorant will dispute that the offence is one of increasing frequency,' it commented. As early as 1822, the utilitarian Richard Carlisle had written that 'the means to destroy the foetus had been practised by many married women'. In 1862, the great investigator of the London poor, Henry Mayhew, reported on 'the immense number of embryo children who are made away with by drugs and other devices'. Gin and gunpowder, lead from diachylon (used for making plasters to heal broken bones and easily available from pharmacies), laxatives and pennyroyal, were taken by mouth to stimulate abortion, often successfully, though no doubt painfully. Colocynth – commonly known as bitter apples – hiera picra (hickey-pikey), tans, turpentine, washing soda and quinine were also applied. These drugs were preferred to interference by instruments, which were known to be dangerous – although instruments might be used as a second line of attack, if the various drugs produced no effect. Sometimes huge doses were taken, the historian Patricia Knight reminds us. One woman took 144 pills before she miscarried seventeen days later. One woman aged forty who already had eleven children took forty pills to no avail.

The numerous women who resorted to abortion frequently had to face illness and sometimes death [Knight continues]. A typical example in 1866 concerned a woman with seven children, who was five months pregnant and who paid a midwife £3 to abort her: her uterus was lacerated, punctured and inflamed and she died a fortnight later from peritonitis and gangrene. There were many pathetic court cases reported in the

> press. For example, in 1868 there was an inquest on Louise Thomas, aged 24, who was two months pregnant and died from an attempt made by a doctor (who was the father of her child) to abort her. The doctor himself had committed suicide by throwing himself under a train . . . Death sometimes occurred from lead poisoning, and women who took lead pills frequently suffered from sickness, abdominal pains, headaches, paralysis of the hands and occasionally blindness. [*Women and Abortion in Victorian and Edwardian England*, History Workshop 4]

Lead poisoning, which was traced by a stain on the gums, was so widely used that women admitted to hospital for miscarriage or stillbirth were commonly examined for the traces of a self-procured abortion. Only in Ireland was there no evidence of this practice. The Irish were noted, too, for not practising infanticide: 'Trodden, persecuted, poverty-stricken often to the verge of starvation . . . seldom do they dash from their breasts the innocent babe,' Knight quotes from a contemporary document about the Irish poor. 'While the crime of infanticide is above, below and around them, they live in a happy exemption from its horrors and an unalterable detestation of its nature.'

Towards the very end of the nineteenth century, attitudes began to change again towards abortion. In the 1890s, the famous scandal of the Chrimes brothers was widely commented upon. Richard, Edward and Leonard Chrimes rented rooms at Ludgate Circus, London, from which they sent out fraudulent messages, purporting to offer women abortifacient pills. 'The Lady Montrose Miraculous Female Tabules are positively unequalled for all FEMALE AILMENTS. The most OBSTINATE obstructions, Irregularities, etc. of the female system are removed in a few doses.' Between 1896 and 1898, they did a brisk business in marketing these pills. It was a foolproof confidence trick because while the pills appeared to work for some women (those who were not pregnant or who might have miscarried anyhow), the women for whom the pills did not work had no grounds for complaint since abortifacients were illegal. The pills, which were a compound of a simple blood tonic, were sold for between three shillings and sixpence and thirty-two shillings for 'extra strength'. Thirty-two shillings was a fortnight's wage for a poor man. Their business might have continued to thrive had they not become greedy and started to blackmail the women who had sent off for the Lady Montrose tablets. Pathetic letters were sent back to the blackmailers. 'Dear Sir – I write in answer to your letter and also enclosing two guineas. I want you to return the paper which you hold against me, and I promise not to repeat what I have done as long as I live. I should not like my missus to know, else I shall lose my situation,' – this from a servant girl. 'Dear Sir, I am very sorry I have done wrong. I did not know I had done wrong to myself or anyone else . . . But if I have done wrong I ask you to forgive me . . . ' – this letter containing the two pounds and two shillings the blackmailers demanded. The brothers were apprehended and sentenced to twelve years' imprisonment each for the elder two, seven years for the youngest.

However, their trial brought much comment on the subject of abortifacients. A long article appeared in *The Lancet*, the historian Angus McLaren tells us ('Abortion in England, 1890–1914', *Victorian Studies*), on the various medications that paraded as abortifacients. Adverts for such pills filled the columns of many Sunday and weekly papers, even including a religious publication, *The Rock*. The blackmailing aspect was particularly distasteful to a contributor to the *Westminster Review*. 'That such practices [abortion] have been common in all classes of society there is a great reason to believe, quite apart from the pathetic and startling evidence to that effect furnished by a recent trial for blackmailing.' At the same time, the first signs that some doctors were beginning to shift their ground on abortion were appearing. In 1899, what is now thought of as the first medical paper justifying abortion where pregnancy threatened maternal health appeared in the review of the Edinburgh Obstetrical Society. 'One physician stated that the foetus had only potential life, and was a "parasite performing no function whatsoever",' reports Sauer in *Population Studies*. 'Although the medical profession continued to oppose abortion for decades to come, this statement seems to have marked the beginning of a change in overt opinion which was to culminate some 70 years later in the legalization of abortion in many cases.'

Abortion was not to become controversial for some time, however. In the early part of the twentieth century, it was almost obscured by the controversy over birth control. When Stella Browne advocated abortion openly during the First World War, even her closest supporters were embarrassed by her boldness, and daunted by her imprudence. The birth control campaigners, Marie Stopes in Britain and Margaret Sanger in America, refused to involve themselves with abortion at all, although letters to Marie Stopes repeatedly requested abortion pills. Stopes and Sanger repudiated abortion for sensible reasons: it was associated with criminality, it was still dangerous, it was bad for women's health, it confused the birth control issues, and neither of them fundamentally approved of it. Sanger still regarded a pregnant woman as carrying human life. Stopes, too, was extra-careful never to associate herself with abortion, and very pointedly told people who wrote to her never to take pills that promised to bring on menses. She, too, believed in contraception – prevention of conception. In Britain and America from 1918 until 1930, the battle over birth control raged and abortion was seldom referred to, except insofar as its practice could be used to advocate contraception. Yet in the 1930s, 400 women a year in Britain were dying from the effects of abortion.

In the Scandinavian countries, however, abortion *was* being discussed. In 1921, abortion was declared a 'punishment-free' crime in Sweden. In 1928 and 1929, abortion was debated again in the Swedish Parliament, and a group of women MPs began to speak about the social perspectives of abortion, about the over-burdened mother, and the need for eugenic abortion. Similarly, in

Denmark in 1929 a delegation of socialist women sought changes in the law. By the Second World War, the Swedes, Danes and Icelanders had legalized abortion on grounds of serious danger to the mother, for rape, criminal acts, inherited genetic disease or serious defects in the foetus, and for girls under the age of fifteen and for eugenic reasons. Insanity or psychological disturbance were also grounds for abortion. Had the war not occurred Britain would very likely have introduced a limited abortion law in the 1940s.

The famous Bourne case indicates that there was certainly a climate of opinion in which some people were ready to accept abortion under certain circumstances. In the summer of 1938, a fourteen-year-old girl was raped by three guardsmen at Wellington Barracks in London. She became pregnant as a consequence and was refused an abortion by a Catholic doctor at St Thomas's Hospital. She was taken by her school care committee organizer to Mr Aleck Bourne, a consultant obstetrician at St Mary's Hospital. Bourne agreed to terminate the pregnancy, though he did wait eight days before doing so, in order to establish that the girl was of a 'genuine' type. Once satisfied with her innocence and good morals, Bourne performed the operation. He then reported himself to the police. He was charged with a criminal offence in a trial that became a *cause célèbre*. Bourne received telegrams of support from the great progressive minds of the time, including Bertrand Russell and H.G. Wells. He was acquitted, on the grounds that it is not really possible to discriminate between a woman's *life* being in danger and her *health* (including, by extension, mental health). In an address which was to influence abortion practice for the next forty years, Mr Justice MacNaghten said to the jury: 'Life depends on health, and it may be that if health is gravely impaired, death results.' This judgement stood as a precedent in case law in England and Wales. Many abortions were thereafter performed because the physician felt it justifiable to equate *life* with health. The outcome of the Bourne case was greeted favourably – except, of course, by Catholics.

David Paintin says that, even without the Bourne case, there would almost certainly have been a eugenic abortion law in Britain had the war not intervened. Certainly eugenics was the great intellectual subject of debate between 1890 and 1940. Eugenics was the so-called 'science' of breeding from 'good stock'. It was passionately embraced by many we would consider the left-wing thinkers of the period. Havelock Ellis, George Bernard Shaw, Sydney and Beatrice Webb, Ottoline Morell, Harold Laski, Dean Inge, J.B.S. Haldane, Julian Huxley, Marie Stopes and Olive Schreiner were all enthusiastic eugenicians, but so too were Alexander Graham Bell, Winston Churchill, John D. Rockefeller and George Eastman. Eugenic societies flourished in Britain, the United States, Russia, Japan, Germany, Sweden, Norway, Switzerland, Poland, France, Italy and Latin America. The eugenicists, whose philosophy was pioneered by Francis Galton and Karl Pearson inspired by Charles Darwin and Auguste Mendel, believed that the stupid, the criminal, the feckless, the feeble-minded and the poor were breeding too much, while the intelligent and the able were breeding too little.

'We know enough about eugenics,' said a leading American academic in the 1930s, 'so that if the knowledge were applied, the defective classes would disappear within a generation.' A large number of papers were produced to explain that the 'defective classes' were ruinously on the increase. Between 1903 and 1918, Daniel Kevles tells us in 'Annals of Eugenics' that more than 300 publications appeared on the theme of 'national deterioration' because of 'dysgenic' breeding. Insanity, epilepsy, alcoholism, pauperism, criminality and feeble-mindedness were all ascribed to bad heredity, and certain races were considered to be particularly undesirable because of their dysgenic breeding habits. 'Nordic' races were considered by the eugenicists to be superior in stock to certain others. Sydney Webb, a founder of the London School of Economics and of the *New Statesman*, wrote in a Fabian tract of 1906 of the alarming increase of population among the Jews and the Irish.

> In Great Britain at this moment, when half, or perhaps two-thirds, of all the married people are regulating their families, children are being freely born to the Irish Roman Catholics and the Polish, Russian and German Jews . . . to the thriftless and irresponsible – largely the casual labourers and other denizens of one-roomed tenements . . . This can hardly result in anything but national deterioration: or as an alternative in this country gradually falling to the Irish and the Jews. [Kevles, op. cit.]

'Race hygiene' and eugenics were very common and indeed very fashionable ideas, and the Nazis took these ideas to their logical conclusion. The eugenic societies especially attracted upper-class women, who saw 'better stock' as part of better motherhood. Defects of character and personality were authoritatively held to be inherited, and moves to sterilize the 'dysgenic' were widely supported. This aspect of the evolution of social thinking has either been deliberately suppressed or deliberately forgotten. When Germany started on an aggressive sterilization programme of the 'inadequate' in 1934, it was applauded in the West, especially in parts of America which had itself embraced such sterilization – notably in California. A 1937 poll for *Fortune* magazine claimed that 63 per cent of all Americans endorsed compulsory sterilization for habitual criminals, and 66 per cent believed it should be imposed on mental defectives. 'Eugenicists on both sides of the Atlantic insisted that sterilization was humane as well as practical,' wrote Daniel Kevles. Once again, the main opponents of eugenics (and compulsory sterilization) were the Catholics, though they were sometimes supported by individual left-wing socialists such as Josiah Wedgwood and John Reed (the American communist and author of *Ten Days that Shook the World*).

The war, however, brought this subject very much into disrepute, as it became obvious to what use Hitler had put the philosophy of social Darwinism. In fact, the reaction was so negative that the word eugenics itself fell into disrepute, and even genetics, its step-sister science (with a valid claim to objectivity and untrammelled by political and social manipulation) was over-shadowed.

Following the Second World War, many doctors were becoming increasingly aware of the farcical situation that accompanied abortion. Poor women were being butchered, while rich or well-connected women got an abortion when they wanted one without too much difficulty. Even before the war, society abortions had been a recognized fact of life: A.J. Cronin refers to them in his popular novels of the time, and Edward James describes in his memoirs the actress Tilly Losch being aborted at eight months pregnancy because she decided she didn't want the child (other guests at this country house weekend included Barbara Cartland and Randolph Churchill). It was the old story of one law for the rich and another for the poor.

A sophisticated account of abortion in the 1950s is found in Bernard Nathanson's autobiography, *Aborting America*. Two or three times a week, as a young hospital doctor, Nathanson would find himself hauled out at two in the morning to go down to the admittance ward.

> There a petrified, shivering creature would be lying on the examining table, bleeding profusely from the vagina and moaning softly to herself. A thermometer registering 103° or 104° would be taken from her mouth and with this, the moaning would give way to loud cries or praying in tongues. Skipping introductions, I would proceed immediately to the ordeal of vaginal examination, often fishing out sizeable chunks of pregnancy tissue lying free among the huge clots. Another victim of a hack-abortionist or of self-abortion. I would sign the admission slip, ordering intravenous antibiotics, blood tests and preparations for a dilation and curettage. I would pass an hour or so watching the 'Late Late Show' on the dilapidated TV set in the residents' quarters until it was time to carry out the D & C, removing the rest of the tissue. If she were lucky, she would be returned to her room, be discharged 48 hours

later, and instructed to return to the gynaecology clinic for a check-up one month hence.

If she were *not* lucky, she might:

- Vomit under anaesthesia, aspirate her vomitus and die of respiratory obstruction and cardiac arrest.
- Continue to bleed from a perforation of the uterus that had been inflicted by the abortionist. Hysterotomy would be carried out without delay.
- Continue to spike high fevers for days or weeks. In that era we had only a few antibiotics available, and most had serious side effects. This might culminate in the formation of multiple pelvic abscesses, requiring periodic drainage of the pus which would collect. The pus was usually fulvous, wrenchingly foul-smelling, and so astonishing in quantity that even those hardened to it had to marvel at the body's ability to tolerate such pervasive corruption. In many cases the infection would be uncontrollable by means short of a hysterectomy.

Occasionally, even a hysterectomy would not slow the steady march of internal gangrene, and the woman would die painfully, her vital organs filthy with the satellite abscesses of her disease.

In contrast to the plight of the poor woman, the rich woman had everything beautifully organized for her, recalls Nathanson. The private physician would telephone the hospital doctor at a civilized hour of the day to say that Mrs Buggins had some vaginal bleeding and was to be admitted with a threatened miscarriage. Mrs Buggins would arrive in excellent form and the doctor would perform the abortion and mark it down as a D & C. The charade was that Mrs Buggins had had a miscarriage which the physician merely completed; in fact, Mrs Buggins had had a medically safe abortion.

Nathanson describes the lengths to which he would sometimes have to go to help poorer women to terminate pregnancies. There was an elaborate procedure about sending them to Puerto Rico – where abortion was as illegal as it was in New York, but where the police could be bought more cheaply. He also describes the widespread, deeply dishonest racket in the 'psychiatric' cases. By the 1960s, 'mental illness' was established as grounds for abortion, and so the accepted charade was that the woman should be seen to threaten suicide if an abortion was not granted. This deception was also frequently acted out in Britain, and in fact it prostituted psychiatrists who were known to attest a perfectly sane woman's mental instability in order to circumvent the law.

Such hypocrisy gradually convinced many doctors of the need for reform, but what particularly influenced them was the number of women admitted to hospital with botched abortions. Doctors were deeply vexed by this as they now had the technology to perform the operation professionally.

'In 1962 we were still admitting large numbers of women who had gone to back-street abortionists and suffered severe pelvic sepsis and haemorrhage as a result,' said Professor Norman Morris of Charing Cross Hospital. 'It was not until the Abortion Bill, pioneered by David Steel in 1967, became law in 1968 that we saw the dramatic reduction in post-natal sepsis and haemorrhage.' In fact, the medical profession was quite ambivalent about changing the law since doctors do not like to be characterized as abortionists. When Dr Nathanson associated himself with abortion law reform he felt a distinct chill from his colleagues, even as late as 1969.

> I was publicly identified with a cause which in the past had been associated with the stereotypes of failed, defrocked doctors or of the filthy old women in grimy kitchens or hotel rooms. Though in the radicalism of the late '60s abortion was crossing over into acceptability, I felt that I was being eyed with the same circumspection as one who had come down with active TB.

In Britain, in the post-war years, between 10,000 and 15,000 women a year were being aborted: nobody quite knows the numbers because, since it was illegal, nobody kept exact records. Women were still dying from clandestine abortion (not all illegal abortion was back-street, and not all back-street abortion was unskilled) but the numbers were gradually being reduced: there were forty deaths in 1964, a dramatic reduction from 400 in the 1930s. But while it was true that the increase in demand for abortion was real enough, the figures were nevertheless vastly inflated. Paul Ferris's book on abortion, *The Nameless*, published in 1966, quoted an estimate of between 100,000 and 200,000 abortions annually; a quarter of a million, half a million were figures often cited. It is now recognized that the upper limit would have been 50,000 and some social historians put it at around 10,000. In his memoirs, Nathanson says that in the United States it was a deliberate tactic to inflate the figures for abortion, and indeed the campaigners always spoke of 'between 5,000 and 10,000 deaths a year', when in the last year before abortion was legalized the number of women's deaths was actually thirty-nine.

Women's deaths were being reduced because of the refinements in abortion technology, and even more because of the use of antibiotics. There is always a certain percentage of infection after abortion, but antibiotics can now nearly always control it, though a few women are still rendered sterile by post-abortion infection. The 1960s' demand for more abortion was part of the spirit of the age. The contraceptive Pill had come on the market in 1961, and sex seemed more free. The relationship between contraception and abortion is a complex one. In some respects, effective contraception does reduce abortion – if the Soviet Union had better contraception there would not be 16 million abortions a year, and Japan's high abortion rate is often linked to its refusal to admit the Pill as a legal drug. Yet, the spread of contraception technology and pharmaceuticals means that more people feel sexually liberated, and there is a general acceptance of the notion that pregnancy can be reversed. The 'contraceptive mentality' is, simply, that you can stop a pregnancy, either before or after it has actually occurred.

Nathanson recalls that the climate of the 1960s was the right one for abortion: 'The war protesters had securely captured the media, male hair was coming down, grass was the white middle-class party drug, all the women were on the Pill. The times, they were a-loosening.'

Although in America – where the abortion battle was to be won by the campaigners in 1973 – the feminist movement did play an active role in that campaign, in Britain feminism was not a key element. (In the 1970s, and thereafter, in France, Germany, Italy and Britain, feminism was actively involved, but not earlier.) The British campaign was animated by social reformers, doctors, politicians, journalists and those who knew that illegal abortion was flourishing. And then there was the case of thalidomide.

In the spring of 1961, it was observed that groups of children with specific deformities were being born in Australia, Germany and Britain. The common factor was thalidomide, which had been prescribed to pregnant women as a sedative and an anti-nausea drug. Taken between the fifth and eighth weeks of pregnancy, it deformed the growing foetus, and the thalidomide babies were born with flipper-like arms and legs. Public reaction was one of horror. 'The impact of thalidomide on the imagination and conscience of the British public and the British press is hard to exaggerate,' wrote Madeleine Simms and Keith Hindell in their book *Abortion Law Reformed.* And it was perhaps the case of Mrs Sherri Finkbine, in 1962, which really illustrated most dramatically the link between thalidomide and abortion.

Mrs Finkbine, of Phoenix, Arizona, was a mother of four children who had taken thalidomide at the start of her fifth pregnancy. She was not prescribed the drug – her husband had brought it home from a European trip where he had got it over the counter to cure insomnia. When Mrs Finkbine feared that her child would be deformed as a consequence, she asked her doctor for an abortion, and he quietly arranged one. However, before the operation took place, Sherri Finkbine told a friend who worked on a local newspaper – deliberately, in fact, because she wanted to alert other women who might pick up thalidomide in Europe (the US Food and Drug Administration had never admitted it into America). The story appeared on the front page, and was immediately picked up by wire services all over the world. The local hospital took fright and cancelled the abortion. Mrs Finkbine tried to go to Japan for the termination, but the Japanese refused a visa, not wanting to get involved in an American controversy. Finally, after a desperate search, she and her husband flew to Sweden, where the abortion was performed in the fourth month of pregnancy. Afterwards the physician told the Finkbines that the baby was so badly affected it would never have survived.

The public sight of a woman flying around the world desperately seeking an abortion in these circumstances was to attract attention and sympathy in Britain. In America, too, it made waves, but as thalidomide had never been put on the American market, it remained, in a sense, a freakish problem. In Britain, hundreds of thalidomide children were being born. Sweden's compassion in permitting abortion in these cases was praised, though in fact Swedish law at this point was still attempting to restrict abortion. Mrs Finkbine was 'granted' an abortion, but a panel of doctors and ethical specialists had considered her case very carefully first. Eugenic considerations were grounds for abortion in Sweden, but the Swedes went through a long period of trying to control abortion by judging each case on its merits. This is nearly always impractical, creates delays, and, as Peter Huntingford has pointed out, is insupportably judgemental of women. Soon after the Finkbine controversy, a Swedish group, led by a newspaperman, made a public issue of abortion by openly travelling to Poland, declaring they were organizing an abortion coach, and inviting the authorities to prosecute. This tactic was afterwards repeated in many countries and was often successful in shaming parliaments into legalizing abortion. French women travelled to Holland and to Britain in open 'abortion coaches', and then invited prosecution. Italians travelled to France, Germans travelled to Denmark. In each case, the authorities found it too mortifying and too unpopular a cause to prosecute, because if women want abortions, for whatever reason, the public does not generally wish to see them punished. And the home legislature is also discomfited that its own nationals have to travel to another country for the operation.

Until the thalidomide disaster, Simms and Hindell reflected, the Abortion Law Reform Association

> had supposed that the general public was hostile to the notion of abortion law reform. Now for the first time abortion was taken out of the context of 'immorality and unmarried girls' and placed firmly in that of public health. With more and more sophisticated drugs finding their way on to the market, married women all over the country became anxious that next time they might be the hapless victims – through sheer misfortune, not sin or irresponsibility. From that moment onwards the reformers sensed that theirs was no longer a minority movement but actually had mass support.

It was, without any doubt, thalidomide which broke the credibility barrier for the abortion campaigners. A cartoon in *Private Eye* by Trog summed up what was seen as the hypocrisy of the situation. A worried pregnant woman is asking a middle-aged doctor for help, and he is saying: 'I'm sorry but the ethical position is quite clear. Thalidomide was a legal prescription, but what you suggest is an illegal operation.' Simms and Hindell dedicated their book to the thalidomide mothers 'for whom reform came too late'. Some of the thalidomide mothers may now find consolation in the knowledge that many thalidomide babies grew up very sane people.

By the 1980s, only a handful of countries in Europe did not have some form of legal abortion – Malta, Belgium, Ireland and Greece. In Greece, illegal abortion continues to be very high. In many Middle Eastern countries, too, there is no legislation for abortion, but it is quietly practised with the now simple abortion technology. In

Belgium, too, although illegal, abortion is carried out in some areas under the guise of protecting a woman's life. Catholic Spain has legalized cautiously for a very restrictive abortion law; none the less it symbolically decriminalizes abortion. Only Ireland, in line with its strong pro-natal, traditional sentiments, went quite directly against the trend and in 1983 by Constitutional Amendment pledged to protect the life of the unborn child. Irish women travel to England for abortions in increasing numbers but Irish public opinion remains resolutely anti-abortion. This is also true in predominantly Protestant Northern Ireland.

History never stands still. Technology never stands still. As abortion freedom has spread, so has an anti-abortion movement. This was dismissed in the 1970s as a historical hangover of diehards, religious fanatics and bigoted old men trying to repress women, and it was expected to fade away. Anti-abortionism was seen as the dying shudder of a dying philosophy. In fact, the anti-abortion movement has remained remarkably robust and in America it has grown phenomenally. It is not only a religious impulse which opposes abortion (though religious people are more hostile to abortion), but it is also the fall-out from yet another new technology – ultrasound and real-time scanning. What changed Bernard Nathanson's mind about abortion was not some new-found mystical inspiration or political conversion; it was seeing a foetus at eight weeks on a television screen and watching a foetus of twelve weeks move, and appear to suffer when attacked by abortion. 'Even if God does not exist,' he concluded, 'the foetus does.' Abortion may be here to stay, for some time yet, but so is the evidence of the existence of the foetus from its conception.

8

OLDER WOMEN REMEMBER

'One of my most vivid impressions was standing at a window of our house in Scrog Road and seeing a pitiful procession of a man in a shabby suit with a muffler and two women and three sobbing children. They were burying his wife who'd had an abortion. She had three children and he had been out of work for years and she couldn't face the prospect of having another mouth to feed. That brought home to me the poverty, the real poverty, under which we were living at that particular time.' – Peggy Murray in 'What Went Wrong? Memories of the 1930s', Channel 4, 1983

'"It's been a hateful evening!" she answered in an icy fury. "The food, the furniture, the way they talked – money, money all the time . . . Smart-set gossip, who's week-ending with who, what the hairdresser told her, the latest society abortion, not one word of anything *decent*."' – A.J. Cronin, *The Citadel*, 1937

Until the 1960s, abortion was very seldom publicly spoken of in Britain. Even medical reference books largely ignored induced abortion, referring only to spontaneous abortion (what we call miscarriage) and, occasionally, to criminal abortion as a marginal issue. Knowledge and experience of abortion varied very much from class to class and from one milieu to another – as did its practice. It might be reasonable to say that the very poor and the very rich had the most knowledge of abortion from the period of about 1920 until the Second World War. The very poor resorted to what was known as criminal abortion because of the shocking poverty they faced – we know that women in the 1920s and '30s died from this. The very rich were thought to practise abortion to cover illicit affairs. It was the solid, upright middle class in between who knew little of such things: they believed in self-control, and to some extent in birth control. Before marriage girls did not usually go 'too far', but if they did and 'trouble' followed, adoption not abortion was the usual solution. Until modern times, young women were seldom aborted in their first pregnancy anyway; the typical candidate for abortion was generally a woman who already had children.

It is nearly always the case that agricultural societies practise abortion less than urban societies; so people from rural areas would very rarely have resorted to it.

Here is how the climate of those times is recalled by some older women.

'Of course I remember people talking about abortion before the 1939 war. I was nineteen when the war began but had five sisters older than myself and naturally we all talked about such things from time to time, as I did with friends of my own age. At that age we certainly did not discuss the ethics of it, it was just the (very rare) but inevitable fate of the unwary. It was either dangerous or very expensive and I certainly would have had no idea whom to ask or where to go had such a nightmare become a reality. People used to talk darkly about Switzerland – but we knew it was done in London, but where or by whom we did not know.

'I am pretty sure none of my friends or contemporaries ever had an abortion. You may say that I wouldn't have known if they had as it was against the law and, naturally, it would have been done in the greatest secrecy. But most of them married very young during the war and were longing to have children so it did not arise.

'The fashion for unmarried women to have children had certainly not started, but you had indiscriminate "love-making". Of course there were exceptions, but as I have already said they were rare, as starting a baby was the ultimate horror for an unmarried girl. It is difficult, now things have changed so enormously, to realize how in awe people were of the law and of their parents and if you were found out you would go to prison and so would the person who performed the operation.'

The Duchess of Devonshire

'No one referred to abortions in the '20s and '30s, as this could involve the police. If a doctor had to be called in owing to something going wrong, the woman would have had to name the person who helped her. So all were called miscarriages, as this was nature's way of getting rid of unwanted pregnancies. This was not talked about openly but my mother "Rose" was a lady who helped people by listening to them and providing a cup of tea and some cake. And as I was usually around – children hear things – as I grew older she explained things to me.

'I was born in 1930 . . . Also various women relations had miscarriages. And my mother being the eldest had to take care of them. Women made some chat, something was done as soon as they "missed". So women just sat on a bucket and then the contents were emptied down the toilet. So no one knew about it. Husbands were not involved, this was women's doing. This was the '30s when life was hard and people just couldn't afford another mouth to feed. There was no social security and no money if you didn't work.

'I personally do not agree with abortion but feel for women who have had to resort to it. I have two children who are now grown up. Women of that time did not enjoy what they did. But when it happened they were released. If it happened naturally that was better, their consciences were clear.'

Mrs Doreen Boyne, Shaston on Mersey

'My experience [1954] trying to get help met with a stone wall. Until I visited an aunt, hoping that she could put me in touch with what was commonly known as a back-street abortionist. No way! But, reluctantly, she advised me to get "Hicra Picra" tablets from a chemist shop.

'I took six and within twelve hours had a miscarriage. Needless to say I finished up in the hospital.

'I still don't know what I swallowed that day, but I remember vividly the quizzical look on the face of the chemist whilst he considered my request. My aunt was an old lady and her knowledge of these things was pre-war.

'The feeling of guilt gets worse as the years go by.'

Anonymous, Manchester

'One thing is certain – abortion was not discussed, and if people were in favour of it they would not admit it publicly. Rebecca West had her illegitimate son openly, I believe, she would not have minded public opinion, even when she was young. I think the usual thing done was for the pregnant girl to be hidden away and the baby given for adoption or fostered. My husband and I, in general practice, were never approached about abortion either before or after the Act, but we retired in 1969.

'We had an abortionist as a patient who was discovered and imprisoned after her own (very beautiful) daughter died of septicaemia following what was probably not the poor girl's first abortion.

'Doctors were of course struck off the register if they were known to have procured even one abortion, but after the Case Law Act in 1939* I think, many abortions were performed openly in hospital for pulmonary TB, kidney and heart disease. The attitude of the public to this was that if the doctors did it it must be right. The TB patients very often died after the abortion because of the devastating effect on their psyche. They felt such a failure in an age when children were expected in a marriage.

'The very condemnatory attitude of women towards pregnancy outside marriage is shown by the ghastly action

* This refers to the famous Bourne ruling, see Chapter 7.

of insisting that the young people should marry for the sake of the child. This was practised in Ireland and I am afraid that parish priests regarded it as the only solution if the father was free. I think it would have been very exceptional for a girl not to know who the father was. If she was promiscuous she would know an abortionist. I think she would feel guilty, probably be sure she was damned, as many people thought adultery and fornication were unforgivable sins, as well as unmentionable.

'I was six-and-a-half months pregnant in 1938 when I had some undiagnosed toxaemia and was not expected to live. The baby was still alive. I was in the Middlesex Hospital under a very senior obstetrician and he told my husband that he feared death for both of us – some hope if he removed the child. A Jesuit priest came to see me and pleaded that it was the only hope for me and we could presume the death of the child. I was horrified and said I could not agree. Twenty-four hours later the baby did die, and it was removed. I gradually recovered. I was never pregnant again but tried hard to have another baby. I lost my first and had two children in 1934 and '35 – the latter a bit of a miracle. I always wanted a big family and in 1932 when I lost my first baby I was told I should never have another – I believe the year after that was one of the saddest of my life. I suppose my own history accounts for my need to save as many children as possible from abortion.'

Catholic woman doctor, now retired

'I am now seventy-three years of age and from birth until I was twenty-five lived in the dockland part of Bermondsey (east London). The birth of a baby there, in my young days, was certainly not a cause for joy, even though most children were loved in my street, an extra mouth to feed meant the family could be on the bread-line. Writing of this in this day and age it seems impossible that this could be so, but a young woman I knew tried desperately to avoid a new pregnancy and not knowing whom to turn to for help, aborted herself. Of course she died, leaving a husband and five children. A few wise women knew who could help, but most times kept the knowledge to themselves, it was not something one talked about.

'My friend, seventy-seven years, has had eight abortions during her married life, and regrets not one, it saved her from living hand to mouth and gave her other children a full table. She gave, by the way, £2 for each abortion. A doctor in the south east of London was well known for the kind of help he would give, believe me, he was much loved and respected by the lucky ones who knew him.

'To my knowledge it was the married women who had abortions. The young women who "got into trouble" quickly married the man responsible.

'I cannot ever remember the words "Birth Control" being talked about in my part of Bermondsey. A few must have known about it, but for most of us we were unfortunately so ignorant, and this was 1935. I was married and two months pregnant, no children but with an unemployed man, one of the girls at work took pity on me and took me to a woman in the back streets somewhere. I still think of that baby, especially as my husband got a good job soon after. We did then practise birth control, and my three children arrived because they were wanted.'

Mrs N.B., Thamesmead, London SE17

'I had an abortion in April 1934 by a doctor in Welbeck Street, W1. £105 in cash, no anaesthetic. It was most terribly painful. I was twenty-three and a half at the time and married to a naval officer. I was desperate to have one as I wanted to be with my husband and would not be able to if I had the baby. Our family doctor would not hear of it. I even went to Paris, but it was more difficult there than in England. I got quite frantic. I was nine weeks pregnant when I had the operation. Naval wives at different ports would tell each other about the local abortionist. The agony women married or unmarried went through no one will ever know. I have never once regretted this. It is the most dreadful trapped feeling in the world.

'My husband knew how I felt and came with me to

Welbeck Street and stayed in the waiting room. He was a dear but had absolutely no idea of money and was always in debt. He knew before we married that I would never have any children. During the early part of the war he met a quite nice respectable girl and made her pregnant, on purpose I think. I divorced him in December 1945 and he married her, but they never had any more children.'

Mrs I.M., Hove, Sussex

'Just before my marriage in 1936 I discovered that I had become pregnant and it was an awful shock as my future husband's family were very strict and uncompromising people. However, I bluffed the whole thing through and got married, but eventually when four months pregnant I had to go to a doctor. He was very worried that I had left the visit so long as owing to trouble in my heart he was sure I could not have the baby. Eventually my mother took me to a Harley Street specialist and after examination he advised a medical abortion as soon as possible. Somehow although twenty-two years of age, the mere idea of abortion seemed like murder and I absolutely refused to have it done. My mother begged me to and so did the specialist but somehow I just couldn't. At the birth things were very difficult and only expertise on the part of the doctors saved us both and I had to stay in bed for months. Eventually the baby – a son – great up a fine healthy man, and has sons of his own. When I see my healthy son and his almost grown-up sons I am so thankful that somebody put so strongly the idea into my mind that abortion was wrong; but of course I was getting married anyway which made things easier in some ways.'

Mrs G.F., Hampshire

'Going back first to Somerville days and for the first few career years after that – the 1930s. I think that young women (and men) were a great deal more careful about contraceptives then than they are now and I can remember only one of my friends getting pregnant before marriage. If one was a few days late with one's period one was pretty alarmed – in my case, it was the terror of my parents – and heaved a sigh of relief when it arrived. It was always said that one could get an abortion legally in Holland, but there were also one or two London doctors who would give the address of a safe, if not legal, abortionist and this is how my friend arranged things. It was very hole-in-corner.

'I can't remember what happened in the working class. I think it depended again on the parental attitude. Very strict parents in the provinces might turn a girl out, and she might go to a back-street abortionist. Village life was different, and in all the villages round here there were always one or two "love children" who were part of the rural scene. When the war came and there were GIs about, there was quite a legacy of illegitimate children, and nobody seemed to mind two hoots. I doubt if the village girls considered abortion. And a baby got them out of the ATS! Ever since 1939, things have been quite different, I would say. In spite of the Pill, girls seem very careless about contraception . . . I do know people who have had children aborted at a very early stage, say after one missed period, but as soon as a girl thinks of a baby as a living creature, she is pretty reluctant to part with it. Personally, I think abortion should be legal, and on demand. All these devices about getting a psychiatrist to say your mental health necessitates abortion are so phoney. I have a friend who, rightly in my view, had an abortion in the 1950s because her husband simply loathed children, and the rigmarole she had to go through was quite absurd.'

Lady S., Wiltshire

'I recall asking my mother what an abortion was in the 1930s. In telling me it was implied it was not altogether a respectable thing. Also, when my mother had a very serious miscarriage, she and my father made it plain to all friends and relatives that it *was* a real miscarriage in case anyone thought it was an abortion. I ought to add perhaps that this was at home – in those days we didn't rush into hospital so automatically.

'For a birth the general thing was it was at home unless

the doctor thought that difficulties might arise . . . If anyone went to hospital for a birth and if it was then announced she'd lost the baby – born dead or miscarriage, etc. – less charitable people might have suspected (in hushed tones) "abortion". It was recognized abortion could be necessary if some dangers to the mother existed but if a doctor advised this it was likely to be called miscarriage or born dead or some such thing. Certainly, better-off people didn't generally speak of abortion – it would have been in confidence only to close friends or relatives . . .

'In 1939, just before war began, a friend of mine became pregnant. Her mother (father was dead) was highly respectable, fairly well-off middle class, and also, as they were Catholics, would have been appalled at an abortion. The man concerned was well known in society and in politics . . . An illegitimate birth would have ruined his social and political status. As he was wealthy and could "pull strings" he fixed up an abortion for my friend at a private nursing home. Socially inconvenient pregnancies were cause for abortions but not talked about except in confidence – or whispered gossip. But whatever one's social class, abortion was not regarded as respectable – though accepted as necessary for social reasons. As the most usual reason for abortion in all classes was that the child would be illegitimate, either because the girl was single or if married a result of adultery, it was not considered respectable. In the war years with standards tending to change and the influx of foreign troops and the "here today, gone tomorrow" feeling in all nationalities, many girls got pregnant who'd otherwise never have done so outside of marriage. It depended on whom you knew and what you could fix up. Doctors generally – many in the forces anyway – were more lenient about conducting abortions.

'But I think in both the 1930s and 1940s, there was more similarity of view between the top and bottom of society. Abortion as an unwelcome necessity was perhaps more casually accepted by upper and lower classes, whether for reasons of social inconvenience or poverty. The very large middle section were far more "moral" in their behaviour.

'My own attitude has changed over the past ten years or so. For a long time I accepted it as on the whole good that it was easily available. But looking back – abortion for all does not seem to have produced a more happy society.'

Miss Evelyn Lister, London SW7

'I am seventy years old and I am one who is pleased that one can have an abortion these days so easy. I was seventeen when I aborted myself. I could not find anyone to do it for me, but I was told what to do. I nearly killed myself. Getting first married I had two girls and could not afford any more, husband out of work, I aborted myself, I had three abortions altogether. My friends were also poor and dreaded every month coming round. They were desperate, they couldn't do it and they were on their hands and knees asking for me to do it. I never took a penny from any one for doing it, but the gratefulness was enough, in those days one would go to hospital for a womb scrape and the ward would be full of women having done the same thing. My husband and family know nothing of all this.'

Mrs H.M., Grimsby, S. Humberside

'I had an abortion in November 1947 at the age of thirty-seven. Two points about this: one is that if I had been pregnant by my lover of many years, nothing would have persuaded either of us to agree to an abortion. To my undying shame I was pregnant by a fellow-journalist whom I didn't even like. I shall never forgive myself for that. But that's how we lived during the war. Second point: three months, as I was, was considered a very late abortion in those days. It cost me 150 guineas therefore. I consider it was safer than a legal abortion today at any stage. *Because* the doctor's fear of prosecution and imprisonment was so overwhelming, extreme care was always taken, and I mean really extreme . . . not the assembly-line job it is today.

'Still, it was quite a terrifying experience. I remember I thought the most humiliating part was the second meeting with the abortionist after it was decided to do it . . . I had to sit in a hotel lobby and when I saw him arrive, *without* looking at him or him at me, I had to follow him out through a back exit; it was like *Smiley's People*. He called a taxi and I just followed. In the taxi he counted the 150 guineas in one-pound notes and some fivers; yes, it took a long time. When he saw it was correct, we arrived . . . Kensington, of course. A block of flats. I believe it was Nell Gwynne House; most of these blocks in the war had either resident prostitutes or resident abortionists. But the supreme humiliation was after all that, when we arrived, I was left to pay the taxi while he hurried inside. I remember that he had forgotten the Lysol and I was sent, hair flying, coat flapping, wishing greatly to be safely dead, to the chemist to buy some.

'The worst worry was for one's job on the *Daily Sketch* in Gray's Inn Road; it was November 1947 and I was to be on duty standing at the door, I think, of St Margaret's for the Queen's wedding, but I had to be sent home because I could not stand up for pain. Yet the shame was even worse than the pain was.

'However, I not only had no ill-effects, but I found all my ailments cured. Before 1947 I was thin and ailing, with a cough. All that went.'

Journalist, born 1910, died 1984. This letter written 1982

'On reflection, it is hard to believe how very innocent we were in those days [the 1940s]. Sex was something to giggle about. I honestly think that the majority of girls were virgins until they married. An unwanted pregnancy for a single girl was an absolute disaster. Immediate marriage was the solution of choice; but this wasn't always possible in wartime with men being posted overseas and getting killed, etc. And, of course, the lass whose boyfriend was going off to foreign parts was emotionally very vulnerable. So, "failing marriage, keep it dark", preferably from the family, certainly from the neighbours. This was sometimes possible for girls in the services, posted away from home. In the pre-welfare state, adoption was much more frequently used. Whatever psychological trauma this may cause the mother I am convinced that this is the wisest course of action, especially in the interests of the child, unless perhaps there are no financial worries and strong family support.

'I spent about nine months of my VAD service in a camp-reception station for the ATS in Camberley, and although unwanted pregnancies were quite commonplace and there were cases of VD and other sex-related complaints, e.g. septic love-bites, I can't recall one case of abortion during my time there. I heard of a girl who was admitted there once, having attempted to procure an abortion on herself by means of a knitting needle. There were rumours about places in London where you could get it done, but I never heard of anyone taking advantage of this.

'When I was a student nurse in the early 1950s, and worked in the gynae ward, there were a few young girls who had had illegal abortions following relationships with members of the US air force then stationed on the Kent coast. You are probably aware that the diagnosis "incomplete abortion" is applied in medical terms, whether the termination is natural or illegally induced. Severe haemorrhage or a septic condition usually indicated the latter, but the nursing staff were not expected to make moral judgements. It was known that the gynae consultant had a former colleague in Harley Street who carried out abortions for £75, but that would be beyond most ordinary people's means in those days. There is no doubt that by the end of the 1950s the incidence of illegal abortions had increased considerably. I would say there were more married women with an unwanted pregnancy resorting to abortion than single girls "in trouble".

'I trained and worked as a midwife in the early 1960s and went on to qualify as a health visitor in 1970. I practised for five years but then unfortunately had a mild stroke . . . However in 1978, I was offered a light job as warden of a church hostel for mothers and babies. Apart from very few exceptions, the girls were pathetic creatures from the lowest rungs of society – the second generation of the permissive society – completely amoral in every aspect of behaviour, because they just didn't know any better, had never been taught anything. They gave me a hard time, including physical abuse.'

Mrs Peggy Hart, former Health Visitor, Northampton

'As a child [1930 to 1940] I lived in a poor district of Manchester. Playing in the street we children would hear the women, sitting on the steps, talking to each other. They once talked of a woman in the next street who had a few small children. "Poor soul, she'll have half a dozen before she's thirty."

'My mother told me later that my friend's mother had done illegal abortions out of pity. The woman with all the children had begged her for an abortion but she had refused until, feeling sorry for her, she agreed to help. The "thing" went wrong and the woman, bleeding badly, was rushed to hospital. Being so frightened she revealed the name of the woman who had tried to help her, in spite of promising she would never tell, and this woman was sent to prison. We were always listening in to stories like this, but this one stayed in my mind and I still feel such sorrow for both women and their families.

'In the past, at least among the poorer classes, I don't think people thought of the moral aspect of illegal abortions. It was a necessary evil. It seemed as though the pregnancy was not thought of as a child, they always said "it". They certainly never discussed the rights of the unborn child.

'As the years passed and they became better educated, or perhaps more enlightened then I think they thought more deeply of the reality of what they were doing. I notice that men seem to be taking more interest in what happens to their unborn child. In those days the worry and problems seemed always to be left to the women.'

Mrs Louise Ellison, Stockport, Cheshire

'We always took it in our stride – it was a natural thing to die from an abortion. You took the risk and that was that. There was an idea in our set that if you dived flat into a swimming-pool you might procure a miscarriage. I remember being in Chelsea swimming-baths and trying to belly-flop into the pool, while an interfering swimming-instructor kept trying to stop me, saying I was "diving" quite wrongly. It was rather funny, because I ended up by diving properly because I was so embarrassed.

'We were far too bound up with other complications ever to *think* of the human aspect – whether "it" was a real human being or not. You just buried that away, and thought about the practicalities. The other thing was that you didn't saddle a man with a child if he didn't want one, and mostly they didn't, not with extra-marital affairs. Men saw children as responsibilities. If you wanted a child, you didn't show your feelings, it was what the young today call "uncool".

Writer, recalling Bohemian life in London in the 1940s

'I look at young women today and think how very lucky they are to be in complete control of their own baby machine. I had one child at eighteen, another, handicapped, child two years later. My husband and I had a furnished bedsit, my parents separated when I was fifteen, my mother could only be contacted by writing to a GPO Box. So I was frantic about the danger of becoming pregnant again. Anyway, I did get pregnant again. When I think back it is like a nightmare. I didn't even enjoy sex, not knowing that a woman had her part to play. One of my neighbours took me to a back-street abortionist, it all had to be hush-hush and would cost £3. £3 was a joke, we didn't even have a pram we could sell. Well, we borrowed £1 from three different people, I went two or three times and nothing happened, so she said she would have to come to my place in case I fainted, well I didn't faint, I went unconscious and was rushed to hospital, and was kept in ten days, being treated very coolly by the nursing staff and me feeling the worst kind of being. I found out that the lady abortionist had vanished and my husband found me unconscious, he had made a convenient exit for the abortionist. Well to cut a long story short I got pregnant dozens of time afterwards. I had to find out myself how to do an abortion on myself, through the patience of a kind friend telling me over and over and lending me her enema syringe. When I think back over what we women went through, it's a wonder we stayed sane. My first marriage broke up after five years, and no wonder. When I see my bank account now, I can't believe that I am the same lady I have been talking about.'

Signed: A Survivor

'All one recollects is a lot of *fear* in those who were about to "have it done". The question of the *baby's* rights in the matter may have been thought about; but they certainly were not discussed. The main thing was, if I remember rightly, that (in the circumstances) a baby would have been "an impossibility" in the *then* life of its prospective mother. The "respectability" angle varied *so* widely – one can't pin it down in a sentence. We ourselves were – as were the friends of mamma and papa – *totally* middle class. "Forsytes" really. So it would have been the end of the world if any daughter of any house had become pre-maritally pregnant – and heaven *knows* what would have happened to the poor thing. (Or maybe it *did* happen – and we never got to hear of it? Who knows? But it would have been muffled up and shrouded in secrecy, of that I'm *sure*.) Aristocratic families are a closed book – or were, then. One *suspects* they might have been more relaxed about it, in the case of the married ladies, so long as "nobody *knew* for certain". But a *daughter* of the house – this would have posed a fearful problem. Marriage in no time flat – or might there have been prolonged stays in some cultural centre – Florence, wherever? – where the poor girl would "study painting" and have the baby in secret and leave it with a family thereabouts . . . *Abortions* took place among ladies who were people's *mistresses* – and who knew all about how to arrange such matters . . .

'At the same age [nearly twenty-five], one of my dearest and prettiest girlfriends became pregnant. She "got rid of" the poor old baby. My reaction was sorry for her: and shock; and I felt that she had been very wise in getting rid of a baby whose father would never have married her. (I *do* know that she was "done" by a proper doctor and that there were no knitting-needles down back streets.) Apart from that people I knew didn't seem to get themselves pregnant before the last war. Middle-class girls were still pretty heavily chaperoned . . . If we got out from under, occasionally (which we *did*!) there was a great deal of canoodling – but we didn't actually go to *bed* with our beaux, to any great extent. It was endlessly dinned into us that "no nice man would marry me" if we "carried on".

'Since the war, I've only had two experiences in the abortion line. An old friend – separated from her husband; one child already; working flat-out to build a career. She fell in love (married man, of course); had the pregnancy terminated – proper doctor, good medical attention. Told me. I was horrified *for her* – because she was so alone, in a way – I mean, her family would have had a *fit*! So, one toddled around, after work, to sort of tidy up around her for a few days, until she felt better. The bleakness of the flat and the weariness of that poor white face, are things I'll never forget.

'And a young relative of my own, who got herself into a muddle; twenty-five years ago, this was. One found doctors who knew doctors – and so on: and it was all straightened out. *To this day*, I don't know how much damage it did, mentally. Maybe none at all? Maybe the scar will never cease aching? One cannot ASK.

Mrs Rosemary Borland, Essex

'I was born in 1925 in a poverty-stricken colliery valley and have lived in such areas ever since, so my experiences are limited to the kind of society that exists in such communities.

'In areas such as this, at that time, every additional child meant an even lower standard of living for the rest of the family. To some, another pregnancy was regarded as a calamity, nothing less; not one of our present generation can have any comprehension of the desperation experienced by so many mothers of over-large families already, and "miscarriages" occurred frequently then.

'It is difficult in retrospect to decide to what extent the practice was accepted in the community – the kind of community in which I lived, I mean. In later years in my capacity as a nurse in a variety of spheres – district, geriatric, acute hospital – I have talked to older women who have confided stories of their younger days and it seemed to me that their individual social standing and financial situation probably influenced their attitudes to abortion. If one could afford children, then one continued to bear them "as the Good Lord sent them" – as one lady quoted.

'Abortion was either self-inflicted or procured by another person. The first method was obviously the most generally employed, I would think. There must certainly have been an element of guilt experienced by the pregnant lady since everyone was aware that it was an offence punishable by law, and obviously, the involvement of another person would add complications and a fear of being "found out".

'An elderly lady whom I nursed was discussing with me a contemporary of hers who had just died. Her friend had been very popular with young women in the 1930s because, said the lady, "she had been always too free with her advice".

'Pressed further, it appeared that her friend "knew all the tricks about abortion" and imparted this knowledge generously to "those in trouble". The lady reluctantly agreed to explain some of them to me; I was not surprised that she had to be persuaded; they were hair-raising.

'(1) Crochet hook or knitting-needle inserted into the mouth of the womb and turned frequently.

'(2) Piece of carbolic soap upon the handle of a long spoon and inserted into mouth of womb.

'(3) Soapy water syringed into mouth of womb.

'Any of these followed by sitting upon a bucket of boiling water.

'Abortion must have been tacitly tolerated, and methods discussed between women, but with a peculiar sort of discretion. Just one woman to another, certainly not in a group. At that time modesty was an important virtue to most, and women were easily embarrassed by personal discussion.

'Great hypocrisy was shown, too, I suspect. When one person whispered behind her hand that her neighbour had "miscarried again", the bearer would probably throw up her hands in horror – but be perfectly capable of miscarrying herself if necessary* . . .

'One particular incident impressed me so that I remember it very clearly. I was probably seven years old or thereabouts, and playing hop-scotch on the pavement outside our terraced houses. My playmate of the same age was the eldest of five children.

'Whilst we played her front door stood open and from the house came the wailing of the younger children. We were used to this, but soon the crying became louder and more persistent, so she went to investigate. Presently she came out, bewildered and frightened because her mother was not there.

'We went into the house together and I saw that the scullery door, which led into the backyard, was open, and there was a big splurge of blood on the step. The blood became a trail which ended in the white-washed privy – where the mother lay on the floor against the scrubbed whitewood boxed lavatory. Pools of blood lay around her and I thought she was dead.

'I ran yelling into our house; my mother dropped her sweeping brush and promptly took charge. The doctor arrived and the children were distributed around neighbours. I presume that the patient was removed to her own bed – it was rare that one was sent to hospital in those days.

'She recovered, and bore no more babies, or, as far as I know, miscarriages; but that was very likely because she died of pneumonia a few years later.

'When I questioned my mother about the blood and the illness, she was most evasive and replied that I would

---

* This is not necessarily 'hypocrisy' but a pattern of behaviour observed by abortion researchers today. Potts et al note that women who have abortions do not necessarily approve of the idea of having an abortion; but individuals often see themselves as exceptions.

understand better when I was older. My playmate later volunteered the explanation that her mother had accidentally sat upon a scissors – which satisfied us both.

'Later, I undertook work as an orderly on a female surgical ward in a cottage hospital which also dealt with gynaecological patients – a number of whom suffered (and sometimes fatally) from uterine haemorrhages and septicaemia. I remember two deaths in particular – a young girl of sixteen and a thirty-six-year-old mother of eight who had both suffered abortions and died within a day of each other. Both lived in adjoining streets in the same village from which an alarming number of women had been admitted to the ward with similar symptoms.

'According to staff gossip, patients were being questioned by police and a big investigation got under way. In spite of non-co-operation from patients involved, suspicion fell upon a certain person, who committed suicide before charges could be brought. Coincidentally, the spate of abortions abruptly ceased.'

Lorna Hubbard, Gwent

'The attitude to abortion, I think, should be considered in conjunction with illegitimacy.

'Pre-1914, fathers and brothers protected girls and men were made to face up to their responsibilities, by marriage or payment. Children were adopted or brought up by grandparents, sisters or aunts. At that time, until the advent of Marie Stopes, sex and contraception was not discussed openly or even at all.

'During the 1914 war attitudes relaxed. After the war during the depression of the '30s, abortions became more prevalent.

'The early part of my life, I lived on the outskirts of York where I was born in 1906, a fifth daughter in a street of 100 or so houses.

'My father was a sheet metal worker in the nearby factory.

'When I was a few months old, we moved out to a country village ten miles away, where we remained for seven or eight years, then we returned to York and lived in a terraced house with a small garden in front and backing on to the backs of the houses in the street where we had previously lived.

'I first became aware of abortion when I was thirteen or fourteen. My mother who was about forty-five gave birth to another baby girl who owing to lack of medical care was born dead. This upset my mother greatly. My parents were loving and caring and were fond of children.

'At that time there was some trouble. A sewer had become blocked and it was found that a baby's body was the cause of it. I saw one woman being taken off to hospital and another had died mysteriously. A neighbour told my mother her daughter was "in the family way" and she had locked her in because she didn't want "that woman to get to her with her dirty instruments". I heard the woman's name, who lived in the street I was born in. This woman practised for years and did several prison sentences.

'After the 1914 war we moved away and I went to work in another chocolate factory. A boyfriend confessed to giving money to a girl who became very ill as was a couple more, and one died. It was the same woman. While employed at the factory my work took me amongst the office and factory workers where I made many acquaintances. Sometimes girls became pregnant and "got rid". I knew two girls in the offices – one became ill and nearly lost her life and the other had three abortions for which her "fellow" paid a doctor, followed by a short spell in a private nursing home. One of my staff got pregnant and her mother took her to a woman. I never asked the woman's name, and I covered up for the girl when she returned to work.

'Now after a lifetime seeing many changes, whilst understanding the trauma and distress of an unwanted child I cannot bring myself to condone abortion only under certain circumstances. With contraceptives being so easily obtainable much of the trouble could be avoided. There is more unhappiness than there ever was with broken marriages and couples living together. So that abortion has solved nothing. Most women who remember our young days hold my views.'

Ada, Manchester

'In my early married life I lived in the Battersea area, near the Junction (this was the early 1950s). The house we lived in was owned by a couple called Elsie and Arthur who had about five children . . .

'When I had the odd afternoon off (I was nursing) Elsie would never let me stay in my own room, I had to come and sit in the cosy kitchen over a cup of tea and she would talk about husbands and usually there was a friend who came in. I was not allowed to feel like an interloper but was treated to a whole afternoon of "operations on the breast" or "veins" or "so and so, just had a baby, or lost a baby" etc., etc. I learned so much about life this way. I saw a drawn-looking young woman of perhaps thirty-five who sat over a cup of tea in Elsie's kitchen and told her miserably that she was having another man's child and her old man would kill her if he found out it wasn't his. When she left that kitchen that woman who had come in absolutely suicidal with worry, was actually laughing at the door and not at all afraid to go home and cook her husband's dinner as if she hadn't a care in the world. All Elsie had done was talk her out of her worries and assure her that all she had to do if her old man turned nasty was pack her bags and come to Elsie . . .

'Another crony of hers was a woman who had at one time worked at the local hospital and although I now know she was never a trained nurse, she had the ability to imbue confidence in Elsie and her friends that she knew how to "get rid of unwanted pregnancies". I asked Elsie once if it wasn't dangerous for her to send people to this woman but Elsie in her usual unworried fashion said, "Oh no, love, she's very clean and particular and always boils the rubber." I have known one or two women who went to this woman and were successful in getting rid of their babies. Although I have heard them say "I wouldn't go through that again", they never got peritonitis or ended up for a D & C in hospital. What used to happen was that Elsie would tell the person concerned that it would cost them about £5. I know for a fact that Elsie never took any of this money. Then she gave them the address of the woman and told the person to go there on such and such a day. The woman [doing the abortion] would be wearing a white apron . . . she would ask the girl questions, such as when did she have her last period and when did she think she had "fallen" for this kid. She then took the girl into her bathroom where she had a zinc bath on the floor and a tall white enamel jug and what I understood to be a large rubber catheter, and a funnel. She asked the girl to undress and she lay on the floor on a towel and the woman pushed the catheter into the vagina and then proceeded to pour some sort of warm soapy water into the funnel slowly. After this the person sat in the zinc bath for varying amounts of time, and when they felt any pain they sat over or in the bath tub. If the manoeuvre was successful the person usually aborted and the woman helped it along and I was told always made sure the placenta was there as well. This could take from anything between two to six hours to occur and then the person was allowed to go and lie on the woman's bed for about an hour and given a hot sweet cup of tea before being sent home.

'The moral attitude to all this was that it was far better for a girl to go through this than to try and brave it out with their parents and risk getting thrown out of the house and to have to face living alone . . . The other thing was that the boy who was responsible more often than not would have nothing more to do with the girl once he found out that she "had fallen" and of course being a male he was able to cover up his part in it . . .

'It all goes to show what agonies the young independent woman went through in the 1950s, when things went wrong. The unbendability of the parents in these matters was very great in that they were still remembering their own, earlier, and even tougher era.

'The only married women I heard of resorting to illegal abortions were usually those who had illicit love affairs. I wasn't aware of the reason being when they had too many children. In fact, most of them carried on as in Elsie's case. If she didn't have her own to care for, there was often someone else's anyway: you rarely found her in the day without a baby on her lap.'

Mrs M.D.T. London SW4

'My first experience of motherhood was, thank goodness, exciting and wonderful, although we were poor and had to bring the new baby back to a rented flat. We managed as young couples do.

'My husband had a job that took him away from home a lot especially at weekends and holiday times, when as a young family we should have been together . . . My husband, I know, did this for the best of reasons, being that we needed the money. However, I was beginning to get depressed and not a happy mum for my baby, and for company used to visit friends a lot . . .

'To cut a long story short, I met a couple of very nice young men from Sierra Leone – they, with my own set of friends, used to make a very interesting, lively evening talking about everything under the sun, which was stimulating. My husband knew all my friends as he was sometimes there and he also liked the two chaps from Sierra Leone and got on very well with them.

'Well, one of these chaps fell in love with me and one fell in love with one of my friends. Mine used to take me out dancing and eating which at the time for me was an absolute luxury, having always liked the high life anyway. He had a flat a few roads away from us and it was so easy to slip around there in the evening for a few hours of talking and playing records. Somehow, I never felt I was doing my husband any harm. However – I did get pregnant. It was as much my fault as his – totally a lack of self-discipline in the matter, but anyway it happened.

'We were both mentally mature people. We didn't spend hours punishing ourselves with remorse, etc., but talked about the consequences long and hard. He was unmarried and I was happily married with a child and intended to stay that way. So . . . it was me who made the break not to see him again. He was very upset and went to live up in Scotland. I couldn't tell anyone about my pregnancy and decided in my own mind that I and I alone had to get rid of the foetus – I couldn't bear to think of it as a baby or I would not have had the courage.

'Knowing the dangers of "doing things to yourself" I did not attempt to stick things into myself, but I did try to make myself sick enough, thinking that it might help. So I drank a lot which of course didn't do any good at all except make me very, very sick and miserable. Babies are very tenacious and have no intention of getting themselves dislodged from their mothers' wombs. I didn't dare tell my doctor as I could in no way explain that it was going to be a coloured child. In the 1950s, unless you had a very sympathetic doctor or there was some disastrous medical reason for not having the baby or perhaps a psychiatric reason it was not possible to get an abortion – except by paying hundreds of pounds at a private clinic. I did seriously think of the psychiatric side of it and wondered whether I should "act" my way through the doctor's surgery and again in front of a psychiatrist, but I was afraid I might fail to convince them.

'So – I have to say "thank God" and mean it – fate took a hand in the form of my getting infective hepatitis – probably through my drinking martinis. I was so ill that I thought I was going to die and my husband had the sense to send for the GP who had me admitted to the hospital within the hour. I eventually had to confess, once I was in the safety of the hospital and a very kind woman registrar sat on the bed talking to me in the middle of the night, it all came out. How worried I had been and what I had been doing to myself. At last the pregnancy was terminated with the reason that it was a danger to the mother (me). I was dying to ask the nurse whether they could tell what colour the baby would have been. I did pluck up enough courage to ask what sex it was and was told it was a boy and it was pretty well advanced – about sixteen to twenty weeks, which was considered pretty late.

'My husband was told that I had been pregnant and he, bless him, was very, very upset that I had apparently lost it through being run down, and I felt thoroughly mortified that he felt partly to blame that he hadn't done enough for me, etc. I swore from that day to never, ever do anything to cause him such distress again. My own daughter who was about three at the time was luckily staying with a friend of ours who also had a daughter of the same age, so I had no worries on that score. This also helped to cure my soul as well, as the place was beautiful and I had the solitude I needed to realize the enormity of what I had done and how it had affected so many people. The registrar who knew the truth about me was the soul of discretion and was very, very kind. We kept in touch for many years afterwards, and she went to work in one of the African countries and eventually died from a tropical disease.

'We never did have another child, however.'

Retired nurse, south of England

There are many, many stories from older women remembering being faced with a pregnancy that dismayed them. But not all such pregnancies ended either with a dangerous abortion, a personal disgrace, or an unwanted child. Many a pregnancy discovered in tears and continued in resignation brought forth a child who was to become the apple of its mother's eye. Lord Willis, the writer, was the son of a London barrow-boy whose mother, back in 1917, did everything in her power to abort him. 'She tried everything possible to get rid of me,' he wrote. 'She carried the tin bath in from the back yard, filled it with near-boiling water and then lowered herself into it, scalding her flesh so painfully that she was in agony for days. She ran up and down stairs until she was exhausted. And when all this failed to check my progress, she procured some gunpowder – enough to cover a sixpence – mixed it with a pat of margarine and swallowed it. This was reckoned in those days to be almost infallible, but it succeeded only in making her violently ill. In the end she reconciled herself to the inevitable and I emerged, none the worse for those adventures, and to add another dimension to her problems. She bore me no ill will for my perverse behaviour: once I was there I was there, to be accepted, fed and loved with the others.'

9

WHAT THE FEMALE PHILOSOPHERS SAY

'Basically, she sees not one, but two moral systems existing side by side. There is the male moral system which views the world in terms of rights and principle, which can be defended and used as the basis of decision-making. By contrast, the female system perceives life as a network of social relationships, in which the woman plays a central role. For women, right and wrong become relative and pragmatic, dependent on the situation. Gilligan calls her female morality "the ethic of care".' – Rosemary Wittman Lamb describing Dr Carol Gilligan's psychological division of male and female thinking in the *Guardian*.

Men have discussed the ethics of abortion since the dawn of civilization. And that is just the trouble, say the feminists: *men* have discussed it. Men, with their theoretical, abstract minds! Men, sitting around in the rabbinical tradition, airily debating women's lives and women's choices! Aristotle, St Thomas Aquinas, St Augustine – what do they know? They've never been pregnant! In her study on women's development and psychological theory, the Harvard psychologist Dr Carol Gilligan put forward the view that women would characteristically approach a subject like abortion decisions in quite a different way from men. Women do not make decisions on the basis of 'abstract' notions about the rights of the foetus (as she tends to characterize men as doing) but on practical assessments about whether they could reasonably raise a child, and above all in the context of their relationship with the father of the baby.

In an inverted way, this itself seems a piece of sexism – as though to say 'poor little women – unable as they are to handle abstract reasoning, they just do the best they can by concentrating on everyday practicalities'. Nevertheless, there is some evidence that men and women do approach abortion differently. Every opinion poll taken on this issue has shown men to be more liberal than women on abortion, and indeed to be more dispassionate. Some explain this by referring to an innate conservatism in women linked to lower educational standards. But women are not 'conservative' on every issue, and in matters such as defence and peace, women tend to be more ready to be open-minded and to take risks. My own experience of interviewing men and women about abortion is that women simply tend to be more ambivalent, more ready to feel (if not always explicitly to admit) the conflicts and difficulties, and sometimes more 'shrill' because they are more involved, and sometimes more upset. The woman who said, reflecting on her own abortion decision, 'I know it was right, but I still think it is wrong just the same', was expressing contradictions which may not fit easily into a rational system, but which are perfectly understandable. An action presents itself as a sensible, a 'right' solution, but the person carrying out the action may still feel that the principle in itself is wrong. The maternal instinct manifests itself in many curious ways: it is not so very unusual to encounter a woman who has an abortion appointment for eight days hence – but who has given up smoking cigarettes for the waiting interval 'so as not to damage the baby'. This might be sensible if the woman was still uncertain as to whether she would proceed with the pregnancy or not, but it occurs even where the woman is certain she will terminate it. Yet there is a feeling that while the foetus is there, it elicits a sense of protection. I suspect that this kind of behaviour may sometimes be difficult for men to understand, though we mustn't generalize rigidly because of the obvious variations in individuals. 'For the first time *ever*, I saw the point of view of the anti-abortionists,' said a father who watched his wife struggle with a threatened miscarriage at twenty weeks. Seeing the baby on the scan and praying for dear life that it would hang on, he realized that he had never before thought through the implications of terminating a pregnancy. It would be unusual for a woman never to have been struck by such a notion. (The baby did hang on, incidentally, and so far as I know is thriving to this day.)

Bearing in mind, however, that a strong criticism of the philosophical deliberations about abortion is that these have been offered by male philosophers, I have consulted nine women philosophers about it. Would women philosophers differ – because they are women – from men philosophers on this issue?

Abortion – and its linked issues of embryo experimentation, new fields in reproductive technology, and the older subject of infanticide – have helped to revive philosophy in recent years, as it happens. In the post-1945 period, philosophy had become concerned with form rather than matter, with linguistics, with structuralism, with ways of thinking and speaking. Abortion, euthanasia, organ transplant, *in vitro* fertilization, surrogate parenting have, as Carolyn Faulder has written, 'created a thriving new industry for moral philosophers'.

Thirty years ago, philosophy seemed little concerned with the old central issues of life and death, what is right and what is wrong. 'In Oxford in the 1950s,' says Mary Warnock (who gave her name to the British Government's report on *in vitro* fertilization), 'the doctrine was that moral philosophy, or any sort of philosophy, had to be kept completely separate from any practical things about what you ought and ought not do. It was a highly analytical affair. And it was quite a long time before I stopped thinking that that sort of moral philosophy – or what you should or should not do – was rather tedious.' In the 1980s, right and wrong, life and death, are once again firmly on the agenda.

In seeking the views of nine women, all qualified as professional philosophers, I deliberately included one Roman Catholic only (thus omitting several distinguished candidates who might have been consulted). If abortion discussions have been heavily weighted by male thinkers in the past, they have surely been even more heavily weighted by male Catholics.

By the feminist criterion of subjective experience, the one Roman Catholic woman philosopher is particularly entitled to pronounce on the subject of pregnancy and abortion. Carol McMillan was, at the time of interview, aged thirty-one (she was born in 1954). Far from being a celibate male who could never be pregnant, Mrs McMillan is in the flower of female fertility and is the mother of four children. And far from being part of the secure middle class from which the 'burden' of childbearing is comfortably distant, Carol McMillan was born in Zimbabwe to a mixed-race marriage. Her personal experience, too, rather confounds the view that people in Africa and other parts of the 'Third World' are bedevilled by childbearing, oppressed by over-population and live in terror of 'another mouth to feed'. 'I was brought up with people who spoke of children as a blessing, and would often hear my mother retort to someone boasting about a new car or whatever, "my children are my riches". I have two aunts who couldn't have children. They could do no wrong because the consensus seemed to be that they deserved special treatment for having to suffer such a fate. As children we were expected to be especially kind and affectionate towards them. At school [a convent in Greenwich, south London] all my friends had loads of brothers and sisters. Wherever you went there were either babies who needed wheeling round the park or chubby toddlers with dirty faces ready for a cuddle and a tickle. And of course the Catholic liturgy and its veneration of the Blessed Virgin totally supported this child-oriented environment in which I was brought up. Consequently, pregnancy, babies, children – they were a part of life, a very positive feature of life, and the discovery that abortion clinics existed, that there were women who wanted none of this, women who went on shopping sprees after abortions, came as a terrible shock. I remember feeling very sad for it had just never occurred to me that things like this happened.'

Coming from Africa where children were very much welcomed, to England, where the advent of a baby was very carefully calculated in terms of costs and benefits (at least among middle-class people whom Carol McMillan met at university in London and Southampton) was bound to be a cultural shock. At the time when she discovered that there was an entire industry dedicated to abortion in England however, she was, she says, a lapsed Catholic. And although she remains an absolutist in terms of abortion morality – affirming that it is the deliberate taking of a human life and that at no stage are we morally entitled to kill a human being in this way – nevertheless she is very critical of the Catholic Church's way of arguing its position. It is sometimes said that the arguments employed by Roman Catholics against abortion are 'emotional': on the contrary, she says, they are highly rational – *too* rational, descending as they do from the traditions of Aristotle and Aquinas. 'The argument goes something like this: what distinguishes human beings from animals? What makes a person a person? The reason always given is because they are rational beings. This is what shows we differ from animals. So people like Peter Singer and Mary Anne Warren come along and say: I agree with you, this is what makes us peculiarly human – our rational faculty. How do we know people are rational? They are self-conscious, they can talk, they can reason, etc. Consequently, Singer and Warren end up with the position that says abortion and infanticide are fine because embryos, foetuses, babies do not show any evidence of being "rational beings".'

But whether foetuses have the capacity to be rational is not the point, she says. Catholics don't need to keep *proving* that an unborn child is a human being – the whole language of those involved presupposes that it is, anyway. And being too legalistic can obscure the intuitive elements. For example, Carol McMillan cites a case in Australia where a pregnant woman died from cancer after having resisted chemotherapy because it would have harmed her baby. 'Catholic theologians would say this woman did the right thing whereas philosophers like Janet Radcliffe Richards and Jonathan Glover would say she would have been totally justified in harming the baby to save her own life.* I dislike both positions because they seem to me to be blind to the fact that *tragedy* has struck this woman's life, her husband's and her existing child's. The doctrine of double effect† and utilitarianism may come down on different sides but neither position seems to understand that what this woman was faced with was really a moral *dilemma*. It was an awful situation and any ethical system which blinds one from recognizing this has missed something crucial about what it is to regard a situation from a moral point of view. What would it have been like for that woman to have carried on living knowing that her baby had died for her sake? What would the baby's father have felt? Think of how it is said that the man saved from death in a concentration camp by Maximilian Kolbe's sacrificial act, went through a period of deep depression because the burden of knowing someone had died for his sake was so great. At an experiential level, Catholicism is well aware of all this. Yet, the doctrine of double effect turns what is in many

* There have been many highly publicized cases of pregnant women with cancer choosing not to have treatment to prolong their own lives at the cost of the child's. However, medically speaking, it is seldom an equal choice – in most of such cases the mothers are actually moribund. It is only when the cancer is in the very early stages and the pregnancy is in the very early stages that the gamble is one with equal odds. (See Chapter 5.)

† The doctrine of double effect is a very famous one classically used by the Catholic Church: if an abortion is the unintended result of another operation (the removal of a fallopian tube, say), then it is permissible, whereas a direct, intended abortion is not. The doctrine illustrates the importance of *intention*. Within utilitarianism, on the contrary, intention is of no importance: an act is to be judged only by its consequences and the amount of happiness it brings, or the amount of suffering it diminishes.

cases a human tragedy into a legalistic issue, and thereby trivializes the problem.' Ordinary people do not react like legalistic advocates weighing one thing up against another, she goes on. They simply think: how dreadful, what a tragedy. And to perceive such an issue primarily as a source of pain, loss and regret makes, perhaps, the most sense.

Abortion is an evil, says Carol McMillan, because life is a gift. And if you want to seek the evidence for that, it is not necessary to consult scholarly theological books; look instead at how various writers have described the *experience* of pregnancy, as for example Simone de Beauvoir in *The Second Sex* and Lynne Reid Banks in *The L-Shaped Room*. In Linda Bird Francke's *The Ambivalence of Abortion*, the women interviewed tell how they feel about their abortions – 'and many of them have ended up by feeling they've murdered their baby'. That abortion is an evil in itself is so hugely obvious, so irrefutably clear that in a way it is odious even to speak about a foetus having a 'right to life'. 'A person's life just oughtn't to be the kind of thing that can intelligibly be up for grabs at all.' And the theological, rational arguments used against abortion can lead towards it.

All the women philosophers that I consulted considered abortion to be inherently an evil, even when they accepted that it was sometimes a necessary one. Mary Midgley and Judith Hughes, who co-authored the book *Women's Choices*, and who would, I think, both be categorized as moderate left-wing feminists, were in agreement on this. Abortion was an evil, though they went on to say that it may be a choice among evils. And they felt, too, with Carol McMillan that the over-intellectualization of abortion – the constant question 'What is a person?', the endless wrangling over conflicting 'rights' – was not particularly helpful. 'I have a general objection to moral philosophy done in that very abstract way,' says Mary Midgley, who is the mother of three grown-up sons. 'I think much moral philosophy here is a kind of displacement activity for intellectual people to reach for some frightfully general concept like "person", or for the row between utilitarians and contract theorists, and they reach for a moral theory, one general theory of morals. And when I read the memoirs of women whose early life has been desperately confused and helpless, like Maya Angelou or Cynthia Payne (who ran a brothel in south London, after a dreadful childhood), or even of people who are better-off than that but who are tossed about in some large city, who are just managing to walk a tightrope, with all kinds of weights on them . . . and then suddenly, they are loaded with this extra, terrifying weight [of pregnancy] . . . Now it seems to me that the choice that any person has then is always a choice of evils. The intellectual philosophers are frightfully unwilling to think in terms of choices of evils.'

Mary Midgley feels that same sense of impatience, or even anger, which feminists often express towards the analytical and philosophical methods of weighing up rights in abortion. 'The fact is that these theories are being tossed about solely among people to whom this has never happened, and to whom it couldn't happen, including respectable ladies, but, still more, men. It kind of disgusts me, so that when I read these articles I tend to feel extremely cross – even by women philosophers whom I respect' – here she mentioned a couple of her contemporaries – 'it seems to me terribly perverse to be starting with these abstract topics such as the doctrine of double effect. The kind of way they think about it – starting from logical issues which already happen to interest philosophers – is too remote from how they'd face some awful thing that happened to them. I want a very different approach and it seems to me the approach that I want would include a great deal of empirical data which show how these frightful dilemmas work from the point of view of the people involved in them. It seems to me that to start always from the question "May you ever kill a foetus?" rather than from "How is somebody to manage this desperate kind of life?" is perverse.'

Mrs Midgley articulates here something of what the feminists would say – and something too which Carol

McMillan (who sees most feminists as child-haters) has also said: that the rational carving-up of the problem is not what we need to think about. She sees the traditional philosophizing about abortion almost as an insult. 'It is of course a general point about judgements passed by privileged people upon the helpless, not only about women. The distinctive point about abortion is just that the unimaginative, crudely abstract approach has been carried much further on this issue than on most others, because it has been particularly remote from the lives of the theorists.' This is no doubt the case: the majority of philosophers have always been removed from the hurly-burly of everyday life, and of the 'desperately confused and helpless' minorities that Mrs Midgley speaks of. But one still finds, among uneducated or modestly endowed people, as strongly-felt 'theories' about abortion as one does among celibate bachelors living in the cloister of a great college. In denouncing the remoteness of intellectuals from ordinary life, one may also be falling into the trap of under-estimating the abilities of ordinary people to be intellectuals: Maya Angelou, for example, is just such a case. But the point remains – and it is a fair one – that abortion is not a theoretical problem, a matter apart, but something wrapped up and related to many other social, moral, political and economic values.

Philippa Foot is a distinguished philosopher – a fellow of Somerville College, Oxford, who teaches at UCLA in California. And although she has never actually pronounced upon abortion before, she has written a celebrated essay on 'The Problem of Abortion and the Doctrine of Double Effect'. It was perhaps such rumination on the double effect doctrine that Mary Midgley had in mind when she spoke of remote philosophical exercise. The essay starts off by outlining the aspect of abortion which worries most thinking people. 'One of the reasons why most of us feel puzzled about the problem of abortion is that we want, and do not want, to allow to the unborn child the rights that belong to adults and children. When we think of a baby about to be born, it seems absurd to think that the next few minutes or even hours could make so radical a difference to its status; yet as we go back in the life of the foetus, we are more and more reluctant to say that this is a human being and must be treated as such. No doubt this is the deepest source of our dilemma, but it is not the only one.' In short, this is what horrifies most people about late abortion, and what makes early abortion much more acceptable: that the late abortus is so evidently a human baby in smaller form, while the early abortus seems to disappear back into mere nothingness.

Yet the point of the essay was not to make a statement about abortion, but to discuss what we think is permissible and what we think is not. 'I was saying – let's sort out what we think is all right to do to people who undoubtedly have full moral rights; when do we think it is all right to kill them and when don't we?' What disturbs Philippa Foot most in the abortion debate is the alarming tendency in recent years for some philosophers to excuse – or to seem to excuse – infanticide on the grounds that most societies now permit abortion. This, she says vehemently, is absolutely unacceptable. She certainly does know what she thinks about infanticide – she thinks it is murder.

Infanticide has arisen in the abortion debate for several reasons. First, in the dilemma of whether handicapped new-born babies should be allowed to die, many respected persons (Crick and Watson, for instance, the Nobel laureates who identified DNA) have advocated that 'the right to choose', as accepted in abortion, should be extended to the post-natal period. Peter Singer, Professor of Philosophy and Director of the Centre for Human Bioethics at Monash University, Victoria, has argued that qualitatively there is no difference between the baby soon to be born and the baby who has just been born, so if we permit late abortions we should permit post-natal termination, as it were. After all, our society agrees that there is nothing worse than having an 'unwanted' baby: and if the baby turns out to be 'unwanted' after birth, why should it not be despatched from a life of misery *after* it has been born as it might have been *before* it was born? Michael Tooley, Professor of Philosophy and Director of the Centre of Human Bioethics at Monash University, has also pointed out that there is no argument for abortion which is not an argument for infanticide, and that historically both have been practised.

It is true, of course, that the Greeks – particularly the Spartans – and the Romans both practised infanticide, by the method of exposing infants to the elements. Abortion was not only dangerous in ancient times, but it was also *less rational*: it carried off the fit as well as the unfit. It is more rational to see what you've got before disposing of it – for this reason, infanticide is still occasionally preferred in China over abortion, which is readily available. And the old Roman principle occasionally holds: if a boy, raise it, if a girl, expose it (though the Chinese method is usually drowning rather than exposure). The Greeks and Romans considered exposure a sporting solution, since there was a chance that the baby might survive: many Greek and Roman legends – Oedipus, Romulus and Remus – begin with an abandoned baby.

Two of the women philosophers I spoke to, Janet Radcliffe Richards in Oxford and Anne Kelleher in London, agreed that infanticide could sometimes be rational and acceptable. 'I certainly do not think there is a sudden cut-off between a late abortion and infanticide,' says Miss Richards. 'And I have the greatest sympathy with people who want to kill deformed children. I wouldn't hesitate, if a new-born child turned out to be severely abnormal . . . I wouldn't hesitate to . . .' yet here, ironically enough, she did hesitate to finish the sentence. On second thoughts, she added later, she might, after all, hesitate to kill the child – 'because taking life is very distressing and always an evil. But I also think that there are times when allowing it to continue is a much greater evil.' Anne Kelleher, a young woman with three growing step-children, almost takes the 'rational' argument *ad absurdum*. 'The *rational* policy would be to allow the foetus to be born (if you suspected it was unacceptable) and then to kill it if it was affected. But probably the better thing to do would be to allow the foetus, the child, to reach a certain age, whatever age that it might be expected to understand these things, and then ask it if it wanted to go on living.' As most people, even handicapped people, don't want to commit suicide, this super-rational libertarianism would very likely end up on the side of continuing life rather than extinguishing it.

Both Anne Kelleher and Janet Radcliffe Richards share the strong utilitarian objection to the causing of suffering. They argue that one very important principle is to avoid suffering, or to cause as little as possible. One of the problems with 'allowing' handicapped babies to die is that until now it has been a prolonged procedure, involving starving the child over a period of many days.

Babies can be extraordinarily resilient – observe, for example, the number of new-borns who, in the 1985 Mexican earthquake, survived for over ten days without sustenance. With the infanticide argument, the utilitarians will have to take their courage in both hands and advocate direct killing, since quick killing certainly does cause less suffering than slow starvation.

Yet that is probably quite unacceptable to most people today. The Swedish-American philosopher Sissela Bok says in an influential paper about the ethical problems of abortion that infanticide is quite unacceptable because, among other problems, the act brutalizes those who do it. (It is possible that this is also true of abortion: experienced abortionists often have a sort of carapace which seems impenetrable.) Her view is different from Tooley's who accepts that infanticide has been frequently practised and who even appears to think it efficient. Bok sees infanticide as the practice of 'a few primitive societies, at the edge of extinction, without other means to limit families . . . But I believe that the *public acceptance* of infanticide in all other societies is unthinkable, given the advent of modern methods of contraception and early abortion, and of institutions to which parents can give their children, assured of their survival and of the high likelihood that they will be adopted and cared for by a family.'

This is something which Philippa Foot also underlined, in interview with me. As far as caring for mothers and children, or children with special needs, we are a very rich society, she said. We don't *need* either abortion or infanticide in any urgent survival sense. 'If we used more of our resources – and as far as caring for mothers and babies is concerned, we have endless resources – we haven't got to abort at all. Mothers don't die of having lots of children – they die of all the work that goes into it; we just don't *want* to help. I think the term "quality of life" is extremely dangerous. When we say "this person's quality of life isn't high enough" – isn't high enough for what? Nobody can judge who is going to be happy. There is a very bad bit of utilitarian stuff here: they think, for instance, that if you are choosing someone for dialysis or kidney transplants, where you haven't got enough dialysis machines and some people are going to have to die – they think that of course you should save the ones who have the best chance of being *happy*. If you ever find someone saying that, you can diagnose that they are a utilitarian, or influenced by utilitarians. Because what they think is, you've got to produce as much happiness as possible. So of course you wouldn't save a blind person or someone who is handicapped because they have less chance of "happiness". This is a bit of utilitarian philosophy that people don't even notice is coming in.'

The mere idea of infanticide, for someone like a Down's syndrome child is, says Philippa Foot, 'atrocious'. Many utilitarians would justify it, however. She is extremely critical of Michael Tooley's book *Abortion and Infanticide* and the respectability it has gained. 'I feel scornful of that man,' she says witheringly. In her own book, *Virtues and Vices*, Mrs Foot writes with a sense of tender appreciation for handicapped children. The only reason it might ever be permissible to allow a handicapped child to die, she has written, is for its own sake. She elaborates on this: 'I have heard paediatricians talk about very young babies on whom they've done operation after operation, and after a time it's been absolutely clear that there isn't anything more but a few weeks' life if they carry on intervening. I think in that case they should stop. The thing is, *there* you are saying "for this child's sake, you wish that it could die". That's not the same as letting Down's syndrome children die because society doesn't want them (or because their parents don't want them). It is absolutely monstrous: not only can you not kill them, but you cannot let them die for your own convenience.'

Mrs Foot really feels outraged about infanticide. And although she still refrains from making any definitive statement about abortion, it is clear that she regards the developed foetus as having an entitlement not to be killed. This is the difficult area of gradualism: that the foetus gains rights as it grows and develops, becomes more complex and sentient.

The 'gradualist' approach to pregnancy and the rights of the foetus is quite widespread: it is not only how most philosophers probably think – that the foetus gains rights as it develops – but it is almost certainly how most people feel. A very young embryo is not given the same weight of moral consideration as a developed foetus, and some abortionists themselves make this point. Malcolm Potts, who has carried out many abortions and who works for International Planned Parenthood, has said that early abortion and late abortion are so different as medical procedures that they ought never to have been called by the same name. It is true that in observing a very early abortion (up to eight weeks) the naked eye can see very little; the foetus is so tiny that it is very quickly turned into undifferentiated matter by the procedure. In watching late abortions it is all too obvious that this is the torso of a human baby.

However, there are enormous difficulties in logic, intuitive reaction and morality, as far as the gradualist approach is concerned. Following the Warnock Report in Britain about *in vitro* fertilization and other linked subjects, there was a fierce public and parliamentary debate about whether scientists should be permitted to do experimental work on very young embryos. The debate continues, moreover. The public, when consulted, seemed to want two things which are considered by some people to be contradictory: yes, they wanted scientists to do everything they possibly could to help infertility and to eliminate genetically transmitted disease or disability; but no, they did not want experiments done on human embryos. Even though abortion is practised in Britain up to twenty-six weeks' gestation, the public does not like the notion of embryos just a few days old being cut up. This is a moral inconsistency, but it is a gut reaction. Mary Midgley, who is also a specialist on animals, says that there is something fundamentally repellent to any creature about an attack on its own species, and this may be why people do not like embryo experimentation. 'This seems to me to be a deep emotional feature of how we're made.' Mary Warnock herself feels the same way – that we owe some special sense of loyalty to our own species. Warnock is a gradualist in that she would not wish to contemplate abortion beyond the first trimester (twelve weeks), except in grave circumstances. So, in principle, are Hughes and Midgley: that is, they consider later abortion a more serious matter than early abortion. So is Sissela Bok, who has a very clear moral view of the rights of the developing foetus. Bok claims that a more developed foetus has rights over a less developed one, but says that even an early foetus has entitlement to consideration. Moreover, she affirms, contraception is always *morally* preferable to abortion. This may seem obvious, but it is by no means universally held. There is a complicated argument for abortion which claims that freedom to terminate pregnancies gives a woman freedom to test her fertility. There are also several successful health guides for women which advise that the most satisfactory form of birth control is a barrier method backed up by abortion when required – since it allows ultimate choice, and freedom from the side-effects of the Pill. There is, moreover, the matter of post-coital birth control – a growing field of research. The morning-after Pill, and the various early abortifacient methods now being developed would not fit conveniently with Sissela Bok's declaration that preventing a pregnancy occurring is always preferable to its *post hoc* extinction.

Janet Radcliffe Richards is a gradualist too, but on characteristically utilitarian grounds – the principle of not inflicting suffering. She regards complexity and autonomy as reasons eliciting respect: the foetus of eight months is more complex than the foetus at four months; but then again a child of seven is more complex than a child of two – and Richards makes the claim that the life of a seven-year-old *is* more valuable than the life of a baby for precisely these reasons, i.e., complexity and autonomy. I would have to interject here, as a mother, that my own instinct is rather the opposite: as the child grows more complex and autonomous, so it requires less and less maternal protection. It is the tiny baby that is more precious in the sense of being more frail, requiring more of our care. By this criterion it is not complexity and autonomy which elicit respect – but tenderness of years, immaturity and human need.

It is of course a notorious consequence of a gradualist view that it is difficult to decide where to draw the line. Janet Radcliffe Richards thinks that as a pregnancy advances the foetus becomes more and more valuable, so that increasingly strong reasons are needed to justify an abortion, but not that there is any particular time after which it would always be wrong. However, she thinks that the point at which the law should start making abortions difficult is when the foetus becomes capable of suffering. This is an interesting, important and new idea in this controversy.

The evidence, so far, is that the foetus can actually feel at twelve weeks' pregnancy. Of course, this is still disputed because it cannot yet be proved that a twelve-week-old foetus feels pain, but there is enough evidence to suppose that it is likely that it does. The organism is certainly complex enough by that stage and the nerves sufficiently sensitive. The foetus also perceptibly moves away from any apparent intervention. In Bernard Nathanson's film about a young foetus being aborted entitled *The Silent Scream*, the foetus was seen to move away from the abortion instruments and to open its mouth and 'scream' when penetrated and dismembered. This has been criticized as being fanciful and bathetic: foetuses open and close their mouths anyway. But perhaps the fact that they do is a good enough reason to give foetuses the benefit of the doubt – that they *might* suffer during the operation.

Even if 'lines' are notoriously difficult to draw in abortion, twelve weeks is a significant turning-point. Between twelve and fourteen weeks, the foetus quite suddenly doubles in weight and substance. Abortion techniques used before twelve weeks cannot be used after this dramatic doubling in size, and second trimester abortion becomes a more complicated operation. So, if we are to suggest the notion of foetal suffering as a criterion for judging abortion, twelve weeks would probably mark the cut-off period. Perhaps not coincidentally, this is the abortion limit in many European countries – Finland, Denmark, Norway, even the USSR, – with other countries choosing a similar time: ten weeks in France, fourteen in Italy.

The criterion of the infliction of suffering is one that deserves respect, but it is not, of course, the answer to moral questions. Is capital punishment more acceptable if it is administered by a painless injection rather than by hanging? Abortionists could themselves do more research on lessening suffering for the foetus – better foetal anaesthetics, perhaps – but that would by no means answer the moral dilemmas of abortion.

Anne Kelleher is a feminist and modified libertarian, but she is not a gradualist. She considers that you cannot really pinpoint the moment when a foetus suddenly acquires rights. But suffering does come into it, she says, and so do aesthetics, as well as psychological aspects. 'It's a very nasty sticky business to abort a foetus at twenty-four weeks and one may be revolted by that without at the same time thinking it is a moral issue. All sorts of psychological factors come into play and I don't think they can be discounted. In trying to create a moral framework in which one acts, one has to take account of how one feels about such things. It is not totally an intellectual exercise.'

Carol McMillan is not a gradualist either, though for different reasons. Indeed, she emphasizes how radical, how strong, how dramatic is the *beginning* of pregnancy – rather than how complex and significant is its ultimate development. 'I totally reject the gradualist approach to abortion. Some people, who include Catholics like Donceel and Mahoney, have made a lot of noise about the first trimester of pregnancy being unproblematic in terms of abortion. Nothing could be further from the truth. From the woman's point of view, the first trimester differs from the later period of pregnancy in that the child asserts itself then in a much more dramatic and turbulent way. The symptoms of pregnancy – the cessation of menstruation, the frequency of micturation, the nausea, the enlarged breasts, the moodiness – leave a woman 'feeling the plaything of obscure forces', as de Beauvoir put it. By the time the rest of the world notices a woman is pregnant, she is just beginning to feel that despite her bump and the baby's movements within her, that her body is at least her own. Whereas, in the first trimester, it is quite different. Again, as de Beauvoir writes, and I think her description is most appropriate for the stages of early pregnancy: 'pregnancy is above all a drama that is acted out within the woman herself'.

Because of this turbulent change taking place within a woman in the early weeks of pregnancy, Carol McMillan states, the young foetus demonstrates its very particular significance. It cannot be brushed aside just because it is immature, small and helpless. Quite the contrary: our moral obligation is to give it shelter because of its unique needs. Dismissing the young foetus or embryo as a 'bunch of cells' is, she says, insulting to *women*, besides being dismissive of human life. A woman carries life within her, and calling it a 'bunch of cells' is what Marx identified as 'reification' – converting people into mere material things.

The feminist view of abortion is, stated simply, that it is for the woman to choose, without any restrictions from outside agencies, and at any stage in the pregnancy. The feminist does not claim that the foetus has no rights: but that whatever entitlements it possesses are always subject to the mother's decision. Women philosophers vary in their consideration of this dogma in the same degree that men vary: some agree with these ideas, and some do not. Secular liberalism has been very much the thinking fashion in our century, so the majority of female philosophers are more inclined to agree than to disagree, as would the majority of secular male philosophers. But there tend to be many quibbles and modifications, too. 'I would support abortion on demand,' says Anne Kelleher, 'not because I am a feminist – although I am – but because quite simply, for me, I would like to live by the principles of the greatest freedom and the minimum suffering. I believe that the quality of life *may* be achieved at the expense of another life. Because there is no doubt that the foetus is alive, but I think that the life of the foetus is not going to suffer in relation to what the woman might suffer if she were forced to bear a child she does not want.' All the same, she would impose certain restrictions on abortion choice, even using authoritarian methods if necessary. In the (true) case of a woman who presented for an abortion at about twenty-one weeks' gestation because her husband had been suddenly killed in a road crash, and she felt she could not have a child as a single parent, Anne Kelleher would have refused to allow such an abortion.

'If you see somebody trying to jump off a building – you try to stop them doing it. There are grounds for being paternalistic in certain circumstances, and I think in that circumstance I would have said to the woman "this is just not on: you are not in a fit state to make this kind of decision". Overriding people's autonomy is a very dangerous game but I think there are circumstances in which one would want to say that this person is not in a position to make this decision. I think in this case the best thing to do is to say – "Look, why don't you sit in this room quietly for a while, and for the next three weeks turn it over, and then we'll talk about it." ' Three weeks, of course, would have brought the baby just up to the threshold of viability. None the less, the National Health Service was more libertarian than Ms Kelleher would have been: it performed the abortion by the woman's choice. It is true, however, that reactions to shock and loss are often dramatic: I also came across the case of a woman aborting her second pregnancy when her first child suddenly died of a virus. A state of shock *is* a poor state in which to make a drastic decision.

Janet Radcliffe Richards is strongly feminist in many respects, and she argues affirmatively that current abortion laws are fundamentally framed so as to have the effect – whether by intention or not – of controlling women, which is a classic feminist accusation against much law and medicine. It is certainly true that the practice of 'allowing' some abortions and of 'not allowing' others is extremely discriminatory, and implies judgements about women. Indeed the only logical way to conduct an abortion policy is either to refuse all abortions or to perform all abortions: anything in between is by definition discrimination. In her book, *The Sceptical Feminist*, Richards make a very clever argument about rape. 'People who oppose abortion on demand usually claim to be concerned about the human rights of the unborn child,' she explains. 'However, when abortion is allowed to raped women but not to others, there is no difference in the status of the *children*, and if the child of the raped woman has no automatic right to life, why have the others? The difference between the two cases has nothing to do with the rights of the unborn child and reflects only a difference of attitude to the *women* concerned.' This proves, she argues, that abortion law and practice are usually framed with the notion of controlling women – 'allowing' the innocent ones (who have been raped) to be aborted, but forcing those less innocent to bear children.

Indeed, Richards's argument about how rape is used to discriminate between the 'deserving' and the 'undeserving' cases in abortion is so persuasive that it has convinced anti-abortionists, who are inclined to waver over abortion where rape is concerned, that you actually cannot make an exception for it. Because if you make an exception for rape, you will then be accused of discriminating against the other women who have not been raped, but who have every much as right to an abortion.

Yet although Richards thinks abortion should be easily available – at least until the foetus can suffer – she does not automatically endorse 'the woman's right to choose'. 'There are lots of things no one has a right to choose. A woman doesn't have the right to choose to murder her seven-year-old, if her seven-year-old gets in the way of her career. The claim to any such right has to be justified in each particular case. But I don't think I'd want to concede a woman's right to choose a late abortion – especially one which might cause the foetus to suffer – just because her pregnancy would get in the way of a holiday, or for some such trivial reason.' This is all very well, but who is to judge what is important and what is not? The feminist argument that the woman in question is by far the best judge of her own needs comes to mind here. But see what shifting sands we come upon when we enter situation ethics. Richards's desire to construct some objective morality, based on criteria of suffering and the proportion of importance is an attempt to give some sort of framework to these judgements.

Judith Hughes, a feminist, rejects the automatic idea that women have the 'right to choose' what they do with their own bodies. Abortion she firmly categorizes as an evil, even if it is sometimes a necessary evil. 'I feel in my guts that abortion is always an evil. Now what I mean by that is not that I always think it is a sin, or the worst thing that somebody could do, or that the evil necessarily lies in the fact that one is killing a human foetus. But for the woman, it is a serious matter. If we are moral beings at all, this is the kind of issue which must seriously concern us. I don't believe that every woman would have regrets – but we must take it seriously. That is the first principle: *take it seriously*. And the idea that only women should have something to say about this is really spurious. "It's my body and I'll do what I like with it" – it's really jolly bad, that. You don't own your body – you are your body. Or at least, it is only part of what you are.'

But the inflicting of pain, says Judith Hughes, who is a mother herself, is not the only reason why the foetus may deserve consideration. 'Foetuses may be important for all kinds of reasons – not just because they are sentient. Something that doesn't feel anything because it is in a particular catatonic state – I still don't want to write it off as unimportant.' Here, for example, one might invoke the taboo against necrophilia. We do not sanction the idea of individuals being free to have sexual intercourse with dead bodies: it does not do any harm, obviously, to the dead body, and the necrophiliac himself is making a free choice, but for some reason we still don't like it, and the taboo against it is very strong.

Thus neither sentience nor suffering nor even the presence of the soul (for those who believe in the soul) tell us the whole story about how we feel other human bodies should be treated. Whether – and when – the foetus has rights is an issue which is endlessly disputed. But Judith Hughes agrees with those who put forward the view that we have carved up the issue altogether too much in terms of rights.

'I think one gets into a terrible confusion as soon as one talks about rights,' says Mary Warnock. 'I desperately try to avoid talking about them because it's only a disguised way of talking about what we think is morally permissible or not. When people talk about the rights of animals, they are really thinking about how we ought to treat animals other than human animals. And so I think to question whether people ought to commit suicide is not a matter of rights at all. Similarly, I think one has got to work one's way very carefully into saying how people ought to treat human foetuses. And it becomes tremendously confusing either where you say the mother has a right to choose or the foetus has a right to life. Neither is demonstrable. Talking about rights makes it sound as though it's more a matter of fact than it actually is. But it's bound to be a matter of opinion – of moral opinion.'

'One of the things that happened in the 1970s was a greatly increased preoccupation with formulating moral issues in terms of human rights,' says Onora O'Neill of the University of Essex. 'That is not new. On the other hand, it is not ancient either – it's eighteenth century. We talk about obligations, virtues, justice – everybody has talked about those since antiquity. Rights come in in the eighteenth century, but they've had this tremendous revival, and I suppose the most public manifestation of them was the 1975 Helsinki Accord, which represents the concern we see about human rights' violations in other countries.

'But I would say a lot of philosophers have got into trouble trying to construct, refine and elaborate theories of human rights and then use them to tackle particular problems. In that well-known article by Judith Jarvis Thomson, people started to construe abortion in terms of rights, so that they were asking themselves "Which *rights* are involved?" And this became a very natural way to pose the question, because, after all, the women's movement was on the same bandwagon, taking up the idiom of rights. So they were talking about a woman's so-called "right to choose". And then people said the obvious thing – "What about the foetus's right to life? Surely a right to life is more important than a right to choose?" So there was a conflict of "rights".' This led to great dilemmas.

The Judith Jarvis Thomson article on abortion is very often cited; written in 1971, it has achieved the status of a minor classic. It is dismissed by several of the women philosophers I have spoken to as totally 'absurd', 'rotten', 'ludicrous', and so on, but, nevertheless, everyone has read it closely. Judith Jarvis Thomson gives us the following analogy for the conflict in abortion rights.

'You wake up in the morning and find yourself back to back in bed with an unconscious violinist. A famous unconscious violinist. He has been found to have a fatal kidney ailment, and the Society of Music Lovers has canvassed all the available medical records and found that you alone have the right blood type to help. They have therefore kidnapped you, and last night the violinist's circulatory system was plugged into yours, so that your kidneys can be used to extract poisons from his blood as well as your own. The director of the hospital now tells you – "Look, we're sorry the Society of Music Lovers did this to you – we would never have permitted it if we had known. But still, they did it, and the violinist is plugged into you. To unplug you would be to kill him. But never mind, it's only for nine months. By then he will have recovered from his ailment and can be safely unplugged from you." Is it morally incumbent on you to accede to this situation? No doubt it would be very nice of you if you did, a great kindness. But do you *have* to accede to it?' And Judith Jarvis Thomson goes on to discuss the rights of the violinist, and the rights of the person providing the kidney support.

It is widely rejected, this analogy, because it really only works as an analogy in the case of rape. Except for rape, women become voluntarily pregnant; they are not kidnapped for the purposes of impregnation. Most women, moreover, have recourse to contraception, and if contraception has not been used, this makes the pregnancy at least to some degree voluntary, and partly the woman's own responsibility. So the analogy is logically poor. Nevertheless, it is a colourful story and it provides a useful context for stimulating ideas about abortion, even if, as Onora O'Neill says, it is largely stated in terms of rights. Moreover, as a sort of *évocation poetique* of an unwanted pregnancy, it captures a certain imaginative accuracy. A woman who becomes pregnant and does not want to be pregnant may well feel trapped and imprisoned. On the other hand, by casting the baby as a world-famous violinist the analogy does not dismiss the child as unimportant, and the inherent value of the child is well illustrated.

Yet Onora O'Neill – whose background is Irish Protestant – agrees with Mary Warnock that 'rights' are not the crucial moral issue. 'I don't think rights are a fundamental moral notion. If we take any theory of rights then the only obligations that we are talking about are the obligation which another has the *right* to have performed, like if I have an obligation not to kill somebody because they have a right not to be killed. This gives us a rather limited set of obligations because there are all those obligations which traditionally have been labelled – though the term means different things to different people – "imperfect obligations". This is where you have an obligation, say, to be kind – but no one has a *right* to your kindness. Now, if we are to take it back to the abortion case, many women would say that they had an obligation to eat well during pregnancy for the sake of the child, but they would bridle at the thought that the child actually has a *right* to this. So that we think there are all sorts of obligations that we have where there are no counterpart rights.'

Professor Peter Huntingford, a gynaecologist who has crusaded militantly for women's freedom to choose abortion, puts the rights issue in a rather poignant way. 'Yes, the foetus has rights,' he says. 'But only the mother can protect those rights.' As a statement of reality, that can hardly be gainsaid.

Onora O'Neill, who certainly considers herself a feminist (but is resentful of the idea that you must be doctrinally pro-abortion if you are feminist), would prefer to start from the notion of obligations rather than a theory of rights. 'It would seem to me to be very interesting to ask – what are our obligations towards others who are dependent on us? There must be some clear line between what a foetus has a right to, and what we *ought* to do. When I am kind or generous, if I am, it is not that someone has a *right* to my kindness; but I may say, and I am not just being coy, "*I could hardly do less*".' From such notions, perhaps, springs the eternal expectation (so often fulfilled) that women will act altruistically. She feels, too, that we have 'de-contextualized' abortion. In a different way, so does Mary Midgley. Midgley feels that abortion is not a subject to be considered on its own, but that it must be related to all sorts of problems such as poverty, deprivation, cruelty, misery and coercion. O'Neill says that we have individualized abortion – and indeed pregnancy – far too much. 'The question I would like to ask – the social question – is "What would be a just framework for reproductive decisions?" Then there might be less emphasis on the actions of the individual procreator. I'd like to ask – how should we arrange life so that people do not experience great pressure, injustice or oppression in reproductive matters? We cut the problem up so that it looks to us as though there is The Problem of Abortion, and then, as a little appendix, the problem of whether adoption in some circumstances is the desirable alternative.

'One might think that the central focus of concern when someone is pregnant is: what arrangements (a) can be made for the good rearing of this child, and (b) should be made? If no adequate arrangements can be made, abortion may be seen in a very different light. My line of thinking would go back to some heavy social criticism of our present arrangements which I think put extraordinary burdens on women, particularly women who are bringing up children alone. If you are really pro-life, it is absolutely clear where you should put your activity – not into stopping abortion, but into supporting people who are trying to do heroic tasks unaided – for twenty years, fifteen years, non-stop, by themselves. I cannot condemn any girl or woman who has an abortion under current social conditions. But there could be societies where the child is born to a community and not to a woman or an individual couple. We don't know how to share the burdens or the benefits of reproduction: I think the childless, too, get a rotten deal in how they are excluded from the lives of children.

'With the size of family we are having now, our children don't have much in the way of aunts and uncles . . . we have no other networks which in any way substitute. And as long as we are putting this degree of pressure on individual couples and occasionally individual women, we are likly to find that some of them simply hold up their hands in horror and say – "I can't!"'

In making this critique of individualism, Dr O'Neill is illustrating that the politics of abortion are not always what they seem. Pro-choice feminists tend to locate themselves on the Left, but in fact the ethic of 'choice' is libertarian, individualistic, and capitalist.

'While technology opens up some choices, it closes down others,' writes Barbara Katz Rothman in *Test-Tube Women*. 'The new choice is often greeted with such fanfare that the silent closing of the door on the old choice goes unheeded . . .' The choice of contraception closed down some of the choices for large families. North American society is geared to small families, if indeed to any children at all. Everything from car and apartment sizes to the picture-book ideal of families encourages limiting fertility. So it is a choice all that contraception gave us, and a choice we may very well experience as being under our control, but it may be a somewhat forced choice.'

The idea that male or female philosophers might by definition think differently about abortion is not one that the philosophers I spoke to endorsed: most believed that their sex was irrelevant. A trained, professional thinker is a trained, professional thinker. Carol McMillan is probably nearer the mark when she says that the religious or the scientific cast of mind is probably the more influential factor in how one sees abortion. The scientific cast of mind wants to plan everything, to control everything, to measure happiness; the religious mentality accepts that there are rough edges to life which may be calamitous, or surprising.

All the same, even if men and women philosophers do not come to any specially different conclusions because they are men or women, only because they are individuals with a particular background and a particular way of thinking about things, it seems to me to be valuable that we now have women's thoughts and women's voices applied to abortion in the realm of philosophy.

Sissela Bok gives what seems to me a very thoughtful summing-up of what she considers the factors a woman should weigh up before having an abortion. They would, of course, be disputed by many different parties, but they are nevertheless rich in reflection and they obey Judith Hughes's wise guideline: *take it seriously*.

The woman should consider:

whether or not the pregnancy was voluntarily undertaken;

the importance and validity of the reasons for wanting an abortion;

the technique to be used in the abortion;

the extent to which it can be regarded as the cessation of bodily life support, rather than outright killing;

the time (duration) of the pregnancy;

whether or not the father agrees to the abortion;

whether or not all other alternatives have been considered, such as adoption;

her religious views.

An 'unwanted' baby may seem a sad or alarming prospect, says Sissela Bok, but studies have shown that in half the pregnancies aborted, the baby was wanted by at least one of the parents. Abortion should be a last resort, she warns, and if we wish to retain ethical standards, it must continue to be seen in this light.

10
MISCELLANY

PART I: POETRY ABOUT ABORTION

Poetry about abortion* is not copious, but it does sometimes explore the intimacy and general air of melancholy surrounding the subject.

NOT TO BE SEEN

No different, I said, from a rat's or chicken's,
That ten-week protoplasmic blob. But you
Cried as if you knew all that was nonsense
And knew that I did, too.

Well, I had to say something. And there
Seemed so little anyone could say.
That life had been in women's wombs before
And gone away?

This was our life. And yet, when the dead
Are mourned a little, then become unreal,
How should the never-born be long remembered
So this in time will heal . . .

---

*Permission to reproduce has been sought wherever possible.

Though now I cannot comfort. As I go
The doctor reassures: 'Straightforward case
You'll find, of course, it leaves her rather low.'
Something is gone from your face.

David Sutton

Most 'abortion poetry', if it can be described as such, is written by men – very possibly because it is a subject men do *not* talk about very much, and so suppress their feelings. This poem was written by a student and published in a Dublin student's magazine. It describes a girl, a lover, taking a boat to England for an abortion.

BARGAIN

We did it
On the quiet.
Nobody knows
We are murderers
Often we debated
With passion
And skilful thrust
How we loved life,
Would sacrifice for life.
But when you are up against it
That's different.
So you told
Your story well
Made your contacts
To break contact
Fifty pounds
From the Mam
And the Dad
The price of
The neighbours' respect
One hundred from me
My freedom; cheap
At the price.
And so to the boat
Tears in your eyes
Your need greater;
Crying as you would

For puppies, kittens, lost birds
The baby within you
Cut out;
Seventy-five pounds
Bargain price.
Bleeding from
London to Dublin
To Mass every Sunday
Your bargain with God
Who saw you through
Your parents pleased
You look so well
In your bright suit
Disco jumping.
In my dark soul
Little hands stretch
Cold eyes
Stare.

Maurice Kearney

Poetry about abortion is difficult to write because it can so easily be mawkish, ghoulish and harsh all at once. In the following poem, Stevie Smith, indeed, is not tender in her judgement.

BUT MURDEROUS

A mother slew her unborn babe
In a day of recent date
Because she did not wish him to be born in a world
Of murder and war and hate.
'Oh why should I bear a baby from my womb
To be broke in pieces by the hydrogen bomb?'

I say this woman deserves little pity
That she was a fool and a murderess
Is a child's destiny to be contained by a mind
That signals only a lady in distress?

And why should human infancy be so superior
As to be too good to be born in this world?
Did she think it was an angel of a baa-lamb
That lay in her belly furled?

Oh the child is the young of its species
Alike with that noble, vile, curious and fierce
How foolish this poor mother to suppose
Her act told us aught that was not murderous.

(As, item, That the arrogance of a half-baked mind
Breeds murder; makes us all unkind.)

Stevie Smith

Where they confront abortion, the poets certainly do not avoid the issues, and D.M. Thomas's poem, 'The Foetus', which first appeared in *Encounter* magazine in December 1979, is as plain as a photograph.

THE FOETUS

A foetus was heard to cry out
while it was being aborted behind screens
the foetus showed signs of being alive
apparently it was human
apparently it was alive
some women wept
the Minister has ordered/the Minister is disturbed.

the foetus did not cry it cried out
it cried out once to the world
with a voice that was human
but that did not make sense
which disturbed the Minister
and the women who were infertile
and the hospital padre

a foetus was heard to cry out
while it was being aborted behind screens
it signalled once its existence
it touched the world for an instant
it was evidently alive
it was evidently human
unlike the foetuses who did not cry out
while they were being aborted behind screens
some women wept

the Minister is disturbed
abortions should not take place

where infertile women are gathered
there is already too much crying
too much crying out
it might disturb the other foetuses
the ones that do not cry out
to hear human cries

D.M. Thomas

This next poem was sent anonymously to the *Daily Mail* when Lynn Reed wrote an article entitled 'Should I Have an Abortion?' Lynn explained in her original article that her lover had been a policeman, a point referred to in the poem.

A REQUIEM

Before
Your lover says: 'Abort it.' You think this may be right.
(A baby will disturb him in the middle of the night.)
Your friends know your dilemma – but most will hold this view.
'Abortion is (with caution) the safest thing for you.'

After
It's done. Go back to work now. Defend the right to speak –
While lover, true policeman, by law protects the weak.
But can you stop your ears now? Shut up that still small voice?
'You claim the rights of others. I died. I had no choice.'

Some do not choose their babies, yet let their seed be grown
For other, barren gardens, who love it as their own.
So save your seed and nurse it. For it will bloom with care
In someone else's garden – Or yours? If love is there.

The black American poet, Gwendolyn Brooks, is a feminist who speaks most affectingly of the ghosts of the unborn in this poem.

THE MOTHER

Abortions will not let you forget
You remember the children you got that you did not
get.
The damp small pulps with little or with no hair,
The singers and the workers that never handled the air.
You will never neglect or beat
Them, or silence or buy with a sweet.
You will never wind up the suckling-thumb
Or scuttle off ghosts that come.
You will never leave them controlling your luscious
sigh,
Return for a snack of them, with gobbling mother-eye.

I have heard in the voices of the wind the voices of my
dim killed children.
I have contracted. I have eased
My dim dears at the breasts they could never suck.
I have said, Sweets, if I sinned, if I seized
Your luck
And your lives from your unfinished reach,
If I stole your births and your names,
Your straight baby tears and your games,
Your stilted or lovely loves, your tumults, your
marriages, aches and your deaths,
If I poisoned the beginnings of your breaths,
Believe me that even in my deliberateness I was not
deliberate.
Though why should I whine
Whine that the crime was other than mine? –
Since anyhow you are dead.
Or, rather, or instead
You were never made.
But that too, I am afraid
Is faulty: oh, what shall I say, how is the truth to be
said?
You were born and you had body, you died,
It is just that you never giggled or planned or cried.
'Believe me, I loved you all,
Believe me, I knew, though faintly, I and I love, I love
you –
All.'

Gwendolyn Brooks

Here we see that poetry so often can express many of the things that rational discussion cannot very easily cope with. Some women write poems to the spirit of the aborted child, and at least one Anglican divine has written an abortion prayer.

A PRAYER FOR ABORTION

Heavenly Father, you are the Giver of Life and you share with us the care of the life that is given. Into your hands we commit in trust the developing life that we have cut short. Look in kindly judgement on the decision that we have made. And assure us in our uncertainty that Your love for us can never change. Amen.

John Vernon Taylor, former Bishop of Winchester

PART II: DOCTORS AND ABORTION

Many doctors, possibly most doctors, changed their minds about abortion between 1960 and 1980. Before the abortion Act, most doctors and most medical colleges frowned upon abortion because it was mostly illegal. Since then, most doctors have swung in its favour, and the British Medical Association today is a strong upholder of legal abortion.

This is partly because doctors are in general law-abiding and conformist fellows who do not have a lot of time to think deeply about ethics, but who go along with practical solutions – and abortion certainly is a practical solution to a crisis. To be fair, it is also because many of them saw, during the 1950s and '60s, a rise in the number of women admitted to hospitals suffering from abortion attempts. Professor Ian Donald once told me that I would hardly believe the instruments he found inside women, and the things they had attempted to abort themselves with. Like Professor Donald, the pro-life pioneer of ultrasound, some doctors have remained opposed to abortion, and it is, to this day, not highly regarded within the medical profession to be known as an abortionist. It is not very advantageous to be seen as anti-abortion either, and gynaecologists who have identified themselves as such often find it harder to get promotion. The smart thing is to be a gynaecologist who is liberal on abortion but who is grand enough not to have to perform very many.

However, the majority of doctors, as repeated opinion polls have shown, are in agreement with abortion, though not necessarily with abortion on demand. Dr Leslie Oldershaw, who has written a book about doctors and abortion, probably represents the average middle-of-the-road GP when he says that most women should be given an abortion when they request one, provided they have talked it over sensibly with their husband or boyfriend – or, in the case of a young woman, with parents – and provided it is not too advanced in the pregnancy. One of his reasons (a perfectly valid one, as it happens) for regarding late abortions unfavourably is that he says he 'wouldn't impose late termination on the nurses'. He does not favour abortion on demand because he has found that patients benefit from thinking over the problem.

On one occasion a patient approached him requesting an abortion. She seemed sure she wanted one and so, she said, did her husband: she knew he didn't want children yet. Dr Oldershaw advised her to talk it over with her husband. The patient did so – only to discover that her husband was thrilled at the prospect of a baby. The doctor recounts this case history as an example of individuals assuming certain attitudes on behalf of their partners, without actually communicating. In this particular case, as her husband was delighted, the woman changed her mind and pronounced herself delighted too and the pregnancy went ahead. Feminists, I think, would query this kind of case; some might say it was an example of a woman bending her will to please a man. If she wanted an abortion, she should have had one. Dr Sheila Abdullah, of the group 'Doctors for a Woman's Choice', says that she thinks abortion on demand is a very good thing. 'Why shouldn't a woman *demand* an abortion?' she asks. Another woman GP from Wakefield in Yorkshire put it this way: 'I always agree to abortion on request because I do not like seeing women having to grovel to try to limit their families.'

But the notion of abortion on demand, or even on request, can raise medical hackles. It is not that most doctors have any objection to abortion *per se*: it is that 'on demand' or 'on request' smacks of consumerist medicine. It is as though the patient is a client, calling the shots, and the doctor merely a technician, or somebody who is providing a service. This is a recent trend in medicine that makes doctors nervous – patients becoming more and more demanding about the services they are receiving generally, more apt to complain, more apt to criticize. Indeed, abortion has played a major part in influencing social attitudes here; the very slogan 'a woman's right to choose' has spilled over into the idea of 'the patient's right to choose' in many areas of treatment. 'Health rights' and the 'rights of patients' are, says Carolyn Faulder, the latest entrants into the 'rights' arena.

> There is a growing consensus of public opinion that medicine, and in particular medical ethics, is too important to leave to the doctors [she writes in her study of informed consent]. If praise or blame . . . is to be attributed for this major shift in society's attitude towards doctors, then there are two post-war movements which can justifiably claim to share out the honours between them. One is the consumerist movement . . . The other – in my view much the more influential because it has encouraged the consumerists to follow in its wake – is the new wave of the women's movement which can be dated from the late sixties.
>
> Right from the start women perceived that the way medical services were being offered to them, the content of these services and the presumptions on which they were based directly affected their rights of choice and therefore their right to be treated as autonomous individuals. The demand to change the abortion laws was grounded in the claim that it is 'a woman's right to choose'. A flood of literature challenging the 'myth of the medical mystique', medical

paternalism and male chauvinist perceptions of women's sexuality has poured out of the movement, both here and abroad.

However, the idea of abortion on demand is rejected by some unlikely sources, too. Diane Munday, founder of the abortion charity BPAS, rejects abortion on demand within the NHS because it implies that the doctor has no freedom of conscience himself – it implies that he may not refuse to be involved in abortion. The doctor must have a right to refuse, in conscience, to do abortion work – though not a right to refuse to refer the patient elsewhere. Though again, Peter Huntingford, the professor of gynaecology who has campaigned so vigorously for abortion freedom for women, thinks there is something cowardly about a doctor refusing to do an abortion himself and passing the patient on to a colleague. Huntingford does not like to do non-medical abortions after twenty weeks; he knows he doesn't like doing them, because he has *done* them. But if a woman presents at twenty-one weeks, begging him for an abortion, will he refer her to one of the London practitioners who will do them up to twenty-six weeks? No, he wouldn't. If he chooses not to do the job himself, he doesn't see why he should ask someone else to do it. Another interesting moral stance.

General practitioners are not really at the sharp end of the abortion business because they seldom, if ever, have to carry them out. All they really have to do is to examine patients and refer them. If they are too 'permissive' about abortion, they become little more than state bureaucrats signing abortion forms. If they are too restrictive, they are accused of 'controlling' women. But they are, for the 50 per cent of women who have abortions on the National Health Service, the first port of call, so their attitudes are relevant. There is no reason to suppose that GPs are in a more special position to advise about abortion than family and friends, since most abortion has very little to do with medical indications, and is a personal and social decision. Yet, in asking doctors about their attitudes to abortion, it is obvious that they still prefer to think of it as having a medical basis. Even when they are liberal, they don't like the idea of abortion as social convenience or as a method of birth control.

'I believe there ought to be real medical reasons for the termination of a pregnancy,' said a woman GP from Greenford in Middlesex.

'I think there should be a medical reason, or at least a medico-social reason,' said a male GP from Lincolnshire. Although he usually agrees immediately to termination of pregnancy for any reason up to twelve weeks and for genetic abortion up to twenty weeks, he still feels more comfortable if there is some medical indication. A little asthma, a bit of blood pressure, the odd depression – any little pain or ache really can make a woman less than wholly fit for pregnancy.

'I tend to agree to abortion on request if the request is reasonable,' said a forty-four-year-old consultant in gynaecology and obstetrics. Ah, but what is 'reasonable'? One person's reason is another person's excuse.

'On request, if I am sure request is genuine and not manipulation from partner or parents,' notes a male doctor from Kilburn, north London.

'There ought to be a real medical reason, but abortion on demand is often very valid,' wrote a doctor from Hertfordshire.

'There should be real medical reasons,' wrote a female GP from south London, adding: 'Contraception is free and readily available – adults should take some responsibility for their actions.'

'First reason should be medical, then age of the mother is she is a minor, then extremely difficult social circumstances,' rules a doctor from Herne Hill in London, concerning his own priorities about abortion requests. So, while many doctors agree to abortion when it is requested of them, in their heart of hearts they like to feel there is a 'good', semi-medical reason for it.

The feminist view that abortion should be available to a woman for whatever reasons under whatever circumstances and without limitation is not one that generally finds sympathetic responses among doctors. The practice of gynaecology, say feminists, is used to *control* women. It is certainly the case that doctors may have moral views about the propriety of a pregnancy, though they are views which are not necessarily anti-abortion. It can happen that it is the doctor who is arguing for an abortion and the patient who is trying to make a case against it. 'I don't really want an abortion,' said a thirty-year-old patient who had contracted German measles in early pregnancy to the registrar at the Hammersmith Hospital. 'It is your duty to the state to have an abortion,' he replied. Doctors tend to be directional, yes. They may be anti-abortion in their directional attitudes; they may also be very pro-abortion. Indeed, since abortion has been legalized, they may be more likely to be pro-abortion, since it is the legal and easy way out of a pregnancy problem. If a woman has a child with the support of her doctor, and the child turns out to have a problem – say a physical or mental handicap – the doctor may afterwards be blamed. Indeed, in West Germany, there have been cases where women have sued doctors for the lifelong financial support of a handicapped child, because the doctor did not sufficiently warn, during pregnancy, that handicap could occur. Whereas if the woman has an abortion, the doctor has no further responsibility whatsoever. Therefore, it can be in the interest of the doctor to lean towards abortion.

'I think it is much worse for an unwanted baby to be born than for an abortion to be performed,' says a male doctor from South Lambeth. He favours abortion as a social as well as a medical policy.

'I fully agree that no woman should be required to give birth to a child she does not want and this as much for the child's sake as for the woman's,' says a specialist in endocrinology. But he adds a moralizing coda: 'On the other hand I do not think that women should allow themselves to have unwanted pregnancies – and this means that they should not engage in reckless sexual adventures and should not undertake deliberately desired and planned sexual activities without taking the trouble to see that adequate and effective techniques for preventing unwanted pregnancies are in operation.' If this doctor is satisfied that a woman has not behaved 'irresponsibly' he is favourably disposed towards her. 'But irresponsible abortion on demand I find particularly obnoxious – the spectacle of feckless women who use no form of birth control, copulate indiscriminately and without thought or care for the consequences. Refusal to terminate would, of course, result in the misery and stress for society of the unwanted children; insistence on sterilization at the time of termination might be regarded as blackmail.'

One doctor who said that he always left the decision about abortion up to the woman or the couple concerned nevertheless had one private rule: he would not abort a young woman who is happily married or in a permanent relationship, who was merely seeking to 'postpone' a baby. This decision was not a judgemental one, but based on an unhappy incident. In the 1960s, a young couple came to him asking him for help; they were students approaching their final examinations, but the girl was pregnant. They felt it would make life very difficult to have a baby so soon – would he oblige with an abortion? In the early 1960s, abortion was theoretically illegal but it was available to those in the know, and these were medical students. The gynaecologist agreed and performed the abortion. The couple qualified, got married, and settled down to their careers. A couple of years later they decided to have a baby, but failed to conceive. And for twenty years they visited every fertility clinic they could to try and find out what was wrong. Nobody was ever able to say what it was exactly, but their original gynaecologist decided he would never again have such a case on his conscience.

A few doctors refuse to be involved in abortion at all, and it is not particularly easy for them to decide this. A consultant in Cumbria became troubled about carrying out abortions; he was a devout Christian, and he gradually came to feel that routine social abortion was inconsistent with his beliefs. He finally made the decision that he would have to stop doing social abortions. But this meant that his colleague, the only other gynaecologist in the hospital, therefore had to do double the number of abortions, which did not please him at all. As medicine is a profession particularly prone to the closing of ranks, and of supporting colleagues through thick and thin, taking unilateral decisions does not make one popular.

Sometimes doctors, however, can be extraordinarily generous to each other. One young doctor was working in a gynaecology ward with Dr Anthony Hamilton (who later became embroiled in a scandal in 1983 when a baby he had attempted to abort survived). On the particular occasion recalled by the woman doctor, Dr Hamilton was very, very busy, and in addition to a lot of other problems, he happened to have a heavy caseload of abortions. Being a Christian, the young woman doctor didn't normally do abortions, but when she saw her colleague so overwhelmed with work, she felt rather sorry for him. 'Look,' she began, 'let me help you out. I don't normally do abortions, but I'll do some of the ancillary work.' He shook his head. 'If you don't believe in doing abortions, don't start. Because once you start, you'll never stop.'

Old-style doctors, doctors who qualified before the idea of 'patients' choice' was articulated, tend to be more paternalistic and more moralistic in their mode of thinking and expression. New-style doctors eschew the paternalism of the old school, and favour a more democratic and egalitarian approach to patient relations generally. Of course, doctors can still lecture patients, but in the matter of abortion a patient is more likely to get a lecture about contraception than about abortion. Occasionally, indeed, the easy availability of abortion makes doctors dismissive. A young woman afflicted by a condition known as oto-sclerosis went to talk to an ear specialist about it. With this condition, hearing is sometimes impaired and when a woman with this disability has a baby, she sometimes goes completely deaf. This girl wanted to know if anything could be done in case of a pregnancy. 'Of course something can be done,' said the medic. 'You can have an abortion.'

It seems to me that Peter Huntingford's view that a doctor cannot sit in judgement on a woman is quite right;

and that, in consequence of this, a doctor should either agree to all abortions, or agree to none. Doctors are not likely to favour that course, because it is hardly practical. A doctor who has an objection to abortion should, however, make that plain to the patient; in that way, he is not judging her personally – he is only making a general statement of principle. It is better to tell a woman outright that you do not refer for abortions as a general principle, than to try to obstruct her request.

But even for doctors who agree wholeheartedly with abortion, it seems to me that Dr Thomas Verney's advice in his book *The Secret Life of the Unborn Child* is not unreasonable.

> I believe the choice to have or not to have a child should be left to the individual woman . . . but I also think a woman must be made fully aware that what is at stake is not a clump of inert cells but the beginning of human life. If a doctor can spend several minutes explaining how he plans to remove a superfluous organ, such as an appendix, shouldn't he be willing to give this kind of decision equal time?

PART III: SOME NURSES' STORIES

Nurses often seem to have to deal with the hardest aspects of abortion: disposing of foetal material, or being left alone with women induced into labour in late abortions. Being a full-time nurse in an abortion clinic calls for a particular commitment to abortion work, otherwise it can become quite depressing.

In the NHS, nurses will usually do some abortion work as part of their training; they may, of course, opt out on grounds of conscience, but in doing so a nurse today loses an essential and technically interesting part of gynaecological experience. All the same, abortion work can set up a conflict in a nurse, who has been trained to preserve life. Moreover, abortion laws in Britain are so anomalous that it is entirely possible that a nurse might be assisting with a termination of pregnancy at twenty-three weeks' gestation in one wing of the hospital while a colleague in another wing is desperately trying to save a baby who has been born prematurely – at around the same stage of development.

The anti-abortion organizations attract a fair complement of nurses, though the large number of Irish Catholic nurses in Britain may explain this. Yet most nurses, at some stage of their career, have some horror story to tell about what they call TOP (Termination of Pregnancy).

'While a third-year student nurse at a London teaching hospital I was sent to work on a gynae ward. Entering the sluice on my first shift I was surprised, not to say horrified, to see a dead foetus of about fourteen or fifteen weeks' gestation in a plastic bowl, and this set the tone of my thirteen weeks on the ward. The staff were hearty but callow: whether they were attracted to the job because of these traits or they resulted from it, I just don't know. It is unnecessary to expound on the cruelty of the juxtaposition of girls having "terminations" and those who have lost wanted babies or who are dying of diseases to their reproductive organs, which may have been useless to them, but it never ceased to be distasteful. Likewise it was an unhappy experience to meet friendly, jolly girls of my own age who put finishing a secretarial course or not ruining their social life above the lives of their expected children.

'Falling pregnant myself while unmarried and not having finished training, while working on the ward, was predictably somewhat embarrassing. The trained staff were inquisitive and aghast, and there were hints that an abortion would be the logical step to take. One houseman who was friendly and whose wife was pregnant suggested he help me get "fixed up" so that I could finish my training without interruption. Presumably his expected baby was a loved individual, and mine simply a barely-differentiated lump of lifeless cells. My only supporter on the ward, indeed the only person who didn't see me as positively weird, was a first-year student nurse who had been adopted – she said she was glad I wasn't having an abortion because if her mother had not taken the same course, she wouldn't be here now. Judy is a good example of the waste of life with abortion.

'Telling all this has been an opportunity for me to exorcize some of the ghosts from that vile TOP ward.'

Amy Quinn, London

'For many women it is the question of the life they can offer the child – it is certainly not a lack of maternal feeling on the part of the woman having an abortion,' wrote another nurse, who remains anonymous. 'Women who have had abortions tend to take better care of themselves during pregnancy, if they later become pregnant. Many children that are born are not really wanted and many adults do have painful memories of their parents struggling to give them some sort of life. And the cold financial truth may be that one abortion may be much cheaper to do than treating for breast or cervical cancer and heart problems from the long-term use of the Pill, not to mention depression from it, or long-term infection or ectopic pregnancy from the coil.'

anonymous nurse

'Post-natal depression has far greater consequences for many women than abortion, unfortunately. When working on a gynaecological ward the attitudes were fairly neutral, or rather you did not know how the nurses felt. Certainly most treated the TOP patients as much like others except with more distance. One or two certainly did not feel any sympathy to the women and resented nursing them.'

anonymous nurse

'I wish people would think a bit more about the quality of life and the great trauma that many people experience because they feel unwanted by their mother.'

anonymous nurse

'I was a staff nurse on a gynaecological ward for a year

and came into contact with many girls and women undergoing abortions. It was always a painful experience emotionally, both for staff and patients, particularly if the abortion was of a wanted baby that was unfortunately abnormal.'

anonymous nurse

'In an ideal society with a perfect method of contraception available, "social" abortions would not take place. Nurses often feel they are not in a position to refuse to deal with a patient who is aborting, despite the conscience clause in the Abortion Act. It is also often not practical due to staffing levels on wards.'

anonymous nurse

'I often found that students were not informed of their right to refuse to help with an abortion before they came on the ward. Roman Catholic students were also not consulted. As gynaecology is not a statutory part of student nurse training, this seemed rather short-sighted and unnecessary of the allocation staff and nurse tutors.'

anonymous nurse

'Although nurses and often the general public would prefer abortions – for social reasons, particularly – not to take place, they can often see that life for the mother and the baby would be less than ideal if the pregnancy continued.'

Jane Wilmott, London

'I was always taught in my training that a nurse's prime duty is to preserve life and alleviate suffering. How on earth does this match up with assisting those who want to destroy life? Many times the Roman Catholic and Church of England nurses have baptized little foetuses gasping their last breath in a kidney dish.'

Carol Tattershall, Plumstead, London

'My own experiences are obviously limited on gynaecology – a period of sixteen weeks and a short period in

Gynaecology Theatre where abortions took place frequently. I admit that although I did feel repulsion for certain characters who presented themselves before doctors requesting terminations, I soon realized that judgement is an extremely delicate business. Many of the "young girls" who came for termination on a first-time basis were frightened and very repentant and quite obviously regretted everything related to the experience of carrying a child. On the other hand, young girls appeared for second abortions, some undoubtedly had little or no responsibility in any form, let alone any sensitivity related to the life of their foetus.

'Such contrasts were clearly evident throughout and of course I experienced artificially induced labour by the use of prostaglandins, this was somewhat upsetting for all concerned, although I came to my final conclusion that distress involved with the patient was accepted for the sake of escaping a normal healthy birth of a child. So this ruled out any sense of blame or regret I personally felt, but I must add that it was not a swift, concise conclusion; more a long soul-searching method of justification.

'Ultimately I would then consider the possibility of suffering involved with the foetus. This again wasn't an easy task, but I did eventually conclude that suffering before actual birth might be less on the scale of 1 to 10 in comparison with the suffering and distress I had seen on my previous geriatric ward where humans who presumably had earned their ticket for an existence on earth long since, had eventually ended up on the "scrap heap" and received the same care and attention as scrap metal, often broken and discarded.

'It was this that made me realize that life, unpredictable as it is, has no room for the already "unarmed and vulnerable". Of course this idea is somewhat restricted to one area, yet to me abortion is a matter of life or death and such comparisons of the unborn, defenceless, the innocent, seem to have the same unique similarities that the elderly and abandoned elderly have. Regardless of personal opinion and experience, none of us, whether nurses or ordinary lay people have room to abandon our consciences. We should stand by our convictions if we believe that they are right.

'However, in my basic nurse training I witnessed once-conscientious colleagues and friends, soon begin to use the same old excuse: "I was only obeying orders", just as habitually they straightened pillows and checked fluid balance charts.'

S.A. Davies, SEN, Manchester

'The hospital where I work is located in downtown Boston and serves a culturally diverse population. My work as a Psychiatric Clinical Specialist involves direct counselling with women wishing to have an abortion and consultation with nursing and medical staff performing the procedures. What has been the most distressing to me is the discouragement that the nursing staff experience, resulting in a very high attrition rate. The staff perform first trimester as well as prostaglandin abortions weekly. Clearly prostaglandins are the most controversial and stressful for all involved.

'Recently, I started working with nurses' groups to help them to articulate their thoughts, feelings and concerns about the abortion process and hopefully channel concerns appropriately. There are numerous occasions where the nuses' own ambivalent feelings interfere with patient care and heighten conflict among staff.

'I recognize that there are no easy answers, that abortion is a very complex emotional and ethical decision for all participants. I continue to be impressed with how long the unresolved pain of abortion resides with so many women.'

Mary Mullany, City of Boston,
Department of Health and Hospitals

It has been said that nurses on abortion wards are capable of taking a punitive attitude towards the TOP patient, even a 'serves her right' approach. Yet it is reasonable to consider the nurses' feelings. Abortion work is not easy. Late abortions are horrific. Nurses doing abortions after the first trimester of pregnancy either seem rather distressed by what is going on, or appear rather cynical and hard. When they are distressed it may be that their caring role and training is still fundamentally at odds with the termination of pregnancy.

Modern gynaecological training tends to emphasize the need for the nurse to be kind to the TOP patient, and not to be condemnatory. But sometimes it takes a personal experience to understand.

'I write anonymously as a nurse who has cared for women having abortions, and as a woman who has recently undergone one,' went a letter sent to the makers of the programme 'Mixed Feelings'. 'Although I am familiar with hospital routine, it was quite different experiencing it from the other side. I find it frightening and bewildering, because no one bothered to explain any of what was going on. Nobody ever stopped to ask how I was feeling. In the hospital, everything was unreal and felt frighteningly out of my control. At one point, a nurse came in after several hours spent on my own to find me crying. She asked if I was in pain. I said no, and she walked out without a word. I think that I have learned that good nursing care means more than efficiently performing tasks. I certainly have never felt more alone and scared.'

11

A WOMAN OF OUR TIME

Women have abortions under many circumstances, and coming from different backgrounds, with different experiences. But Liz Davis seemed to me to speak for a whole generation of Western women. A cosmopolitan girl, with an Australian background but an experience of life both in the rich and the poor world, she was thirty-eight when we talked – a vital, attractive and articulate woman who had been a supporter of the feminist movement since the 1960s, and had seemed to live through, even to personify, so much of what has happened in our time. She welcomed the Pill, went straight on to it as a young woman, had problems with it, went through the 'whole supermarket' of contraception, fell pregnant a couple of times, had a couple of abortions. She began by recalling her most recent abortion, which took place in New York in the late 1970s.

It was so easy to arrange. It was so quick and efficient that it was very easy to turn off from the fact that you were having an abortion. It was probably less painful and less anxiety-making than a trip to the dentist. And in a way, almost because of the ease and the quickness, and the fact that it was accepted as right and proper and your own personal choice – you could kind of go on automatic pilot about it. It was only later that I got to thinking about how I had taken this decision.

At the time, I was working on a film. This film was really complicated – there was one day when it had to be set up with nine crews and God knows what else. I was starting to feel very sick and rather bloated, and I thought, ooohhh, and I knew I was pregnant. Somehow or other it seemed impossible, but I knew that I was. So I thought I'd phone up several of these abortion clinics which advertise in the *Village Voice* and elsewhere. You *really* get a choice in New York. If you ask around. If you ask someone about such-and-such a one they'll say 'Oh, this one, mid-town, on the east side, very plush, six-inch pile carpets, fresh-cut flowers and everything' and I thought, Oh God, I can't be doing with that. So I went to this place on 13th Street and Park.

It was on the eleventh floor and there was a Puerto Rican doctor and there was the nursing staff. They were terribly efficient. They did a urine sample and it was positive. 'Would you like to stay now or would you like to come back tomorrow?' It was getting a bit late that day so they said why didn't I come back tomorrow. That was convenient as it would be a Friday, it'd give me the weekend to relax.

Well, I went back the following day at about six o'clock in the evening. I waited. It was reasonably pleasant. I waited for about three-quarters of an hour, and you get moved along to the next room where you take off your clothes, put on all the paper gear, and paper slippers. Then we're all sitting about rustling in our paper. And there's this black girl sitting next to me who then started crying. And I found that I was in a position of having to comfort her and tell her that it was going to be all right. She was really shaking and trying to keep it under control, and I concentrated all my energy on her.

They called my name. Went in. Lay down. Feet in the stirrups. Not a local anaesthetic – a general. He wouldn't do a local. In fact, just before I went in there was another drama, because they are very insistent that you don't eat food beforehand. There was a slight emergency because one of the girls had come around from the anaesthetic and was vomiting. She had eaten. The anaesthetist was going crazy. The anaesthetist was a real Brooklyn lady – she used to come out and have a cigarette in between abortions. She had steel-grey hair pulled back in a bun, glasses perched on the end of her nose and a trail of things like stethoscopes falling out of her pockets, so she was a real slob. But terribly sort of nice. And she was reading the girl the riot act. 'You silly little bitch! You could have killed yourself!' They were obviously very scared because abortion clinics in New York are big money. But they are very strictly licensed. And if there is a whiff of anything dramatic – bang goes the licence.

It only took three minutes. You came around virtually immediately. Just feeling a bit woozy. And then, there we were in the next room, in a row, like factory farming, everybody sort of groaning because the one thing they don't tell you is that there is a degree of pain afterwards. They give you something like two Panadol and you stay for a bit. At least half a hour. I stayed about thirty-five minutes. It cost $125 at the time – fantastically reasonable. Abortion is a competitive business in America and that keeps the prices sharp.

All of us were given antibiotics which you were told you must take, and to come back in a week's time for a check-up. I went back and I asked how many others did. Very few did. For the check-up you had to pay an extra $20. Maybe it was an emotional thing too – quite difficult to go back to the same place. There was no question of counselling or anything like that: it was purely physical.

When I calmed down, after the film, I came back to London. I didn't actually tell the man involved that I had taken this unilateral decision to have an abortion, and I felt guilty about that. I anticipated his reaction would be 'You bitch! How could you do it without even telling me?' He'd say, I thought, 'We should have discussed it.' And then I felt a bit like a female chauvinist pig, thinking this goes against everything that I've always felt about men and women and their relationships. But still, I felt I had had the abortion for all the right, sensible reasons. It was too early on in our relationship – we had only been together about five months. I thought that a pregnancy would make Andrew feel trapped. I just felt the pregnancy was a dreadful mistake, and I cursed my own fertility which has been – well, I suppose now I don't think of it as a curse – but then I suppose I felt it had bugged me throughout my adult life.

My experience of contraception – well, I've been through the whole lot. I took the Pill in the 1960s – I was virtually a pioneer of that, even though I really shouldn't have taken it because I had a kidney condition. I stopped using it for a while because the doctors like you to come off it every now and then. I got pregnant. I have used the cap – and got pregnant on that, though the pregnancy miscarried. Then I went back on the Pill again and never stopped using it until I hit thirty-five. And then, leading a rather stressful life and smoking the odd cigarette, and also because I was suffering from what seemed an ever-increasing depression, I stopping using the Pill around then. Within a fortnight, the depression had gone altogether. And it never came back in that same gloomy, black-shroud way. So then I had the coil. And so I got a pelvic infection. I was seriously ill with that. And after that I was told that I would probably never conceive again. Absolutely appalling. That was quite appalling.

From my mid-twenties, I had lived with one person – it was a very stable relationship – for nearly ten years. And I was aware that I wanted to have children, though it never seemed quite the right time. And Jim used to say 'Oh yes, we're going to have children', and I believed him, simply because he was wonderful with children, on a sort of equal-to-equal basis. Till one day, we were at a party and I heard him pronouncing in his confident, flowing, Welsh tones, 'Oh no, Liz and I aren't going to have children – it would ruin our social life.' And something inside me just – well, I was completely *outraged*. And I don't think we ever resolved this. Ultimately, it was probably the main reason why I left him.

I know that if I had pushed it with him, if I had accidentally-on-purpose got pregnant, it would have been all right. He would have indulged me. But I really felt I couldn't do that. I felt I couldn't possibly let him ever say 'You tricked me' or 'You wanted the child, so get on with it'. I didn't want that. With Jim, it would have had to have been a partnership.

All this is quite ironic when applied to the circumstances that I am in now. Because in getting pregnant with Sam [her two-year-old son], well, as it turned out, I had to do it alone. There was no partnership. Getting pregnant with Sam was a disastrous accident at the time – though I feel dreadful about talking about it as an accident now. I wouldn't be without Sam for *anything*. And it has in many ways completely changed my thinking about everything. And it has also made me rethink the whole business of abortion. Very much so. As a general issue. Because I found that when I became pregnant with Sam that abortion was used *against me* as a real weapon. I think it's rather odd and somewhat ironic that if easy abortion did not exist, then more than likely Sam's father and me and Sam would be living together in probably quite happy circumstances. But because it does exist, he was able to say 'I want you to have an abortion and if you don't, I don't want to have a child with you' – to say appalling and dreadful things to me to try and force me to have an abortion.

And I felt, then – all the years of struggling uphill to try and attain some sort of equality and pull my own weight and to be an equal with men! It was as though I had landed on a snake and gone right down to the bottom of the board, with a man saying to me, exercising a supreme male prerogative, 'If you don't do this thing, you will be punished and you will always realize that you are being punished.'

After Liz left Jim, she commuted between London and New York working on film and television production. She met Andrew, in London, and they had begun to live together. They got on very well. for a whole year, there wasn't a cross word. She didn't tell him about the abortion in New York, because she felt it was her fault, even though she had been told she would not conceive again due to the pelvic infection. When she had the post-abortion check-up the gynaecologist told her that the pregnancy was a fluke, it was still unlikely she would conceive again. Though she continued usually to use a cap, just in case. When she became pregnant with Sam – about eight months after the New York abortion – it was an accident, though Liz admits to a certain degree of devil-may-care feelings about it, alongside a feeling of awe for her own ability to conceive.

I got pregnant again really for embarrassing teenage reasons. I got rather drunk and went to bed without cleaning my teeth or putting in my cap, and in the middle of the night . . . I didn't even remember it the next morning. I said to him 'Did something happen last night?' And he was all rather sheepish and boyish and 'you-seemed-to-enjoy-it' sort of thing. And I said, 'But I think that's a really bad time for that to have happened.' And then I said, 'Well, never mind, I'm sure it will probably be all right.'

Two weeks later I was being violently sick all over the place.

If Liz thought she was protecting Andrew from feeling trapped by terminating the first pregnancy without his knowledge, she had somewhat misjudged the situation. Informed of the second pregnancy, he was furious. He did not want the child. He did everything to persuade Liz to have an abortion.

He was going on at me up until I was seven months pregnant. When I was nearly seven months, he phoned me up and said he had found some place that would do abortions at this stage. He was all the time going on about it. Seven months pregnant!

In this, Andrew – who was involved with a left-wing

political scene – was aided and abetted by feminist friends.

Part of Andrew's personality is a desire to be approved of. When I was pregnant with Sam, he spoke to a lot of women about it. Mostly a lot of women in their early thirties with no children. And I was terribly hurt. I felt: these young women who certainly say they believe in equality, yet somehow they fail to understand what equality means – it does mean sharing the responsibility. But there was an acceptance by them that abortion was the only thing.

But my instinct was powerful. There was no way I could have had an abortion this time. I knew that if I had another abortion, I would not have survived. I don't think I could have lived with it. It would have been enormously self-destructive. I would have been destroying a really important part of me, and probably the better part. And that was my self-preservation, in knowing that I couldn't have an abortion now.

Also, in between-times, I had decided that I wanted to do a series of films about women and their fertility. I decided that fertility was very little examined as the mainspring of the female. It was something that was taken for granted, looked on as a problem. Complete infertility is looked on with some degree of sympathy or understanding. But fertility – well, it was like oxygen. It was there. But a problem. World fertility is looked on as a problem. Over-population. We are always shouting loudly at Third World women that they have got to contain their fertility – either to be sterilized, or for the men to have vascectomies, and it's all a great problem. Your children, your wombs, they are draining the world – you women and your fertile wombs! So I started to get interested in this. I started doing some research. I went around the hospitals and I started to see all the latest equipment and scans and all the rest of it.

And suddenly, it was as though the *biological* me, to whom I'd said 'Shut up – sit down! I don't want to know you! You are a problem' all these years, replied, saying,

'Move over! I'm sick of all this head-wanking that you indulge in and everything else – *I* want my time in the world as well.' I started seeing tiny little embryos and foetuses. And they didn't look at all like lumps of tissue. And something was gnawing away. And that's when I went through some enormous guilt about that last abortion. I just became incredibly miserable about it.

It's very complex for women, especially when they get into their thirties, especially for women who have flung themselves into a career and interesting work. And I think they are inclined to ignore that side – the female side of their lives – or only confess to it among close girlfriends or perhaps their close male friends, but I have my doubts how much men can really comprehend. I think women in their thirties march to a different beat of time than men. Men in their thirties are young and thrusting and dynamic, but when a woman gets to thirty-five she's seldom described as young. And suddenly the biological self is there, saying, 'Wait a minute, *I* have a right to a place in the sun as well.' And I think that's probably the greatest dilemma for women who have waited, who have sought a life outside the traditional woman's place. Everything that we put on the back burner for so long – it suddenly rushes out and wants attention.

Somehow, I just knew about this pregnancy. I knew that I wasn't going to abort it, I knew that I wasn't going to lose it. I knew that I couldn't have an abortion because I knew this time I would be killing a baby. It wasn't just getting rid of foetal tissue. I had almost like that real Catholic feeling – *the sanctity of human life.* As though – this life – it was meant to be. My background was, in fact, Scottish Presbyterian. Heavy on guilt. Heavy on sin. The moral sense is still there. Very much so. And strangely enough, now, I wouldn't be without it.

I was in my youth in the 1960s and I did it all, over the top, loved it all, don't regret any of it whatsoever – and put guilt completely out of my mind. My first job in television was on a pop music show and I thought, 'This is *work*? This is one long party!' But deep down I was always this very moral girl who wanted to be monogamous, and wanted to have a family. My own family are still a terrific support to me. Even though they are halfway across the world, I feel their loyalty.

Although I knew I wasn't going to lose the baby, I had a physically ghastly pregnancy. I was sick all the time for about four months. Then I had about three weeks when I felt vaguely all right. And then it got worse again, and I ended up with toxaemia. In the last week, I put on eighteen pounds in one week which was fluid. And then Sam was at risk when he was being born – I had a haemorrhage the day before, in Kensington High Street. People carefully stepped around me, and I had to get myself to hospital as best I could.

But ever since he was born, he has been the most perfect child. Absolutely perfect. No problem whatsoever. It's almost as if I knew – the world would be a dimmer place without him. A sunny nature, a funny little boy, bright, absolutely charming and delightful.

Andrew treated me like no man should ever treat a woman during my pregnancy. At any time, indeed. Left alone, except for the nagging calls about abortion. If a good friend hadn't offered me a place in her home at the time I don't know what I'd have done. Yet this was the man with whom I'd got on so well. It wasn't a great passion, we just liked each other so much. And I think, now, in my dotage, that this is by far the best basis for any kind of relationship. It just seems a pity that it was all wasted.

Andrew is thirty-five, thirty-six. Very spoilt and indulged. Eldest son of elderly parents. His parents had given him a blueprint for his life: prep school, public school, Cambridge. They live in rather genteel thrift in Hampshire and are rather proud of him because he's done terribly well.

When I was about three-and-a-half months pregnant, his mother phoned me up. I had met her – I had stayed in her house. She is of rather rigid opinions, of Tory persuasions. A rather keen churchgoer in a Church-of-England, social way. It's Lady So-and-So's benefit for the bell tower, and the bridge club, and this sort of thing. And she phoned me and said, 'I shall be coming up to London on such-and-such a day, and would you meet me for tea at the Charing Cross Hotel?' I thought this sounded like something out of the 1940s, but along I went. And there she was. But it wasn't like out of the '40s; they didn't have cucumber sandwiches, just the odd soggy digestive biscuit and they were doing up the tea-room so there were ladders everywhere.

Andrew's mother was in her early seventies, and opened the conversation by telling me that she knew what had happened, and asking me, quite cordially, what I was going to do about it. I said, simply, 'I'm pregnant, and I don't understand what you're getting at.' She asked me if I would consider having an abortion. And I told her, 'I'm sorry, I really can't.' I explained that I had already had had two abortions, one when I was younger. You know, my mother wasn't here in this country with me and I thought she might be a little bit motherly. She had two children herself. Instead, she launched into a confessional of her own. She had been married before, she explained, to a man who had been an alcoholic. She had got pregnant. 'You have to understand,' she said. 'I couldn't possibly have had that child because the man was an alcoholic.' She was talking about the 1940s, before Andrew was even born. So there I was patting her on the hand saying, 'Of course I understand.' And she was telling me this story to say 'All sorts of people have abortions. The most unlikely people. Why, *I myself* have had an abortion.'

I was saying – 'Well, that's all right, you know, I *quite* understand. But you subsequently remarried and you went on to have two children and rebuild your life. Please try now and understand *me*.' I did actually say to her – 'I can't say that I am madly in love with your son, but I love your son, we get on very well together, but please understand me that I can't have an abortion and I would really like you to respect my reasons for it. Not that I am trying to thwart your son in any way whatsoever. I really do understand what he is going through, but I wish you could understand what *I* am going though.'

Then she tried a different tack. She said how much she had enjoyed meeting me in the past, how much her daughter, too, had liked me and wanted me to go and stay in Scotland. And finally, she made it clear that if only I would choose abortion, everything would be paid for, the best doctor in Harley Street would do it.

As we were about to leave, I told her that I was booked for an amniocentesis test. She showed keen interest. I told her that the only circumstances in which I *would* contemplate a termination would be if there was anything wrong with the baby. She perked up in hope. Perhaps there would be something wrong with the baby and an abortion would ensue! Her son let off the hook! She took out her diary and enquired as to the date of the test. I told her. Then, she said the family would love me to come down to the country and stay with them after that. We parted then, and I thought, 'Well, even if Andrew and I aren't together, you will be our baby's grandmother.' I felt this was rather important as I had had a very close relationship with my grandmother.

As the pregnancy progressed, Andrew was silent, most of the time, but his mother did phone, asking about the amniocentesis test. It was done, as usual, around the sixteenth week and a couple of weeks passed before the result was through. As soon as the news came through that everything seemed fine, Liz phoned the woman she thought of as her child's grandmother.

I told her everything was fine. The baby was healthy. 'Oh,' she said, and there was a long pause. I asked her about the weekend I was supposed to come and see her. 'Oh I'm terribly sorry,' she said, 'but there's a bazaar at the church that weekend and we've got some relatives coming over to stay, so it won't be possible.' And that was the last I ever heard from her.

When Sam was nine weeks old, I sent her a photograph of him, thinking that she was obviously dying to see him, her first and only grandchild, but she feels she can't because she's behaved so badly. I was so thrilled with him that I thought I would be magnanimous and make this gesture to her. I remembered that when I had stayed with her previously how she had brought out all the baby pictures of Andrew, how she had told me the whole story of his birth, how he was born in the Middle East because they were stationed there, how she doted on every picture, how she was looking forward to having grandchildren. So I wrote her this letter after Sam's birth and I described him, and said how brilliant he was and handsome, and all those other modest things that mothers say. And I said, 'If you would like to see Sam, please don't hesitate to get in touch with me – I'm sure we can arrange something.' I didn't even get an acknowledgement. I asked Andrew about his mother and he said, 'Well, of course she'd want grandchildren, but not this way.'

For heaven's sakes – what do you have to do to be accepted by your grandparents?

In a way – and I'm sure that this is what it is all about – the fact that I didn't have an abortion is a reproach to her, for her own abortion. She is the sort of person who is so deeply repressed that, at seventy-two or three, it's too late for her to admit this, to come to terms with it. But it's sad for *her*. Because she is denying herself one of the supreme pleasures in life as a woman – of being a grandmother. You ask any grandmother. My mother, though she's at the other side of the world, and she has four other grandchildren, just idolizes Sam already. It is so sad that his paternal grandparents won't even acknowledge him. Andrew's father, too, is denied the chance of knowing the child. He's in his eighties. He's such an old potterer – I don't think he has ever taken a stand about anything really. But Sam is *his* only grandchild too. Their daughter, Jane, she doesn't look as though she's going to produce any children. *She's* had an abortion. I had to hear all about that as well. Jane went to Greece, met a Greek and came back pregnant. That had to be got rid of, of course. Not respectable, you see.

Admittedly, I was not easy to deal with when I was pregnant because I was unwell. I felt ghastly, I was under such stress, and I used to have hysterics every time I spoke to Andrew. I used to always end up in floods of tears. And I know that's dreadfully off-putting for a man. But I couldn't bear his going on and on about an abortion. I really feel in a way there should be a code of conduct in pregnancy. Men should learn it as they learn common manners. I don't think it is up to the man to go on and on about abortion to the woman. For the woman, it is her body, it is not his body. He has done his bit. She is pregnant. If she says 'I think I should have an abortion' or 'I'm thinking about it' and invites him into the discussion about it . . . and I think women should do that too. I recognize now that the way I treated the abortion previous to Sam, it was bad behaviour, too. I should have consulted.

Liz felt really and truly fulfilled by motherhood, and by the birth of the perfect Sam, who was an everyday joy. She took a lot of time off working, just because she wanted to enjoy motherhood. When I last saw her, Andrew was still not really reconciled to fatherhood. And his parents had still not acknowledged their grandchild, though they were continuing to work in the cause of the local church.

Liz is not bitter but she is sad on Sam's account, that the child might be rejected by his paternal family, especially since her family is so far away. And she is very reflective, too, about the spirit of the times which has made us all what we are.

We were so arrogantly cocky in the 1960s and '70s! We thought we knew it all. And yet, we accepted things so easily. We accepted the Pill without question. And we thought it was marvellous. It meant we could go out all the time and go to bed with whoever we pleased. But we didn't really want to go to bed with whoever we pleased. We just wanted to try it on, to see how far you could go. Real maturity is realizing that you don't have to go to bed with people, that you can just as well have a cup of tea with them and, in some ways, it turns out just as nice.

Men like you just as much for *not* going to bed with them, funnily enough.

And then there was this thing about abortion, in the '60s and '70s. Abortion became so much easier. I remember Germaine Greer wildly proclaiming to the women of the world that here was another new thing that was going to liberate women further, and that was the lunchtime abortion. In at noon, out at two.

I don't renounce or denounce women's liberation as it happened to my generation. It was quite revolutionary and it was exciting and you get carried away by the momentum and you want things to happen quickly. It is only as time goes by that we start to see that some of the things about it were a bit off-the-wall or a bit ill-informed. We thought contraceptive freedom, abortion freedom were the be-all and the end-all. But it is all a lot more complex than that. Contraception and abortion can be used *against* women just as much as it may be used for them. Contraception is complex because most women actually want to know if they *can* conceive. The Pill has done this to women, in a way, because the Pill puts women into a biologically infertile state. And then women come off it . . . and I know some extremely intelligent and clever women who have behaved like idiotic sixteen-year-olds – Russian-roulette style – because they want to know if they *can* get pregnant.

Feminism began by claiming abortion as a great thing, but it's a personal matter and very complex. Most people who I know who have had abortions say that. I have a friend who is extraordinarily tough and terribly masculine in her sexual conduct. Doesn't give a damn, you know. She became pregnant – she is also very ambitious and has a very good job. There was no question whatsoever of continuing the pregnancy. It was an immediate abortion. And she went to this abortion clinic in Brighton.

She told me she took the train to Brighton, thinking 'Oh, jolly day down at Brighton, go on the beach, get a silly hat and a stick of rock, have an abortion' – I mean, she's like that. Outrageous. She got down there and she went to the clinic, and suddenly, it started to dawn on her that it wasn't really very funny. Ridiculous, she thought, babies, who wants them? That's for other silly women – not for me. And afterwards, she was completely shattered. Walk on the pier? – No. She took a taxi to the station, cried all the way back to London. It just tapped something inside her she hardly knew was there. Actually, it broke her heart. She never suspected she would take it that way. She only told me about it recently. Otherwise, nobody would ever know.

That is the story of abortion, really. Most of the time, nobody ever knows.

12

THE FUTURE OF ABORTION

'"So you are going to have quads the year after next . . ." said Jacqueline slowly. The implication was left hanging, questioningly; and when David and Angela nodded, everyone present drew the obvious conclusion. The young couple had had their genetic material frozen, to be stored for a year or so, when it would be nurtured by ectogenesis . . . Like David and Angela, modern-minded couples were avoiding pregnancy by arranging for their future family to spend its first nine months in a laboratory.' – Peter Singer and Deane Wells, *The Reproduction Revolution*

'She finds all the talk about "the right to control our bodies" (she pronounces it in a mocking American drawl) rather silly. "Nobody has a right not to feel pain. We should have been talking about the right to choose our reproductive destiny."' – Germaine Greer, interviewed by Frances Cairncross, *Guardian*

What will the future of abortion be? In the 1980s, we are in the middle of a dynamic reproductive revolution which touches so many aspects of pregnancy, conception, procreation, termination and birth. From the moment the first test-tube baby was born, on 25 July 1978, we entered a new era in human fertility and the way in which we regard it.

In retrospect, it is obvious why the social pressure for abortion arose. By the time we entered the twentieth century, abortion was becoming medically possible as an operative procedure. However strong the moral taboo was against abortion – and it was, and remains, considerable – such a double standard was bound to become unacceptable in an increasingly democratic age. And with so many other social changes in the wind during the 1960s – liberalization of divorce, recognition of prostitution, legalization of homosexuality, availability of the contraceptive Pill, the rise of post-war feminism with its new, bold style – abortion seemed an inescapable part of the picture. By the 1960s, too, the technology of abortion, with the introduction of the vacuum aspirator, had become remarkably easy.

However, history does not stand still, and social events and innovations change perspective. Lecky reminds us in his history of morals that certain oppressions, such as slavery, started out as enlightened measures.

And technology will almost certainly alter our perspectives on abortion. Many people today consider abortion humane and sensible – indeed, they consider it inevitable. At the very least, better to have safe and legal abortion than dangerous and criminal abortion; and it is, many would say, finally, for the woman to decide whether her body is to be pregnant or not. But if we develop half the technologies that the reproductive engineers are predicting for the future, will this not alter abortion again? Supposing, as seems very likely, a commercial test were available which could discover whether an egg was fertilized the day after sexual intercourse took place – would that not make abortion at eight, ten, fourteen, sixteen or twenty weeks seem obscene? Supposing better techniques of viewing the growing foetus from a very early stage are developed, so that we could see the six-week foetus – which looks like a very tiny human form – on a colour television screen, would that change our view of abortion? Supposing embryo transfer became a reality: supposing a doctor could 'wash out' a small embryo from a woman's uterus, freeze it and store it for possible future use, or transfer it to another woman who offered herself as a host mother? Since the birth of Louise Brown we have already seen formidable developments in the area of reproductive techniques: embryo freezing, commercial surrogate mothers, sperm banks, egg donation.

What has all this to do with abortion? The answer is that the reproduction revolution is redefining the whole framework of abortion. In his book about this, Peter Singer prophesies that in our lifetime, ectogenesis will be a reality. Ectogenesis means the possibility of developing a foetus outside of the womb – in a laboratory with an artificial womb and placenta. In 1971, Singer and his co-author Wells note that doctors in Australia were working hard to save babies weighing 1,500 grams at birth. 'Those weighing under 1,000 grams were allowed to die because nothing could be done for them.' By 1981, he learned, a baby weighing just 470 grams at birth had been born and treated at the Queen Victoria Medical Centre: though three and a half months premature, the child pulled through, survived and is healthy and normal. Thus the authors foresee the day when smaller and smaller babies survive a very early birth, and it will be possible to keep the immature foetus alive in laboratory conditions from almost any stage in pregnancy.

Some regard the immediate prospect of ectogenesis as fanciful. It is absolutely true that babies have now survived from a pregnancy of twenty-three weeks' gestation – while babies who have died at twenty-three weeks are still regarded as a miscarriage, and cannot legally be buried, since anomalies in the law mean that it is considered impossible for a child to survive before twenty-eight weeks. But, for the moment, there is no system available which will keep an immature infant's lungs artificially working below this twenty-three-week mark. So ectogenesis is not, for the moment, on the agenda. Yet Singer and Wells welcome its future prospect. Ecotogenesis, they believe, would bring together pro-abortionists and anti-abortionists in happy unity.

If the feminist argument for abortion takes its stand on

> the right of women to control their own bodies, feminists at least should not object. Freedom to choose what is to happen to one's body is one thing; freedom to insist on the death of a being that is capable of living outside one's body is another. At present these two are inextricably linked and so the woman's freedom to choose conflicts head-on with the alleged right to life of the foetus. When ectogenesis becomes possible these two issues will break apart, and women will choose to terminate their pregnancies without thereby choosing the inevitable death of the foetus they are carrying.

Ectogenesis would, in fact, present a huge new set of ethical problems, but it would indeed change the specific ethical problem which at present surrounds abortion: do we have the right to take another life, however small, because we personally do not want it? Ectogenesis would mean another alternative to abortion, as in embryo transfer: a woman with an unwanted pregnancy may then be faced with such questions as, 'In terminating your own pregnancy, would you care to donate the embryo to someone else who *does* want it?'

But what is already taking place is that the technology now being used in pregnancy is subtly changing the way we view foetal development. 'Usually, a mother first experiences parental bonding when she feels her child move,' wrote the woman's magazine *Options* in November 1983, reiterating what has always been historically an important moment in pregnancy – animation.

> But technology is pushing back this experience to a much earlier stage of pregnancy for both parents: when they see the image of their unborn child on the ultrasound screen. This is becoming a routine procedure and is an excellent checking device.
>
> Ultrasound is a 'non-invasive' technique – the image is produced by bouncing sound waves off the foetus, with the shape of the child drawn by patterns in the reflected sound waves – which doesn't interfere internally with either mother or child.

> But although there seem to be few purely physical effects, judging from the correspondence columns of a recent issue of the *New England Journal of Medicine*, the emotional and social implications of ultrasound are far from limited. The letters provide evidence of how parental bonds can be formed by seeing this image of the child. The most charming letter is from a father who first saw his son of seventeen weeks on screen, then proudly showed the pictures to his colleagues, saying 'You wanna see a picture of my kid?' Another correspondent maintains 'visualization' of the child should make health education easier – the dangers of smoking, drinking and the benefit of a healthy diet make more sense if related to this early image.
>
> So it seems that ultrasound can provide a window on the womb and has, therefore, far-reaching social and emotional consequences.

'Far-reaching social and emotional consequences' – yes indeed. The American philosopher Richard Wasserstrom once wondered if the uterus had been transparent, if we could *see* the foetus developing – would our attitude to it be different? And many physicians working in this area say that when people can see the foetus, their attitude is different.

'Recent advances in medical technology have revolutionized our understanding of the intra-uterine life of the foetus,' wrote consultant radiologist Patrick Gill of West Glamorgan. 'This has been, until lately, an unknown being in an opaque womb. Ultrasound scanning has changed all this. As early as twelve weeks of age, the foetus can be seen, by doctor and mother, with its obvious human form and beating heart, visible in the womb. Even earlier, at six weeks, with this technique, it is possible to see the foetus, though not as clearly as at twelve weeks due to lack of sensitivity of the current machines. Yet even here the foetal heartbeat can be noticed.'

Not only is the effect on women that of a new sensitivity towards foetal life, but the effect on men is immeasurable. Fathers do not normally 'bond' with their children until a baby is weaned or even beginning to talk. The new technology can bring it home to a father what it is to have a child. 'I must say, seeing Edward on the ultrasound screen at twelve weeks' pregnancy did make me think again about abortion,' says a man who has always taken an open and liberal view of abortion. 'It certainly presents you with rigid evidence of the living reality of the unborn child.' He is still, he says, not anti-abortion. But he is now in little doubt of what exactly it entails.

There will, I think, be fewer serious arguments about the foetus being a 'blob of jelly' in view of our modern technology.

The changes which have taken place are part of greater changes within the whole field of obstetrics. In *The Captured Womb*, the feminist writer Ann Oakley expresses a certain amount of anger that the limelight, in obstetrics, has moved from the mother to the baby. At least until the Second World War, in childbirth the mother was basically regarded as the important unit. Earlier, this was even more so. In Edmund Gosse's autobiography, *Father and Son*, he tells that as a new-born baby he himself was all but forgotten. The advent of his birth was recorded thus in his father's diary: 'E. delivered of a son. Received green swallow from Jamaica.'

> Long afterwards, my Father told me that my Mother suffered much in giving birth to me, and that, uttering no cry, I appeared to be dead. I was laid, with scant care, on another bed in the room, while all anxiety and attention were concentrated on my Mother. An old woman who happened to be there, and who was unemployed, turned her thoughts to me, and tried to awake in me a spark of vitality. She succeeded, and she was afterwards complimented by the doctor on her cleverness. My Father could not recollect the name of my preserver.

In days when babies were plentiful, and often accepted

with resignation, less attention was paid to the infant, be it inside or outside the womb. It was a great source of Victorian grief that many mothers died in childbirth. However, now that maternal mortality has been so dramatically reduced (see page 121), the focus of attention has passed to the baby, since it is still a mystery why babies die *in utero*, why pregnancy develops complications, why habitual miscarriages occur.

The technology which enables physicians to visualize the foetus has also made its impact. 'The foetus is being looked upon as a patient now,' Dr Alan Fleishmann, a New York specialist in the care of the new-born, told the London *Standard* correspondent Jeremy Campbell in 1985.

> That is the big difference and it has come about suddenly. In the recent past we treated the mother. Today, we think of her as a vehicle for treating the foetus. This has increased the moral standing of the unborn. It has changed the way we think about abortion. People will decide that the foetus has a moral status as early as the first ten weeks of pregnancy. That is when we can do a biopsy, screen for genetic defects. Irregular heartbeats and vitamin deficiencies can be corrected at fifteen weeks.
>
> The question now is, if some foetuses have the same rights as a patient, should all foetuses have those rights?

Dr Ernie Young, of Stanford University's School of Medicine – where they specialize in caring for very premature babies – also pinpoints the development of foetal technology as undermining abortion rights. 'Gynaecologists are sensitive individuals and many of them are beginning to feel a revulsion about abortion procedures. And abortionists are being somewhat looked down upon in the medical profession. And the major reason for this is the astonishing progress made in being able to see the unborn child moving about in the mother's body.'

In a sense this is ironic, because the feminists of the late

1960s and early '70s who looked forward to more technology in reproduction, foresaw it as a means of relieving women from the burdens of physical pregnancy. It was not foreseen as something which would re-evaluate the rights of the foetus. In her influential feminist prophecy, *The Dialectic of Sex*, written in 1969, Shulamith Firestone looked forward enthusiastically to the artificial womb and the foetus in the laboratory as a means of advancing *women's* freedom.

When the Warnock Report on *in vitro* fertilization and other linked issues – artificial insemination by donor (AID), surrogate parenting – was published in 1984, it became the basis for intense discussion, and parliamentary debate, on the ethics of the new reproductive technologies. The Warnock Report gave its blessing to experimentation with the human embryo up to fourteen days' development. This was fiercely and bitterly disputed. Warnock had finally settled for fourteen days because this is the point at which the 'primitive streak' appears in the embryo – the point at which, scientifically speaking, the embryo manifests individual human characteristics. Critics of Warnock replied by saying that it was unethical to experiment with human embryos at all – a viewpoint which has quite strong public support, as the idea of scientists playing around with human material has overtones of Frankenstein. Scientists, including the original *in vitro* pioneers, Patrick Steptoe and Robert Edwards, have pleaded that they must work with embryos to solve certain problems. In order to discover the cause of Down's syndrome, to find out why many genetically-transmitted disabilities occur, to research miscarriage and to save women from distressing late abortions, Mr Steptoe has argued, it is necessary to do experimental work on embryos. The editor of the *Journal of Medical Ethics*, Dr Rannon Gillon, has said that: 'It is irrational to prevent research on early embryos if one accepts that abortion is permissible. The human embryo becomes relevant gradually. Early on in its development one doesn't have to treat it with respect.' Various scientists and scientific journals claim they would draw the line at experimenting, or even interfering with, the embryo at twenty-two or twenty-three or perhaps thirty days' development. Certainly nothing after six weeks' gestation, when a rudimentary consciousness as the embryonic specialists say, is present in the unborn. Yet we abort at twenty-six weeks! All this is inevitably moving towards a position where abortion will be less and less acceptable in the middle and later stages of pregnancy.

I do not think that abortion will go away – certainly not in the immediate future. It is highly convenient, it is widely accepted as a fact of life, and it is institutionalized in the health services and in the private sector. Moreover, the notion that you can now reverse a pregnancy has been stamped into public consciousness. A woman who recalled going to her doctor in 1966, distraught with the knowledge that she was pregnant, remembers the doctor saying to her firmly: 'You are pregnant – and *there is nothing you can do about it*.' She looks back now on this episode as though from another age – which indeed it is. We know that there is plenty you can do about it. Abortion technology is there to be used, and it will not be dis-invented. It is not so much abortion in itself that is regarded with a feeling of welcome and relief by wide sectors of the population: it is the idea that pregnancy can be reversed. 'We are here,' said a counsellor at Marie Stopes to me, 'to give women the chance to put the clock back.'

In a sense, contraception itself is now changing to *include* early abortion, or as some people put it, 'retrospective contraception'. The word 'contragestion' is also used to conflate preventing pregnancy before coitus, and preventing the implantation of pregnancy after coitus. The IUD and the 'morning-after' or post-coital pill are steps which blur the division between preventing conception taking place before the act and dissolving it after the fact.

In the early days of the birth control battles – in the 1920s and 1930s – contraception campaigners such as Marie Stopes and Margaret Sanger were emphatic about never confusing abortion with contraception. Marie

Stopes took great care never to advise abortion, and Margaret Sanger was committed to the view that preventing conception was the key to health for overburdened mothers, but added: 'Do not take life.' These views are now considered outdated by the successors to Stopes and Sanger. Contraception and abortion are regarded as a 'package' – and indeed the 'package' generally now involves sterilization as well. Dr Timothy Black of the Marie Stopes clinic actually believes that some aspects of the traditional advocacy of contraception is now hopelessly middle-class and fuddy-duddy. 'All this "family planning" is very middle-class and very Western. Poor women in poor countries do not have an opportunity to "plan" their families. To take the contraceptive Pill every day – you have to have an obsessive personality anyhow.' For him, 'retrospective contraception' – that is, very early abortion as part of the 'package' is the way forward. 'In future, women will be able to discover very quickly whether they are pregnant, and if they are and don't want to be, will very quickly have an early abortion. Walk in, walk out, no big deal.' Restrospective birth control is more satisfactory for many women, he points out, because it helps them to keep a check on their fertility. Some women have taken contraceptive measures for twenty years – only to discover they were infertile anyway. What a lot of time and trouble they might have been saved if they could have relied instead on early abortion!

Some of this may sound perilously close to the 'abortion chic' advanced by some American feminists in the 1970s – the decision to get pregnant and have an abortion just to prove solidarity with the abortion movement, to prove one's absolute freedom of decision-making. But many women – they would not even need to be ardent anti-abortionists – would regard the notion of getting pregnant deliberately just to check your fertility as having a cavalier approach to human life. Moreover, the 'walk in, walk out, no big deal' view of abortion may diminish the importance of the decision in the eyes of so many women. A spokeswoman for the National Abortion Campaign emphasized, in speaking to me, that while they supported the woman's right to choose an abortion whenever she thought best, they appreciated what a very serious decision it was for many women. To diminish the seriousness of it may not be serving women's interests best at all.

However, the quick and early abortion points to the way things are going. The next most important step in view is the abortion pill, which has already been tried in France with some success.* Once the abortion pill is perfected, Dr Black believes, it will truly revolutionize abortion. When the abortion pill gets on to the black market – no pun intended for the aforesaid doctor – it will make much of present legislation about abortion redundant. At present, the law says that a pregnancy should be established before it is terminated. When the abortion pill arrives, women will quite simply be circumventing that, so that the entire legislative structure may have to be revised. On the other hand, the law may become irrelevant. Early abortion by the method of the prostaglandin pill may just enter the realm of private behaviour – much as, today, is the smoking of marijuana. (Theoretically, smoking marijuana is illegal, but de facto it is tolerated. Where people are charged with the possession of cannabis it is nearly always as a cover for some other crime which cannot be proven – rather like Al Capone being sent to jail for tax evasion.)

Abortion will not, therefore, go away – but it will change. With all these new techniques, there will be easier access to earlier abortion. Screening for genetic defects in the unborn will become technically possible earlier and earlier in pregnancy. And by the same token, better techniques for visualizing the unborn will make later abortion more and more unacceptable. This has been a

---

* The abortion pill, named the RU 486, in French trials showed that 70 per cent of women aborted completely at five to seven weeks; 20 per cent had incomplete abortions which had to be completed surgically; 10 per cent did not abort. At eight to ten weeks, 50 per cent aborted completely, 35 per cent had incomplete abortions (completed surgically) and 15 per cent did not abort. For this report I am grateful to Miss Anna Flynn, MB, FRCOG, of Birmingham Maternity Hospital.

progressive trend anyway. In the nineteenth century, babies under one year old were not regarded as proper human beings – until 1850, they were not registered for 'birth' purposes until they had completed twelve months of life outside the womb. The whole drift of child-care during the twentieth century has been to regard babies more and more as individual human personalities, not only after birth but in the last months of pregnancy. And technology is pushing back this recognition of the early human form for its unique personhood earlier and earlier.

Many European countries already draw the line at routine abortion after the first trimester of pregnancy – between twelve and fourteen weeks. In Britain there is no political will at the moment to alter the law which allows abortion so much later than most other countries because of the way abortion politics divide up. That is to say, on the right-to-choose, or pro-abortion, side of Parliament (and outside of it), *any* move to alter abortion freedom is seen as an attack on women's rights. On the right-to-life, or anti-abortion side, any mere amendment of abortion legislation is regarded as conceding the moral point that abortion should be permitted at all. So both sides are committed to an absolute situation. The usual English notion that you can always find a compromise just does not apply here.

At the same time, there are a lot of people who are vaguely in the middle – who feel that abortion is sometimes justified, but not really acceptable as an everyday occurrence just the same. (An *Observer* poll of September 1984 showed that only 5 per cent of the British public thought abortion was 'too difficult' to get, and 33 per cent thought it was positively 'too easy'. As is usual, substantially more women than men thought the abortion laws too lax.) And there would probably be widespread support for the utilitarian view put forward by Janet Radcliffe Richards that abortion should always be done before the stage where the foetus is capable of suffering. And that, again, would pitch it at around twelve to fourteen weeks.

Of course, there will always be women who are

unlucky, who find out only quite late on in a pregnancy that they are pregnant, whose circumstances change and who suddenly discover, in the middle of pregnancy, that they don't want a baby after all. But as society today says to a woman who presents for abortion at twenty-four weeks 'sorry – you're too late' – so society will simply draw that line earlier on in future times. When the technology makes it possible, indeed doctors will say instead: 'You can terminate the pregnancy, yes – by offering a foetal transplant to a woman who cannot conceive.'

'Don't you accept abortion, nowadays, on any grounds?' a friend asked me when I spoke about my own odyssey through the dark forest of the abortion conflict. All I could reply was that I understand wholly why women want to reverse pregnancy, and I could think of so many cases where a woman had excellent reasons for wanting to do so. But an anti-abortionist is in the same position as an anti-vivisectionist: even if it can be shown that experimenting on live animals brings useful results, the anti-vivisectionist has to stick by the principle that experimenting on live animals is wrong. And even where abortion can be shown to be useful and sensible, if you feel in your bones that it is wrong, you have to adhere to that conviction. It is not a Roman Catholic principle; it is a Lutheran one. 'Here I stand. I cannot do otherwise.'

I can think of one very compelling case in particular where a woman had every good reason for an abortion. She was forty-one years of age when she discovered she was pregnant for the fourth time. Her two oldest children were fully-grown teenagers, and her third child was ten. Her husband was in his sixties. Her elderly mother was living with her, and ailing. Times were hard. There was a war on, and rations were modest. She really was in despair as to know how she would cope with another child. She wept for weeks when the pregnancy was confirmed, and felt deeply depressed. But in those days, women generally accepted pregnancy with resignation, so she just gritted her teeth and carried on.

The baby was born in due course. And that baby was me. 'I remember a priest saying to me – "Never mind, that child will be a consolation for you when you are old,"' my mother told me when she recounted the story. And then she added: 'And you are.' I am very glad I was born, and what is far more important, so is she. Not every unwanted pregnancy turns out to be an unwanted person.

I do not say the foetus has a right to life – none of us has that, since we must all die. Perhaps a chance of life is the appropriate phrase. 'I didn't ask to be born,' the Irish novelist Kate O'Brien once wrote to me. 'But had I been consulted, and whatever the difficulties and pain I was to face, how could I possibly have refused?'

BIBLIOGRAPHY

Anstruther, Ian, *The Scandal of the Andover Workhouse*, Bles, 1973.

Ardetti, Rita, et al., *Test-Tube Women*, Pandora Press, 1984. A radical feminist perspective on test-tube and new reproduction technology.

Badinter, Elisabeth, *The Myth of Motherhood*, Souvenir Press, 1981. A French feminist dissects the maternal instinct and finds it wanting.

Benet, M.K., *The Character of Adoption*, Jonathan Cape, 1976. A description of adoption laws and practices.

Berger, Brigitte & Peter, *The War over the Family*, Penguin Books, 1983. Abortion, feminism and similar issues placed under a cool and ironic socio-political analysis.

Bok, Sissela, *Ethical Studies of Abortion*, Institute of Social Ethics and Life Sciences, Vol. 2, No. 1, January, 1974. A very thoughtful discussion on the ethical problems associated with abortion by the respected Swedish philosopher.

Borg, Susan & Lasker, Judith, *When Pregnancy Fails. Coping with Miscarriage, Stillbirth and Infant Death*, Routledge and Kegan Paul, 1982. Case histories about foetal loss and neo-natal loss, including sections on abortion after amniocentesis.

Burtchell, James Tunstead, *Rachel Weeping and Other Essays on Abortion*. Andrews & McMeel Inc., 1982. A rigorously intellectual examination of abortion by a Catholic priest.

Callahan, Daniel, *Abortion: Law, Choice and Morality*, Macmillan (New York), 1970. Still regarded as a classically objective examination of law, choice and morality.

Cheetham, Judith, *Unwanted Pregnancy and Counselling*, Routledge and Kegan Paul, 1977. A social-work approach to counselling in pregnancy.

Dally, Ann, *Inventing Motherhood: The Consequences of an Ideal*, Burnett Books, 1982. A psychiatrist and a mother examine the pressures of motherhood through the ages.

De Mause, Lloyd, *The History of Childhood*, Souvenir Press, 1974. A grim catalogue of some of the horrors, including infanticide, which characterized childhood in the past.

Draper, Elizabeth, *Birth Control in the Modern World*, Penguin Books, 1972. An experienced family planning expert examines the whys and wherefores of birth control.

Faulder, Carolyn, *Whose Body is it? The Troubling Issue of Informed Consent*, Virago, 1985. A medical writer examines patient choice.

Ferguson-Smith, M.A. (ed.), *Early Prenatal Diagnosis*, British Medical Bulletin, 1983. The medical papers on pre-birth screening.

Ferris, Paul, *The Nameless*, Pelican, 1967. An examination of the abortion scene just before the law was changed in England and Wales.

Firestone, Shulamith, *The Dialectic of Sex*, Women's Press, 1979 (first published 1971). The fiery feminist radical's prescription of women's liberation, which included, prophetically, glass wombs.

Foot, Philippa. *Virtues and Vices*, Basil Blackwell, 1978. A discussion of moral problems by a professor of philosophy at UCLA, humanitarian, anti-utilitarian.

Francke, Linda Bird, *The Ambivalence of Abortion*, Penguin Books, 1978. A revealing description of the ambivalence of women's feelings in abortion, as reported by a pro-choice feminist.

Francome, Colin, *Abortion Freedom: A Worldwide Movement*, Allen and Unwin, 1984. A factual description of changes in abortion legislations by a polytechnic sociology lecturer.

Friedman & Gradstein, *Surviving Pregnancy Loss*, Little Brown. A psychological and biological exploration of miscarriage, including ectopic pregnancy and the impact on men.

Gardner, R.F.R., *Abortion – The Personal Dilemma*, Paternoster Press, 1975. A doctor with a Christian commitment and a liberal approach to his patients discusses abortion.

Gibran, Kahlil, *The Prophet*, Pan, 1980. Words of wisdom about birth, death and other eternal values from the Middle East.

Gill, Derek, *Illegitimacy, Sexuality and the Status of Women*, Basil Blackwell, 1977. A social analysis of why single women have babies.

Gilligan, Carol, *In a Different Voice*, Harvard University Press, 1982. A study of the differences in psychological and moral attitudes between men and women.

Glover, Jonathan, *Saving Life and Causing Death*, Pelican, 1981. An Oxford professor gives the utilitarian analysis of life and death.

Gorman, Michael J., *Abortion and the Early Church: Christian, Jewish and Pagan Attitudes in the Greco-Roman World*, Intervarsity Press (Dublin), 1982. A careful study of antiquity.

Gosse, Edmund, *Father and Son*, Penguin Books, 1982 (first published 1907). A celebrated recollection of a religious nineteenth-century childhood.

Grant, Dr Ellen, *The Bitter Pill*, Elm Tree Books, 1985. A swingeing indictment of the 'Perfect Contraceptive'.

Greenwood, Victoria & Young, Jack, *Abortion in Demand*, Pluto Press, 1976. A feminist analysis of abortion politics which irritated doctors and moderate reformers.

Greer, Germaine, *Sex and Destiny*, Secker and Warburg, 1984. Germaine Greer's maverick personal survey of attitudes to fertility.

Hall, Ruth, *Dear Dr Stopes*, Penguin Books, 1978. Letters sent to Marie Stopes from people desperate to control fertility.

Hamblin, Angela (ed.), *The Other Side of Adoption – Natural Mothers Tell Their Stories*, Jigsaw (84 Oakfield Road, London N4 4LB).

Hann, Judith, *The Perfect Baby?* Weidenfeld and Nicolson, 1982. A scientific guide into the choices that will be available for babies in tomorrow's world.

Hardymen, Christina, *Dream Babies*, Jonathan Cape, 1983. How fashions in child-care have altered, from Locke to Spock.

Harris, Harry, *Prenatal Diagnosis and Selective Abortion*, Nuffield Provincial Hospitals Trust, 1974. A slim volume considered a minor classic by geneticists.

Hensley, Jeff Jane (ed.), *The Zero People*. A poignant plea on behalf of the unborn.

Higham, Flores, *Lord Shaftesbury, a Portrait*, S.C.M. Press, 1945. A short biography with particularly heart-rending accounts of child labour in the 1830s.

Hodgson, Jane E. (ed.), *Abortion and Sterilization: Medical and Social Aspects*, Academic Press, 1981. A medical textbook for the specialist.

Huntingford, Peter, *Birth Right: The Parents' Choice*, BBC Publications, 1985. A methodical guide to conception and pregnancy intended to be terminated in birth.

Hutter, Bridget & Williams, Gillian (eds.), *Controlling Women. The Normal and the Deviant*, Croom Helm, 1981. In several different areas, develops the feminist theme that laws are often devised to control women.

Huxley, Aldous, *Brave New World*, Granada, 1982 (first published 1932). The futuristic novel that predicts test-tube technology.

Kevles, Daniel, *Annals of Eugenics, New Yorker* magazine, October 1984. An account of the eugenics movement in the United States which reveals how enormously influential were the 'race improvers' in England and America from 1890 to 1940. Subsequently published in the US as a book.

Kremer, E.J., & Synan, E.A., *Death before Birth: Canada and the Abortion Question*, Griffin House (Toronto), 1974. An account of how a puritanical society altered from being anti-abortion to favouring it. Contains a section which claims that 'wanted' babies are as likely to suffer child abuse as the 'unwanted'.

Kupfermann, Jeannette, *The Ms/taken Body*, Robson Books, 1979. An anthropologist examines the relationship women have with their bodies, with insights such as that Maoris regard menstrual blood as a human being *manqué*.

Lasch, Christopher, *The Culture of Narcissism*, Abacus, 1980. An essay on modern life and its 'Me-Me-Me' ethic.

Leatherd, Audrey, *The Fight for Family Planning*, Macmillan, 1980. The development of Family Planning Services in Britain 1921–74. The story of how birth control won acceptability, with references to death from illegal abortion and to Marie Stopes's somewhat astonishing 'race improvements' theories.

Lehmann, Rosamond, *The Weather in the Streets*, Virago, 1981 (first published 1936). The definitive novel about a 1930s Bohemian love affair and illegal abortion.

Llewelyn Davies, Margaret, *Maternity: Letters from Working Women*, Virago, 1978 (first published 1915). Eye-opening and extremely literate letters from poor women about the circumstances of their lives, just before World War I.

Luker, Kristin, *Taking Chances: Abortion and the Decision not to Contracept*, University of California Press, 1975. A milestone of a book, examining the whys and wherefores of contraceptive failure. A very influential book now causing some experts to consider that for some individuals, the 'costs' of contraception are just not worth the 'benefits' – in fact, some folks would just sooner take the risks than contracept.

Luker, Kristin, *Abortion and the Politics of Motherhood*, University of California Press, 1984. A description of how perspectives on abortion altered from anti to pro.

McAll, Kenneth, *Healing the Family Tree*, Sheldon Press, 1982. Christian healing applied to abortion, miscarriage and other feelings of loss.

MacIntyre, Sally, *Single and Pregnant*, Croom Helm, 1977. Investigations into the attitudes of young women who discover themselves to be single and pregnant.

McMillan, Carol, *Women, Reason and Nature*, Basil Blackwell, 1982. A philosophical critique of feminism.

Mahoney, John (SJ), *Bioethics and Belief*, Sheed and Ward, 1984. A Jesuit of liberal inclinations looks at bioethics.

Mall, David and Watts, Walter, F., *The Psychological Aspect of Abortion*, University publications of America, 1979. A Catholic approach to psychological problems, dealing with difficult subjects like rape and incest.

Marsh, David & Chambers, Joanna, *Abortion Politics*, Junction Books, 1981. Political shenanigans at Westminster on how the abortion battles were fought. Written from the pro-abortion point of view. The villain is definitely the Catholic Church.

Midgley, Mary and Hughes, Judith, *Women's Choices: Philosophical Problems Facing Feminism*. Two women philosophers indicate how complex these problems are.

Mitterauer, Michael, & Sieder, Reinhard, *The European Family*, Basil Blackwell, 1982 (first published Munich, 1977). Patterns of family life mostly in Austria and South Germany in the nineteenth century.

Miura, Archbishop Domyo, *The Forgotten Child*, Aidan Ellis, 1983. An astonishing little book about how the Japanese cope with post-abortion therapy and still-birth through *mizugo* or ritualization. An ancient Eastern answer – a modern problem.

Mohr, James, C., *Abortion in America: The Origins and Evolution of National Policy*, OUP, 1978. A history of nineteenth-century abortion in the United States, with special emphasis on advertising and the drug-quacks.

Moore, George, *Esther Waters*, Everyman, 1977 (first published 1894). A dated, but still heart-rending account of single parenting in the 1890s.

Mount, Ferdinand, *The Subversive Family: An Alternative History of Love and Marriage*, Jonathan Cape, 1982. A maverick view of sex, pregnancy and family politics, showing how durable the family unit is, having been attacked by every agency from Christianity to feminism.

Nathanson, Bernard, MD, with Richard N. Ostling, *Aborting America*, Life Cycle Books (Toronto), 1979 (available from SPUC). A personal and at times, strangely wry story of why a doctor felt moved to do abortions, and then why he changed his mind about the status of the foetus.

Nathanson, Bernard, MD, *The Abortion Papers*, Frederick Fell (New York), 1983. Continuing Dr Nathanson's story about the inside of the abortion debate.

Newson, Gina and Neustatter, Angela, *Mixed Feelings*, Pluto, 1986.

Nilssen, Lennart, *A Child is Born*, Faber and Faber, 1977. Extraordinary photographs of how life develops in the womb with accompanying text. The pictures were very influential in advocating the humanity of the foetus.

Noonan, John T., *A Private Choice. Abortion in America in the Seventies*. Free Press (New York) and Collier Macmillan, 1979. One of America's leading theologians discusses the moral problems of abortion, from the Catholic point of view.

Oakley, Ann, *The Captured Womb*, Basil Blackwell, 1984. A careful and thorough examination of how male medics have 'managed' women's wombs.

Oldershaw, K. Leslie, *Contraception, Abortion and Sterilization in General Practice*, Kimpton, 1975.

Petchesky, Rosalind Pollack, *Abortion and Women's Choice. The State, Sexuality and Reproductive Freedom*, 1984. A feminist and left-wing view of 'choice' in reproduction which would be 'right-wing' and monetarist if it applied this 'choice' to economics.

Petersen, Candida, *Should We Have a Baby?*, Rigby (Australia), 1982. The anguish of a modern couple trying to decide whether or not to embark on parenthood, revealing how difficult the decision can be.

Pizer, Hank & Palinski, Christine O'Brien, *Coping with a Miscarriage*, Jill Norman, 1981. More about miscarriage with special reference to genetic links.

Potts, Malcolm, et al., *Abortion*, 1977. Three experienced doctors examine the medical, legal and historical aspects of abortion, from a liberal point of view.

Raynor, Lois, *The Adopted Child Comes of Age*, Allen and Unwin, 1980. A very serious-minded summing up of available studies on adoption.

Reidy, M., *Ethical Issues in Reproductive Medicine*, Gill and Macmillan (Dublin), 1982. The ethical problems in genetics. Who needs genetics counselling.

Richards, Maura, *Two to Tango*, Ward River Press (Dublin), 1981. A story of a pregnant young Irish woman and her struggle to be a single parent.

Richards, Janet Radcliffe, *The Sceptical Feminist*, Penguin Books, 1980. Analysis of feminism by a clever utilitarian academic.

Rubin, Sylvia P., *It's Not Too Late to Have a Baby*, Prentice-Hall, 1980. Genetic counselling from a very well-informed author.

Scorer, C.G., *Life in Our Hands*, Intervarsity Press, 1978. A gentle, Christian consultant's guide to human relationships and responsibility.

Shapiro, Howard, *The Birth Control Book*, Penguin Books, 1980. Produced as the most comprehensive birth-control book and discussions on abortion – it dismisses any post-abortion reflection as neurotic.

Shorter, Edward, *A History of Women's Bodies*, Allen Lane, 1982. The horrors of the bad old days when midwives were ignorant old crones.

Shostak, Arthur B., *Men and Abortion: Lessons, Loss and Love*, Praeger Special Studies (New York), 1983. Sensitive US study which shows that most men are pro-choice, many actively pro-abortion but they can also be hurt.

Siggers, D.C., *Prenatal Diagnosis and Genetic Disease*, Blackwell Scientific Publications, 1978. A medical guide to chromosomal genetic abnormalities.

Simms, Madeleine & Hindell, Keith, *Abortion Law Reformed*, Peter Owen, 1971. The definitive account of how the abortion law was altered in England and Wales in the 1960s.

Simon, Julian, *The Ultimate Resource*, Martin Robertson, 1984. This book argues the population increase is usually an optimistic sign and that population worries are overdone – written from an economic viewpoint.

Singer, Peter & Wells, Deane, *The Reproduction Revolution: New Ways of Making Babies*, OUP, 1984. Brave New World again.

Smith, Carole, R., *Adoption and Fostering: Why and How*, Macmillan, 1984. Another methodical compilation of studies done on adoption with the overall conclusion that adoption can be very successful.

Smith, F.B., *The People's Health 1830–1910*, Croom Helm, 1979. Misery and starvation in Victorian England.

Stevas, Norman St John, *The Right to Life*, Hodder and Stoughton, 1963. Abortion, suicide, capital punishment, euthanasia, killing in wartime – regarded as a minor classic.

Stone, Lawrence, *The Family, Sex and Marriage in England 1500–1800*, Penguin Books, 1980. Extraordinary stories about attitudes to babies in former times. Sometimes the child under two was scarcely regarded as a person.

Storkey, Elaine, *What's Right with Feminism?* SPCK, 1985. A Christian philosopher defends feminism but concludes that abortion cannot be squared with Christian moral theory.

Sumner, L.W., *Abortion and Moral Theory*, Princeton University Press, 1981. A philosophical treatment of abortion which comes to a middle-of-the-road conclusion.

Tooley, Michael, *Abortion and Infanticide*, Clarendon Press, 1983. An Australian professor claims that infanticide is as common, historically, as abortion. Moreover, he doesn't seem to see much wrong with that. Most tribes adjust to infanticide quite well, after all.

Turnbull, Colin, *The Human Cycle*, Picador, 1974. An anthropologist's description of how horrible people can be to one another, and to their young.

Verney, Dr Thomas (with John Kelly), *The Secret Life of the Unborn Child*, Sphere, 1982. How the unborn baby develops. The doctors are not against abortion, but they are in no doubt that what is in the human womb is a human being.

Vosnesenskaya, Julia, *The Women's Decameron*, Quartet Books, 1986. Fictional accounts of Russian women's lives based on the author's experiences.

Wagner, Gillian, *Children of the Empire*, Weidenfeld and Nicolson, 1982. How poor English children were sent to Canada and Australia.

Walters, Williams & Singer, Peter, *Test-Tube Babies: A Guide to Moral Questions, Present Techniques and Future Possibilities*, OUP, 1982. A forward and sometimes frightening look at what the reproduction revolution could bring.

Walvin, James, *A Child's World 1800–1914*, Penguin Books, 1982. A social history of English childhood, with emphasis on the misery.

Warnock, Mary, *A Question of Life*, Basil Blackwell, 1984. The substance of the Warnock Report with a foreword by Mary Warnock.

Weldon, Fay, *Puffball*, Coronet, 1980. Extraordinary novel about a woman who talks to her foetus – and gets a reply.

Willke, J.C. & M.S., *Abortion – Questions and Answers*, Hayes Publishing, 1985 (available from SPUC). An exhaustive compilation of facts and arguments about abortion, all carefully documented. The authors are American pro-life activists.

Wood, Clive & Suitters, Beryl, *The Fight for Acceptance: A History of Contraception*, Medical and Technical Publishing Co. Ltd., 1970. Birth control from Plato to NATO.

HISTORICAL PAPERS

Knight, Patricia, *Women and Abortion in Victorian and Edwardian England*, History Workshop 4, 1977.

Langer, William L., 'The Origins of the Birth Control Movement in England in the Early 19th Century', *Journal of Interdisciplinary History*, Vol. 4, Spring 1975.

McLaren, Angus, 'Abortion in England, 1890–1914', *Victorian Studies*, Summer 1977.

Sauer, R., 'Infanticide and Abortion in 19th Century Britain', *Population Studies*, No. 32, 1978.

INDEX